RECESSES OF THE MIND

Recesses of the Mind

Aesthetics in the Work
of Guðbergur Bergsson

BIRNA BJARNADÓTTIR

Translated by
KRISTJANA GUNNARS

McGill-Queen's University Press
Montreal & Kingston • London • Ithaca

© McGill-Queen's University Press 2012

ISBN 978-0-7735-3910-5

Legal deposit first quarter 2012
Bibliothèque nationale du Québec

Printed in Canada on acid-free paper that is 100% ancient forest
free (100% post-consumer recycled), processed chlorine free

This book has been published with the help of a grant from the Department
of Icelandic Language and Literature at the University of Manitoba.

McGill-Queen's University Press acknowledges the support of the
Canada Council for the Arts for our publishing program. We also
acknowledge the financial support of the Government of Canada
through the Canada Book Fund for our publishing activities.

Library and Archives Canada Cataloguing in Publication

Bjarnadóttir, Birna, 1961–
   Recesses of the mind: aesthetics in the work of Guðbergur Bergsson /
Birna Bjarnadóttir; translated by Kristjana Gunnars.

Includes bibliographical references and index.
ISBN 978-0-7735-3910-5

   1. Guðbergur Bergsson, 1932– Criticism and interpretation.
   2. Guðbergur Bergsson, 1932– Aesthetics. 3. Icelandic literature –
History and criticism. 4. Aesthetics in literature. 5. Aesthetics,
Modern – 20th century. I. Gunnars, Kristjana, 1948– II. Title.

PT7511.G78Z63313 2012   839'.6914   C2011-905652-6

This book was typeset by Interscript in 10.5/13 Sabon.

To my daughter Ása

Contents

Acknowledgments

It was a stroke of luck to have Mark Abley consider the manuscript for publication, and it was a source of great pleasure to work with him. I would like to express my sincere gratitude to him. The same is true of Kristjana Gunnars, the translator of this book. In addition to her knowledge of Icelandic culture, and the translation of cultures, she is no stranger to the writings of Guðbergur Bergsson and his position in modern and contemporary Icelandic literature. Given the nature of the book's subject matter, the translation was a demanding task. All the more reason for the two of us to join hands, and that we did, time and again. Five of my graduate students at the University of Manitoba's Department of Icelandic Language and Literature enter the picture of the translation–in–progress. Adam Kitchen read the entire manuscript. He is also the translator of *Flatey–Freyr*, Bergsson's book of poems, excerpts from which appear for the first time in English in appendix 2. Elin Thordarson, Christopher Crocker, Becky Forsythe, and Andrew McGillivray read chapters of the manuscript in a course on modern Icelandic literature, and Andrew also assisted with the book's index. I thank them all dearly. Darlene McWhirter, the department's office administrator, assisted graciously. I would also like to acknowledge Joanne Richardson, the book's copy editor, without whose epic editing the text would read very differently. Her contribution is invaluable. As stated in the preface, I am responsible for the end result.

The Icelandic Research Council, Science Fund, supported the writing of this book. It is the University of Manitoba's Department of Icelandic Language and Literature – the only Icelandic department outside of Iceland – that has fostered the publication of the English

version. The adventure started with David Arnason and Timothy
Samson's support shortly after my arrival in Winnipeg. That is when
I received a translation grant from the University of Manitoba's
Icelandic Language and Literature Fund, which enabled me, in turn,
to hire Kristjana Gunnars as the translator. Thanks to Richard
Sigurdson, dean of arts, the same fund has supported the publication
of the book. I have also received a publication grant from the
University of Manitoba's Faculty of Arts. Thanks to Ron Goodman,
two Icelandic clubs (one in Calgary and one in Edmonton) enter at
this stage of support. The University of Iceland's Rector's Fund is
also hereby acknowledged for its generous support. I am deeply
grateful for all of this.

A few other people have made a difference. Despite the geographical distance, Ingunn Ósk Sturludóttir is a friend like no other. The
continuous support of my former supervisor, Ástráður Eysteinsson,
is no less valued. Gunnvör Daníelsdóttir, who was born and raised
not far from the Florence of the North (Guðbergur Bergsson's hometown) and who immigrated to Canada decades ago, is my only rela-
tive here, and I cannot thank her enough for her support. George
Toles, the collaborator and my daughter's teacher, is a precious
friend. The same is true of Cliff Eyland, another collaborator, and
Guy Maddin, the Icelandic department's distinguished filmmaker in
residence, not to mention Matthew Patton, a fellow traveller in the
sublime Westfjords and the department's honorary composer. Last,
but not least, I would like to thank my students for being right here,
right now.

Finally, I am indebted to my parents, my late father Bjarni Ólafsson
and my mother Fríða Ása Guðmundsdóttir. Without their support,
this adventure could easily have turned into a nightmare twice over.
The same can be said, although in a different way, about the novelist
and poet whose writing is the subject of this book. My daughter Ása
Helga Hjörleifsdóttir was a child when she travelled with me to
Warwick and only a few years older when we moved to Canada. She
is a young woman now, living in a city in another country. This book
is dedicated to her.

Preface

Many years ago, when I was deciding where to go to conduct my research on aesthetics in modern literature, my time at the Nordic Summer School in Comparative Literature at Helsingør turned out to be a decisive moment. Simon Critchley's lecture on Blanchot was significant. That is also where I heard about an upcoming conference on the soul and Augustine to be held that same year at the University of Warwick. Along with that university's centre for philosophy, literature, and the arts, and its centre for translation and comparative studies, it was the conference on the soul that fascinated me. A couple of months later, I found myself waiting for a bus. It was early in the morning, the autumn winds were blowing, and I saw a priest and a nun approach the waiting line. We rode the same bus to the university, and later that day, I saw them again in a crowd of secular people. We were all attending a conference on the soul held by the University of Warwick and organized by Gillian Rose. The organizer did not make it to the conference, though: she lay dying.

The year at Warwick turned out to be essential for my research on aesthetics in modern literature and how it bears on the subjects of love, faith, and beauty. That is where the path to what follows revealed itself. The courses in Continental philosophy, Blanchot and modern literature, and translation and literature were adventurous. Gillian Rose's book *Love's Work* still holds a special place and was published around the time of my arrival at Warwick. The same is true of Hannah Arendt's *Love and Saint Augustine,* which appeared later that same year. Arendt's book offered much support for my own studies, as, generally speaking, did my stay in England that winter. In the years that followed, I enjoyed the supervision of Ástráður Eysteinsson, professor of comparative literature at the University of Iceland. His knowledge of modernism was essential to my study. The supervision of Vilhjálmur Árnason, a professor of philosophy, was no less crucial with regard to the writings of Kierkegaard and Nietzsche.

This book was originally written as a doctoral dissertation on the aesthetics in Guðbergur Bergsson's work and was published by the University of Iceland Press in 2003. What I could not have foreseen at Warwick was that the writing of this book would take seven years. As if on the path of Teresa's *Interior Castle* twice over, I had no idea that it would take another seven years to ferry this book into the English-speaking world. Kristjana Gunnars, the translator of this book, took on a demanding task. Together, we have revised the translation, I have edited fragments of the original text, my graduate students have read chapters in translation, and Joanne Richardson, the book's copy-editor, has worked wonders on the final editing front. The author of this book is and remains responsible for the end result.

But there is more to this story. The novel *Hjartað býr enn í helli sínum* (*The Heart Still Dwells in Its Cave*) awakened in me a serious interest in the writing of Guðbergur Bergsson. I read that book over Christmas in 1982, when I was studying at the Freie Universität in Berlin and was absorbing poets and philosophers like Novalis and Nietzsche. Perhaps my fate was determined there: in the present work, not only is the writing of Bergsson in the foreground, but a great deal of consideration is also given to Nietzsche and Jena romanticism. What inspired this study in particular, however, was another of Bergsson's novels: *Sú kvalda ást sem hugarfylgsnin geyma* (*The Mind's Tormented Love*). I also read that book over Christmas during my final year of MA studies in Icelandic literature at the University of Iceland. Guided by the late Matthías Viðar Sæmundsson, professor of Icelandic literature, existentialism, and history of ideas, that winter I was reading two other books, both by Augustine: *The Confessions* and *The City of God*. Aside from *The Mind's Tormented Love*, the novel that could be called the heart of the present study, Augustine's *Confessions* assumes special significance. Nor do I wish to forget the long-standing admiration I have had for the writings of Kierkegaard, and explorations of these are to be found here as well.

Whatever the sources of this book, my interest in the writing of Bergsson has taken me into a study of aesthetics in modern times, especially as it bears on the above mentioned subjects, namely, love, faith, and beauty.

Ever since the publication of Guðbergur Bergsson's first books in 1961, the poetry volume *Endurtekin orð* (*Repeated Words*) and the novel *Músin sem læðist* (*The Mouse That Skulks*), readers have had to orient themselves to a creative force that reaches across a huge spectrum: fiction, poetry, translation, the philosophy of art, aesthetics, criticism, and epistolary writing. With the novel *Tómas Jónsson metsölubók* (*Tómas Jónsson Bestseller*), Bergsson secured his place as one of the chief modernists in Icelandic literature and, simultaneously, as one of the leading inheritors of the modern Icelandic literature of Halldór Laxness, Þórbergur Þórðarson, and Gunnar Gunnarsson. Bergsson is also a much respected translator of Spanish, Portuguese, and Latin American literature. With his translations he has enriched Icelandic culture with timeless classics like Cervantes' *Don Quixote* and Juan Ramon Jimenez's *Platero and I*. He has introduced Icelanders to streams of twentieth-century literature, among them works associated with magic realism. In addition, many of Bergsson's own books have been translated into several languages. In *Recesses of the Mind*, I discuss the aesthetics of Bergsson's writings.

But what is the aesthetics of Bergsson's writings and how does one approach it? Is Bergsson's home town of Grindavík, in southwestern Iceland, perhaps the Florence of the North?

Grindavík was not only a garden of gardens, a ring of rings, but the sea also encircled the land with a white fringe of surf to throw on the black hue of lava and land. All this had the effect that, in the village and in its neighbourhoods, life was as colourful as in that other heavenly comedy by Dante. Our deportment was not lagging behind his creation either, and the contents were often more colourful than his. The only one who can render a description of it is someone who wants to tread in his footsteps, go into exile and die far from his Florence.[1]

In his fictional autobiography *Faðir og móðir og dulmagn bernskunnar* (*Father and Mother and the Mysterious Power of Childhood*) (1997) the poet again returns to his Florence and searches out stories of life and mannerisms that rival Dante's *Divine Comedy* in picaresque structure. Here we are introduced to Bergsson's perception of beauty, love, and faith. We also find him engaged in a dialogue with the principles surrounding beauty, love, and faith, not only as they pertain to art, both structural and narrative, but also, and no less so, to life. In brief, Bergsson's fictional autobiography could be described as a meditation on art from the point of view of life.

What makes Bergsson's aesthetics challenging is that it involves doubt about the possibilities of scientific investigation into the matter. The very concept of a *fictional autobiography* reveals the depth of doubt we face: not only are the boundaries between art and life uncertain but we also see how fiction shapes the latter from two directions: life originates in fiction and becomes narration. What follows is nonetheless an attempt to interpret the narratives of Guðbergur Bergsson and, in so doing, to conduct an inquiry into individualistic aesthetics in modern literature.

The aesthetics of Bergsson's works involves a dialogue not only with Icelandic society and culture but also with certain writers and philosophers in Western intellectual and literary culture. As the above quotation indicates, in Bergsson's creative universe, not only is Grindavík a village on the southwestern coast of Iceland but the life of the town and its inhabitants is also evocative of Dante's *Divine Comedy*. The questions, therefore, are: What is the nature of this dialogue? How is it invoked? The subjects of Bergsson's stories bear witness to social and cultural realities his readers recognize. As a result, we can speak of a resonating reader response. On the other hand, we can discern in his stories and essays positions of and requirements for a readerly engagement beyond that of recognition, for another kind of participation in ideas concerning life and art. The main purpose of *Recesses of the Mind* is to explore this adventurous dialogue.

But what is the aesthetics of modern literature? Does an understanding of modern art and the experience of modernity in the Western world not require a grasp of Continental European philosophical movements?[2] Aesthetics is not only a branch of philosophy: it also touches directly on various other disciplines as well. The domain of aesthetics, some argue, is an area of inquiry that ties together, rather than separates, the different disciplines within the arts.[3] That perspective is the one I adopt here. I also agree with the notion that the philosophy of aesthetics has undergone significant changes within the last century or so. Within philosophy itself, in fact, aesthetics has always been on the margins. This is because the realm of aesthetics encompasses those areas of human experience that least lend themselves to classification: subjects like art, beauty, the emotions, and the ever-changing ability of the human senses to experience pleasure.

Aesthetics has undergone serious changes, as have other disciplines, for refinements in classification have affected all the sciences. In the wake of what has been termed the "industrialization of experience," a new way of thinking has developed concerning the relationship between the individual and phenomenological reality. The subjective self is no longer thought to affirm an independent mental existence; rather, we speak of the connection between consciousness and reality. As a result, aesthetic experience has been redefined and is now seen in relation to the question of how mind and world are conjoined. After being on the sidelines in philosophical inquiry, aesthetics is now edging towards the centre, not least among those thinkers who wish to consider the possibilities of thought and the senses in opposition to an increasing tendency in contemporary theory to move towards objective classification. In the absence of truth, it is also said, we have only art (Cazeaux, Introduction, xiii–xvii).

RECESSES OF THE MIND

1

Aesthetics in Modern Literature:
The Mind's Tormented Love

In a book dedicated to god,[1] one can read the following warning inscribed on the flyleaf:

> Every event in this story is to some degree true, and everything
> here that is turned into letters on a page has at some time hap-
> pened, according to various methods of understanding. For this
> reason, if anyone seems to recognize himself in the work, that
> will be more than right; the author has no doubt used that per-
> son as a model. It is not unlikely that the model will feel that he
> has sole proprietorship over himself and will wish, if possible, to
> sue and have the author charged for the offence. But in that case
> it is good to remember that words that have been spoken or
> written, even though only one time, can never be taken back,
> especially not by a judge or a court of law.[2]

This warning might concern those readers who, by putting two and two together (i.e., life and art), recognize themselves in the story. Unless the reference is much broader and concerns the reception of the story of creation itself. If that is the case, then it is possible to see this warning as an allusion to Christian culture and to the fact that no one can thwart god/the author's sole ownership of the biblical story of the creation of humankind. The reader may therefore recognize him or herself in the book but will be unable to do anything about it.

But who has ownership of what is "to some degree true?" And what events take place "according to various methods of under-standing?" What does the author mean? Perhaps there are still

people who are at home in the mystery of the creation story. Those
people, lost as they are to direction and time, can hardly be considered representatives of the modern era, this time in history, which,
in its essence, is characterized by godlessness – an era of glittering
progress in science and technology.

In the afterword to his Icelandic translation of Gabriel García
Márquez's *One Hundred Years of Solitude*, Bergsson discusses the
function of original sin in modern writing: "It is a strange thing that,
for radical authors, original sin is more relevant than reason as an
explanation for the human condition" (364). In the same afterword,
Bergsson also discusses the scriptural atmosphere that hovers over
the narrative of *One Hundred Years of Solitude*; how Knut Hamsun
was the first author to rewrite the Book of Moses "in modern guise
and down-to-earth language"; how Halldór Laxness has rehashed
the Old Testament in his novel *Independent People*, as have other
authors in "manifold ways with manifold results." These stories,
Bergsson claims, have been "especially well loved in countries that
were once New Worlds but later became spoiled. These are family
tales inspired by pure Lutheran or communist thought, but fiddle in a
strange and degenerate way with sin, and have the objective of being
national symbols, a form of punishment, and a declaration of love to
the fatherland, all at once. The best known authors of such love-hate
fiction are Hamsun, Faulkner, Laxness, Rúlfo, and Marquez" (361).

In his afterword, Bergsson claims to have no ability to delve into
comparative literature, to compare *Growth of the Soil*, *Independent
People*, Rúlfo's *Pedro Paramo*, "the characters in Faulkner, and the
arrogant rascals in Marquez's *One Hundred Years of Solitude*" – fictional worlds that he calls closed, male worlds that smell of rutting
and biblical tragedy. Those works are not part of my discussion either,
and no comparison with them is offered. However, if original sin is
more relevant than reason for the authors of the above novels, could
the same perhaps hold true for the author of *The Mind's Tormented
Love* – a novel not inspired by pure Lutheran or communist thinking
but one that does smell of rutting and of biblical tragedy. Is the universe of Bergsson's fiction similar in kind to what he, as a translator,
found in *One Hundred Years of Solitude* – a world that is closed,
circular, like time and "the eternal return"? a world that includes
"many floods, because life and time are circular" (364)?

The subject of the novel *The Mind's Tormented Love* is, in rough
detail, as follows: One summer in Reykjavík, Iceland, a man sits in

his basement and records in his journal his mental and physical search for the path to love. After having lived an exemplary life as a husband, father, teacher, and employee of the government's Ministry of Culture and Education, he inherits an apartment and his childhood friend's lover, and throws himself into a love affair with another man. As if human emotions remained a serious subject in modern inquiry, he wonders about the possibilities of love: Is marriage the real road to love? If so, why do so many relationships thrive outside its bounds and on its margins? Is love more suited to the emotional life of members of the same sex? If the answer is yes, why does this man not find contentment? Why is death always so close at heel to love? Is it AIDS that marks the continuous presence of death? Or is the connection between love and death much older in the annals of humankind? The protagonist's search produces profound questions regarding the relationship between death and love and modern art. It is tempting to construct a theory on the subject, but that will not be done here. In this novel – which is not dedicated to human beings but to god – the question of human emotions is too enduring for an interpreter to draw doctrinaire conclusions. If nothing else, the protagonist and writer of the diary serves as a kind of warning to the reader: in his tireless search for love, he makes a fruitless attempt – in his mind – to nail himself to his lover. The only option, it seems, is to join the protagonist and embark upon a search for the possibilities of the emotions – which appear at once real and unreal, alive and dead. The story is seen to harbour an existential sensibility that is hidden but not forgotten and that awakens, here and now, the boundary of life and art in a creative repetition on the stage of Western culture.

A MODERN PRELUDE TO THE PROSPECT
OF THE EMOTIONS

The diaries that make up the narration of this novel (written by Bergsson's protagonist) are seven, penned between 1988 and 1993. In a foreword, written on 16 October 1993, the narrator, as he looks back on his life, reviews what led to his journal keeping. He explains that he chose his working space in order to enjoy a love affair with his childhood friend, telling his wife that he needs a room in which to write. He finds a convenient basement room with an entrance at the back and a kitchen nook in the corner, which he rents from an elderly woman who is described as having "an old-fashioned style rather than the formless, artificial style of the modern kind, which smudges out all eras in its continuous rush" (12). In his basement lodging, "old-fashioned" as it is, the journal writer plans to carry out his affair with the man he has inherited from his childhood friend and to do so in the following manner: "Every individual has to take stock of his own emotions; to live the life he has chosen and stand or fall as the tides turn and as armies of resistance arise for him to combat – more likely from within himself and from his own doubts than from outside – in fact, few people are so sickly that they cannot defend themselves from their own onslaughts" (13–14).

However, it is not long before the diarist discovers the restless presence of death in the proximity of love. He mentions superstition – an anxiety he claims is primitive in nature and that becomes evident in the suspicion that love will be the harbinger of "disaster, torment, and death, or at least very bad news" (14). The diarist confesses that he himself harbours this superstition. Reason and rationality hold no sway in this matter; he simply knows that "love is the harbinger of death and we (probably myself) will sooner or later have to sacrifice our lives – perhaps not for love, but because of love" (14). Such superstitious feelings are not lessened in a situation of same-sex adultery in the era of AIDS. Instead, this disease emphasizes such superstition – a nagging suspicion lovers have that "love and its consequences are immutably connected to tragedy" (14). Nor does it mend matters that his contemporaries think some kinds of lovers are inherently guilty:

> Ever since the disease was first identified, it has been in the eyes of the Christian a punishment for the fact that certain degenerate and ungodly people made love, and the need for physical intimacy, into a physical relationship that served their own sole purposes – love and intimacy were pleasures enough in themselves. This particular kind of person – pre-judged and socially rejected – untied love from its ideological shackles, and sought pleasure and satisfaction in the flesh, for its own sake – and to make matters worse, with members of his own sex.
>
> The disease, that flaming sword, was therefore sent to the world from god, who created a virus as punishment on the flesh of the degenerate, so he would die a terrible death for the sin of enjoying the fruits of love in an unhealthy manner, and not in

marriage, as Christian law requires, with the requisite procreation from a mother's womb in order to populate the earth. The
disease has sprung up because someone has offended woman's
holy sanctum, which is the wellspring of life, and this same someone insists on lusting after a baser and darker ravine or hole on
the body, where no light is sparked from the darkness and the
seed is expelled from there before a child is conceived, as it is
with the most primitive peoples. (14–15)

The diarist continues by discussing the fact that Christians have had
to come face to face with the reality of this disease and how it is "im-
pervious to sorrow and steals into any and all caverns." AIDS did not
play out "according to the desired tenets of Christian men and
women" but, instead, went its own way, "answering to no laws but its
own, and it did not come as punishment to those who break god's law
and his preferred procreation cavities. It was one against all, just like
all other forms of death" (15). In the diarist's opinion, this view of the
"deviance" of AIDS has helped neither "Christians" nor their aesthetic
sensibility when it comes to their ability to judge: "To enjoy the pleasures of love and die for its sake from a real and threatening disease is
not tied to philosophy or economics or the gods but, instead, to an
ambiguous and uncontrollable desire that Christians claim to be
wrong – a desire that in fact expires as soon as it is satisfied" (15).

It is possible that the main factor in the connection between love
and death in which the reader participates is simply the imminence
of death in the relationship between two homosexual men. As we see
in the foreword, the narrator is consumed by the subject of love in
the time of AIDS. He is also a man who throws himself uncondition-
ally into a sexual relationship with another man. The connection
between death and love can therefore be thought of in this way: two
men defy Christian morals and deal a mournful blow to the notion
held by Christian men and women that there is some sort of difference between the sinful love of the homosexual and the normal love
of the heterosexual. The radicalism of Bergsson's novel is here – if
not in the rewriting of a biblical tragedy, then in its realistic treatment of gender analyses in a story in which the main emphasis is on
the impending doom of two male lovers.

This reading is not just taken out of thin air. The novel has also
been interpreted within gay studies and has been analyzed as being
an exploration of the plight and condition of homosexuals in modern

Western society, as is evident in Geir Svansson's essay "Unspeakable Love." Svansson argues that, in this story, love suffers so much "social prohibition" that it cannot thrive and so takes on "the most harmful and anguished damage to be found in contemporary life: illicit love metamorphoses into pathological love!" And he continues: "The teacher, and probably the sailor, most likely has HIV or AIDS. This confession is presented towards the end of the foreword, and death hovers over the narrative ever after and cannot but colour it. Any interpretation of the story must necessarily take this fact into consideration" (510). I agree with Svansson that death is always present in the narrative. The question is, however, how the critic defines or interprets death. I am in accord with the view expressed by Álfrún Gunnlaugsdóttir, writer and professor of literature, that scholars need to be careful when they use novels as sociological sources (490). Such a reminder can be viewed as auspicious when considering the relationship between love and death, as we see in the details of Svansson's argument concerning society's response to homosexuality and the prevalent view that it is unnatural. He argues that the realism of Bergsson's theme arises from its references to the social and medical condition of its setting. In other words, the love in question is doomed not only because it is socially condemned when viewed from a "healthy," "Christian" vantage point but also because of AIDS.

But what if the torment expressed in Bergsson's *The Mind's Tormented Love* is not completely explained by such socio-cultural references? Is Bergsson's subject perhaps broader – is it death in life, and how we are all doomed? "We are not only doomed on account of this, but on account of everything, from the day of our birth," (17) the narrator says to his lover when discussing AIDS. The same character also utters the following to the same listener:

> If I were Christ, and Roman soldiers were going to crucify me and told me I could have one wish like other prisoners, then I would wish for the executioners to crucify me on your body and that your nail were hammered right through me.
> "Is that what is written in the Bible?" he asked, shyly pleased that there might be something about him in print.
> "No," I answered. "We haven't known each other that long." (63)

In a discussion of this man's search for love – the existential sensibility that search awakens about the things known to be real in the story and the events that take place through various modes of under-standing – one could argue that the part played by AIDS in a story of the sexual relationship between two men is more a modern fore-word to the prospects of the emotions than it is a central theme. The palpability of this observation may be illustrated by another novel written near the end of the twentieth century. This novel is Edmund White's *The Married Man*, which, at first glance, appears to be about something very similar. In both stories, the love bond between two men who are infected with AIDS is foregrounded, and in both stories one of the men is married to a woman. However, unlike *The Married Man*, Bergsson's novel, when it comes to the relationship between two men in the time of AIDS, is not based on social realism. White's novel deals with serious issues concerning love. Its central theme involves the effect this disease has on the two men, and clear and powerful lines are drawn concerning both their emotions and their social position. However, Bergsson's novel circles around different issues. He does not write about the disease as such, or about the re-sponse to it, or about its effect on the lives of his characters. Nor does he write exclusively about the feelings characters in relation-ships with other characters experience. Rather, his novel is more existential in nature and, first and foremost, concerned with the pro-tagonist's passion for *thoughts on life*.

What I call "a modern foreword to the prospects of the emotions," therefore, has to do with the themes of love and AIDS in Bergsson's novel. What follows, however, is an exploration of the narrative's deep–seeted questions concerning the relationship between love and death in modern times, and how this relationship can be viewed as a creative repetition on the stage of Western culture. One other twentieth-century Icelandic novel engages similar themes: Gunnar Gunnarsson's *Sælir eru einfaldir* (*Blessed Are the Simple*) (1920). His narrative takes place in Reykjavík in the first half of the twentieth century, and an epidemic is raging in the town. As in Bergsson's novel (which is a diary in seven parts), Gunnarsson's story is a perverse Genesis: for seven days, the devil walks freely about and burns the lives of simple people to the ground. In both novels it is possible to see a passionate search for a way of life. In both the search becomes more intense as we near the end, perhaps because both narrators ferry the reader through the fire and brimstone of an existence stripped of its delusions. These are philosophical stories and both, in their own way, are based on existentialism.[3] However, the differences between them are also significant. Gunnarsson's narrative is concerned with the embodiment of death in the form of an epidemic and the inevitable derangement that results from a crisis of faith. Bergsson's narrative, on the other hand, takes as its subject an enigmatic and modernistic treatment of the human condition in matters of love and faith.

Perhaps it is the times we are in that decide the outcome of things. If we are to believe the childhood friend of Bergsson's narrator, modern humanity has created for itself a "nasty time to live in, where there is no longer any wholeness, but only an education that leads to division, segregation, and a tiresome and killing specialization" (59). Bergsson's narrative reveals the experience of modern times and, simultaneously, may be perceived as an aesthetic duel against them.

LOVE AS MARTYRDOM

The first part of the diary begins with the words: "I had gone to bed at the set hour in the afternoon because he said he would 'appear' between one and two. I had already taken a bath so I would be clean and he could fondle me for a good while in holy uncleanliness, defile me with passion, toss me in his surf and tend to my ecstasy with what is probably simply lust for him, but for me is more like tormented, unblemished love" (20). In what could be termed an introduction to the course of events in modern fiction, a strange setting emerges: the body and its pleasures are unequivocally foregrounded. The imagery, however, has echoes of Christian dualism, even though it is expressed oxymoronically (for example, as "holy uncleanliness"). Here "lust" and "love" are separated, but this is a separation that has been cherished in Christianity, in the spirit of the ancient Greeks. If the narrator-diarist is after physical pleasure, why does he not simply throw himself into that bottomless well that is plainly in the offing? Instead, he desires something beyond the physical, which his partner is unable to give – something involving the torments of the spirit.

Unlike his partner, who grabs what he needs and uses it to satiate himself physically, the diarist has not parted with ideas about the sins of love, which have remained prevalent in Western society. While everything is physical for his friend, the narrator struggles with spiritual matters – as if he is determined to contemplate the fundamental problem of the separation of body and soul, that persistent dualism. This conflict of opposites is taking place in the diarist's mind: "I had intended, like a man who is raised in moderately strict Lutheranism and in a belief in its ideas, that I would leave this life as clean, pure and naked as when I was born into the world. Now I have decided to reject it, because of another kind of faith" (23). In the strength of a new love and a new faith, the man is prepared to give his former life over to death – that life of half-baked Lutheranism he has created for himself, along with his wife and children.

What happened to this man?

As he says himself, it all started with the death of an old school-mate, a death that launched him into "unexpected flight": "When he cut the thread of his life, I took what was hanging on his post and what he abandoned: I took his lover. It was just as though I were rejuvenated by his death; a terrible thirst for life engulfed me and limitless optimism as well as joy and hunger for fulfilment. That is how one man's death can become another man's vital force, or manna in the desert of life" (33–4). It is because of another kind of faith that this man decides to put an end to his life as he knew it. This man who has lived, sexually and emotionally, according to the precepts of Lutheranism, which concern, first and foremost, the body and its purity. When the diarist bites into death's lure, there-fore, he is starving, and he devours his partner's body. Consequently, one could say that the "terrible thirst for life," "limitless optimism," and "hunger for fulfilment" that the diarist experiences set in motion not only creative struggles within but also a process wherby his con-version is finally realized. It also becomes evident that the body takes on not only material but also spiritual dimensions. References to his "new-born" state can be found in passages such as this one:

> When I nestled my face against his neck, I felt the warmth and scent of the pleasure that loving brings; the sweet odour of love itself. His flesh was everywhere, both physically and mentally. We lay that way like two beings who have been nailed each to the other of their own free will, so they might die on a common cross. I lay in a dream until I could sense how our bodies slowly melted together the way a worm crawls into moist soil, I discov-ered how flesh grew into another flesh and we were glued togeth-er with the only glue that can fasten everything and was now outside of our bodies but had been inside before. This position describes in its own way the feeling and longing we had to die in each other. (35)

The religious task this diarist has set himself is, in other words, no small matter. He has started a relationship that, from the vantage point of the Lutheran faith (or what is left of it among those who claim to be Christian), is based on *atheism*. In this matter, seen from the perspective of the history of culture, the diarist is not unique, however. Right after the above fragment comes the following:

> Then I quickly thought:
> "No, this is just wishful thinking."
> We dozed like this, crucified on one another, or perhaps I only dreamed it. I think people's dreams should be seen as an investigation into the deep; that the dream should follow the winding path through the labyrinth of the only certainty there is, which is the sporadic existence of the body. While we linger, the only thing that exists for sure is the body, and at this moment I have no confession but this one:
> If someone offered me with enticing words to step off the cross and return to the society of others, so no spear would be struck into my suffering flesh and body and no blood or liquid would run from the wound as a symbol of the flood within, and if I were offered Paradise with untold dwellings, security with my father and continuous feasting at his home, and if I were allowed to live beneath the gentle, protective wing of my mother for all eternity and in this way end up in the embrace of the holy family, then I would choose rather to hang crucified on my friend, though the world considered it to be a deadly sin and stoned me and ostracized me for preferring to die in the scent of my lover rather than live my life content with what I married fifteen years ago but had my first child with twenty five years ago, then a young man of just twenty. (36)

We are reminded of this same development in the Christian tradition: in the first century AD, Saint Stephen, arch-martyr, was accused of heresy and stoned to death by his Christian compatriots. In the name of "another kind of faith," Bergsson's diarist reawakens the image of that ancient martyr. He would rather die in the dust of his friend than live his life according to Christian ideas about the holiness of marriage and, as a consequence, of love. But what is the staging of this martyrdom? Is someone stoning him or do the onslaughts come from within?

As has been seen, the protagonist has no illusions about family love. But he is afraid that love will fail between him and his friend. He knows that the kind of love that flourishes "naturally" is thought to "threaten the family, even though the family is mostly finished and has helplessly exhausted itself" (190). Nonetheless, he seemingly nourishes the same desire as others for a home, this small image "of the coveted society one is prepared to enter and live in all of one's life, enclosed in the mild and suffocating embrace of the kingdom of father and mother who fight grimly for power and struggle noisily behind the screen with their heads full of mildewed rules and who sometimes emerge, either on the stage itself or in front of the curtain, and invite everyone to good manners and peace. I have done my duty to the family and I am gone, I am free but afraid. I will go my way and choose to be terrified rather than free but locked inside a jail" (190–1). This is his confession and also his inner struggle. For even though he says he has done his duty to the family and has departed "free, but afraid" from this stage play, he still, by his own admission, does not dare to throw off the "invisible collar" but, instead, returns, like a dog, back to his suffering and crawls into his dog house to "sleep away the dreams instead of dreaming new ones" (191).

The diarist only hangs on a cross in his own mind. This matters not only when considering the martyrdom that this man's need for faith generates but also when considering the progress of his search for love. The martyrdom he speaks of is more about the relationship between love and death, within himself, than it is between society and the individual. In other words, his martyrdom rests on the undefined boundary between dream and reality, imagination and actuality, the present day and eternity, life and art. And, by setting out on a narrative journey in search of what is attainable – sometimes real, sometimes unreal, living and dead – the reader is able to participate in a search for the possibilities of human emotion.

Modernity is overpowering in this narrative. As the protagonist's friend says: "Now I have lost two wives, have had five common law wives, I have parted in all seriousness with two women, have conceived seven children with them all, and I am only just forty and in the prime of life as far as that goes. Would you like to be in my shoes?" (188). The diarist does not know how to respond to this. He thinks the story of his friend's problems in his private life is "a little comic" (188). There are many sides to this issue, in fact, and they do not necessarily concern "sexual" martyrdom; nor do they concern ideas about how society creates a kind of two-part tragedy for modern humanity in matters of love – one for straight relationships and another for gay relationships. On this occasion, the diarist claims to be greatly relieved when his friend exits the basement apartment. He does find, however:

> that his presence stayed with me more powerfully than when he was here, so I did what I sometimes did after not having been satisfied with the wife, and masturbated so I could be with him and with both of us exactly as I liked.
>
> My need for physical intimacy grows with the years, and I hardly care what it is, it grows at the same rate as my powers and intellect diminish. This simple healthy man I have inherited is therefore not only a physical need for me, and compensation for my waning strength, but he also becomes more and more the focus of my thinking and a riddle for me as time goes on. My spiritual pleasure and astonishment over his appearance and behaviour have outgrown the physical. (188)

Who is this man in a basement in modern Reykjavík who is playing with his prey at will? This man who finds his spiritual enjoyment deepen and his wonder grow on account of his friend's behaviour?

LOVE AS A CREATIVE REPETITION

With a new kind of faith in love, the diarist awakens not only an ancient image of martyrdom but also a creative repetition on the stage of Christian culture. This relationship between love and death in a basement in modern Reykjavík is not all that meets the eye. The narrative also bears traces of a dialogue with ancient ideas about the viability of the emotions, a topic that may be said to be constant in Western culture, though it takes varying forms in different times and places. This topic is what might be called the continuous recurrence of the spirit's limitations in the face of the imminent volatility of the emotions. In the first diary, the protagonist asks questions such as: "Does love discover itself only in love that exhausts itself, or was it originally a single gender in the same way the whole of life was created from one cell that divided in the living world where everything is continuously searching for its origins by obliterating itself?" (39).

The man is also a hunter in the game of love:

> We meet and are often physically as one without being together
> spiritually. It could be, though, that the spiritual is also some-
> thing physical, but we don't know it yet. We only know each
> other on this level, which is a small part and unrelated to other
> parts of daily life and our activities. Therefore I hover expectant-
> ly over this breathing hole in my life the way the hunter does, or
> the curious man who listens in secret for answers to things he
> knows little of himself, and asks: "Is man satisfied to join with
> another only physically if that is all? Will simply touching satisfy
> us in the long run, or simply flailing about like a foetus without
> tongue and no sufferings other than what the body generates,
> although we know it has to bear us out of the warm pleasure of
> the womb into the cold of humankind and of the world?"
> (39–40)

The diarist's quest ferries him between worlds: he is no sooner born
from the pleasant warmth of the womb than he finds himself out in
the cold world, among human beings. What are the uncertain paths
he is travelling? And his prey? Is his private journey something to be
found in life or on paper? Is it an idea or is it made of flesh and blood?

The diarist is not a neutral explorer of the realms of love and death.
He is in some ways reminiscient of Søren Kierkegaard's protagonist
Constantin, the imaginary author of *Repetition*, a man who does not
believe in the systems constructed by philosophy and wants to see for
himself all the possibilities of life, leaving his hometown of Copenhagen
for Berlin. Once there, he settles in a guest house, wanting "a safe hiding place to which he can retreat and devour his booty in solitude – "
this privacy being something he values highly, "since, like certain
beasts of prey, [he] cannot eat when anyone is looking on."[4]

That is also partly the situation for Bergsson's diarist-protagonist.
He settles down in his basement hovel in modern-day Reykjavík,
where he hunts and then devours his prey, again and again – not out
of sheer promiscuity but because he is exploring the unknown. Now
those who have read the Reykjavík story will say that the diarist is
not always alone in his basement. Is that not where he meets his
lover, over and over? What does Kierkegaard's Constantin have to do
with it? He who wishes to be alone with his prey in Berlin well over

150 years earlier? Who is this "prey"? Constantin has no connection to this basement tragedy played out in the Reykjavík of today, his love of the idea of the repetition of life and art notwithstanding.

In other words, Kierkegaard's narrator is the man who sets himself the goal of exploring the philosophical notion of *repetition*.[5] The ancient Greeks, Constantin says, believed that all knowledge was memory, that all that exists has existed before. When people say, however, that life is repetition, they are saying: the life that exists now is at this moment coming into existence. If the concept of remembering or repeating is not to hand, then life becomes an empty struggle and is all for nothing. According to Constantin, repetition is the signal word for all moral perception; it is an unavoidable requirement of all theological problems (149).

Kierkegaard's notion of repetition can also be described as *the possibility of reality*. What matters in relation to the present discussion is the way in which this notion concerns the general, on the one hand, and the particular, on the other. The universal is the concern of traditional ethics, but Constantin claims not to have any faith in systems of moral philosophy. The particular is, however, dual-natured and is about both the theological and the aesthetic. The problem deepens as, for Kierkegaard, the theological is tied to the individual's inner truth, or reality, while the aesthetic is more concerned with the observable, or the external, form of phenomena.

But how does Constantin come to play a part in this basement tragedy of modern-day Reykjavík? Is his love for the idea of repetition in life and art able to cast light on the boundaries between faith and aesthetics in modern narrative?

It is Constantin who conscientiously tests in himself the idea of the singular, or the unique, in life, both aesthetically (where the test fails) and theologically. This examination takes place on the border of creative narrative. For besides being himself the imaginary author of *Repetition*, he also creates the character of a Copenhagen youth in love and struggling with a serious problem: no sooner has he fallen in love with a woman than he has "lived" through the whole relationship. In the blush of a beginning love adventure, this young man finds himself regarding it with the eyes of an old man. Constantin tests the young man's love in his mind and thinks: "It may be true that a person's life is over and done with in the first moment, but there must also be the vital force to slay this death and transform it into life. In the first dawning of erotic love, the present and the future contend with each other to find an eternal expression, and this recollecting is indeed eternity flowing back into the present – that is, when this recollecting is sound" (137).

In this spirit, Constantin advises the young man to engage with repetition in life instead of being the prey of memory; to say yes to the everyday activities of the passing moment instead of seeking poetic shelter in a by-passed happiness; to give himself "time to live" and not be tempted to "find an excuse to sneak out of life again" (131). If repetition is truly possible, it will make the man happy, unlike memory, which awakens unhappiness, Constantin asserts. What is remembered is passed and is repeated in a bygone time; but what is repeated is a memory of a time that is yet to come.

The young man does not stand the test and disappears without a trace from his project and from the city. Time passes, and suddenly Constantin receives a letter from the same young man in which he describes his mixed emotions towards his advisor. How do you reasonably prove the possibilities of the emotions? How do you live in your mind? Do people not lose their entire lives in that sort of obsession?

> Is it not, in fact, a kind of mental disorder to have subjugated to such a degree every passion, every emotion, every mood under the cold regimentation of reflection! Is it not mental disorder to be normal in this way – pure idea, not a human being like the rest of us, flexible and yielding, lost and being lost! Is it not mental disorder always to be alert like this, always conscious, never vague and dreamy!(189)

Constantin claims that he has himself given up his notion of repetition in life and that the young man will not find an explanation with him. Fortunately, Constantin says further that the young man is not seeking knowledge from any world famous philosopher or "professor publicus ordinarious." No, he

> turns to an unprofessional thinker who once possessed the world's glories but later withdrew from life – in other words, he falls back on Job, who does not posture on a rostrum and make reassuring gestures to vouch for the truth of his propositions but sits on the hearth and scrapes himself with a potsherd and without interrupting this activity casually drops clues and comments.

He believes that here he has found what he sought, and in his
view truth sounds more glorious and gratifying and true in this
little circle of Job and his wife and three friends than in a Greek
symposium. (186–7)

And what is it the young man finds in the story of Job? "Job's greatness," the young man says in one of his letters to Constantin, is that
"freedom's passion in him is not smothered or quieted down by a
wrong expression. In similar circumstances, this passion is often
smothered in a person when faint-heartedness and petty anxiety
have allowed him to think he is suffering because of his sins, when
that was not at all the case. His soul lacked the perseverance to carry
through an idea when the world incessantly disagreed with him"
(207). This is something the advisor understands. It is also Constantin
who says: "There must be screaming; it is beneficial, like bleeding
with a bruise" (216).

In consequence of the very serious questions raised by the young
man from Copenhagen shortly before the middle of the nineteenth
century concerning the danger implied in ice-cold reason, one may
wonder whether it is thinking about the emotions, in and of itself,
that brands the lover of life with the mark of death. Is this perhaps
what has happened to the diarist in Bergsson's novel of modern
Reykjavík? Has his love for thinking about emotions become excessive? Is this why he perceives a rift between what is possible in life
and what he may do in his mind and on paper, emotionally speaking? The diarist and his lover have not known each other long when
the former's search produces the fruit of solitude:

That is how I can be with him in the spoken word and we can
agree, because I can distinguish events and their nature when I
am alone with my imagination, but I become confused and vulnerable when I am in the midst of the shifty and simple physical
needs of my friend.
    As soon as I took up writing, it was instantly easier to be with
him in word than in act. Words can only give you what might be
called the dust from the drumbeat. They do not serve us the
drum itself, its girth, its weight, nor the palm of the hand that
pounds hard on the skin, because words are signs for the mem-
brane with which we satisfy ourselves when we lack what they
refer to. They warm the mind but are hardly more than

compensation for the fact that one cannot – fortunately – attain
the object or the world. That is simply impossible. If we were
granted everything without a struggle, language would be lost
and we would grunt instead, ceaselessly drawl and curse the
same way animals do, especially the bull.

With words, almost everything is possible but not obtainable.
(Bergsson, *Mind's Tormented Love*, 48–9)

It appears as if the prey can only be dealt with in the mind. Such is
the solitude of the diarist, which he puts into words. But what is
gained by compensating for life by writing? Is the diarist himself
only an idea rather than a frail and fragile human being? Where does
this search, which seems to subjugate "every passion, every emotion,
every mood under the cold regimentation of reflection," lead?

It is clear that the diarist does not follow the path to the particular,
which is bound up with faith. But if we consider the diarist's choice
to reject his life, we may ask whether this choice is his determination
to live the "passion of freedom" and its call in the spirit of Job. The
diarist wishes that the man he has inherited from his childhood
friend would become "real in an intimate, tactile manner," and he
must be

neither a sour nor a sweet desire, nor a weakness that would
have sprung from my words in plain solitude, nor the emergence
of an inclination I have inherited and then suppressed, nor a ven-
geance for the betrayal of my origins, nor a fictionalized diary,
but rather an ordinary man, dressed in firm flesh that age will
mark and eventually conquer, a desirable vicissitude. (50)

And love?

Is not love the talent to be able to roam endlessly on light feet in
the dim shadow without security, rather than the determination
to find the solution to things at any cost and to gather up arms
under the banner of certainty?

And I answered according to these arguments:

In love nothing is certain. Is this love of mine then an
exception?

No, not at all, I answered and curled up comfortably in the
shelter of my friend. (50–1)

This is also a man who asks: "Why has life struck down my body, and what has it done to my years and what has it left to do to me before it is all over?" (71) He asks this because he feels he is "innocent and not in control of [him]self against the unquenchable urge" that has burst forth in him. It appears that his quest takes him from these ponderous concerns about the sin of love to the incomprehensible possibilities of the love of freedom. He is also reminiscent of Job among the ashes when his search for the path of love lands him on the floor of the storage shed of the apartment block in which the diarist and his wife live. In among the rubble of the shed he feels the urge to merge with the "mould of the books." There he questions humanity's need to "be an observer of [its] own mental suffering, and at the same time be contemptuous of it" (172).

Regarding the question of the particular, the here and now, Kierkegaard's Constantin chooses repetition and, thereby, the path to faith, while Bergsson's diarist chooses aesthetics: the average human being, "with firm flesh that age will mark and eventually conquer." This is the difference between the existentialism of these two protagonists. Yet, we can see how the "surface matter," or the aesthetics, is unquestionably tied to the inner reality of the Reykjavík diarist, in the same way that the issue of faith, for Constantin in Berlin, awakens a deep sensibility for what cannot be easily attained. In light of this, we may surmise that the boundary between the theological and the aesthetic in these works of Kierkegaard and Bergsson are of equal intensity, different though they otherwise are.

But what are the possibilities in this man's life?

ON THE BOUNDARIES OF FICTION

Another fictional hunter in the realm of love comes to mind in connection with Kierkegaard and Bergsson. This man is French and is the protagonist of Maurice Blanchot's novel *Death Sentence*.[6] He dwells in a hotel room (or rooms) in Paris for the most part, where he is immersed in his own inner world, while the events of the Second World War are blowing everything to tatters around him. As with Constantin in Copenhagen, and the unfaithful one in Reykjavík (who is not only unfaithful to his wife with his friend in the basement but also with Sigga, a friend of him and his wife, as well as with another woman whom he describes as "well read and lovely" and who tempts him into her bed, which smells of arthritis cream), the protagonist of Blanchot's *Death Sentence* knows no moderation in his contemplation of what is possible in matters of love. And death? That is just as pressing a subject for Blanchot's protagonist as is love. Obsessed with his inner urges, the man in Paris again and again comes up against what might be called death's sign of life, if not in language, then in connection to an idea that intrudes upon him repeatedly in his hotel room – in the guise of a woman. He reminisces about a relationship that is confusing to him:

> For some time I lived with a person who was obsessed by the idea of my death. I had said to her: "I think that at certain moments you would like to kill me. You shouldn't resist that desire. I'm going to write down on a piece of paper that if you kill me you will be doing what is best." But a thought is not exactly a person, even if it lives and acts like one. A thought demands a loyalty which makes any slyness difficult. Sometimes it is itself false, but behind this lie I still recognize something real, which I cannot betray.[7]

Here we see the results of a quest that is just as paradoxical in nature as is the one discussed earlier. As far as the emotions go, an idea is not quite the same as a person. The *prey* is therefore only dealt with in the mind, and, as a result, the man's solitude is amplified. Here we are also reminded of how a person's loyalty to his/her own thoughts, his/her emotional honesty, makes any kind of shiftiness or cunning impossible. But is this not good for something? Is not this loyalty to the self, which the mind requires and which makes cunning impossible, a kind of recompense? Why are the possibilities of the emotions not thereby made tangible?

The quest of Blanchot's protagonist takes place – as with Constantin and the diarist – on the edge of literature. He steps into the story as its declared author and into the world of the imagination. It is in this imaginary world that he relentlessly attempts to take on the possibilities of the living. The story's realism, if realism is the right word, is thereby not made up of the sirens that sound the alarm of bombing raids in Paris during the Second World War but, rather, of the painful friction in the inner life that is brought about by the consciousness of a confrontation with the possibilities of the emotions.

Perhaps it is the world of the imagination that brings the quests of these three protagonists together. Their inner world is marked by the relationship between creativity and death, and between excess and danger. In this relationship, language is continuously in a state of creation, just as the life of the person is continuously in danger. Constantin in *Repetition*, the diarist in *The Mind's Tormented Love*, and the narrator in *Death Sentence* are not the same person, that is clear. But if there is any basis to the aesthetic connection discussed here, then clearly unconfirmed suppositions concerning love have travelled unhindered between cities in Europe for a long time. Are emotions possible? these hunters ask. And restless death in their wake, what is that?

It appears that the passion these fictional men have for the life of the mind, on the one hand, and their recognition of the limits of mental activity, on the other, are key issues. These elements concern not only their criticism of general patterns of thought in modern times but also their loyalty to the particulars of existence – the inner possibilities of the human being. They all put the possibilities within themselves to the test, and they all do so on the edge of literature. Perhaps here we have combined the friends of "the great hunt," or those who are "born psychologists" and, as Nietzsche discusses in *Beyond Good and Evil*, those who do not fear "dangerous hunting grounds, where courage, intelligence and subtlety in every sense are needed." Nietzsche talks about the need for hunters of this type in the "primeval forest" of the soul and how scarce such people are. The problem with sending scholars into these "new and dangerous hunting grounds," he says, is that they "stop being useful the very moment the '*great* hunt' (but also the great danger) begins: – this is just when they lose their sharp eye and keen nose" (*Beyond Good and Evil* 43).

Clearly, the search for the possibilities of love is not without risk. And the fruit of this quest can be viewed as paradoxical: the more passionately these hunters love the idea of the possibilities inherent in humanity's inner life, the less prosperous their own possibilities in life become. Their quest has been realized. But where does it exist? In life, in the mind, or on paper? What are the *possibilities* of the quest itself?

It is the Reykjavík diarist who, at one point, discusses what his companion terms the "grain of salt" in his heart and how terrified he is that he might have to live the rest of his life without it. Immediately thereafter he talks about the obsession of writing and says: "I have the superstition or the suspicion that if I write unrestrainedly about my companion, he will be in danger of becoming mere words" (Bergsson, *Mind's Tormented Love*, 70). He also talks about how the fixation with writing is a battle with the mirage of words and claims this fixation is a capitulation before the real task of living. In this connection, he remembers his childhood friend's words about mirages in the desert; that they can be stupendous and tower high against the still sky but that, "if you should venture to look closely at what this illusion arises from, then you will find at most some scrubby plants or a small leaf of grass in the desert" (70–1). But for the diarist, there is more than one kind of writing:

> He who writes out of passion alone can never curb the mirage that arises from words and sentences and it is useless to tell my students about such things, they think like most others that words and language have specific meaning and that when they speak, they also mean what their words say. But most often it is the exact opposite: words can only offer those who know how to read them an opportunity to interpret their content from the mirages they give rise to.
>
> That is perhaps true of my work, and perhaps also of my companion and his grain of salt: what he does with me is an illusion. (71)

Perhaps it is passion that finally determines the outcome of the search for the possibilities of the emotions, if not in life and in the mind, then on paper. Writing that cannot quell the ghosts of the mirage is in fact writing borne of passion and excess. Such writing is nourished by the "heart's grain of salt." The search for love can in this manner become real in writing, which – in its mortal way – activates not only the always incomprehensible task of mortality but also the creative boundaries between literature and life. For this reason we can distinguish an important context, aesthetically speaking, in the diarist's quest. This context manifests itself as a creative repetition on the stage of Christian culture, revealing a certain thread that runs throughout the Western narrative tradition. We can, at the same time, see the indisputable part played by modernism, or the idea of *the aesthetics of language*, in this literature. I now discuss this in greater detail.

THE LANGUAGE OF FICTION

The distinction between the language of daily use and the language of fiction is of concern for the present discussion of the search for love. We can discern in Blanchot's *Death Sentence* the protagonist's passion for thought and its contradictory consequence: beset by the primitive urge from inside him, the protagonist comes up against death's sign of life, if not in its connection to *the idea* (disguised as a woman or women), then in its connection to language itself. This narrative engages in deep thought concerning the connection between humanity and language, a topic Blanchot discusses not only in fiction but also in essays, articles, and fragments. In his essay "The Language of Fiction," he deals both with this topic and with those writers who make the experience of death their subject and then, in particular, *the experience of the connection between death and the unknown.* In this context, he refers particularly to the writing of Kafka.[8]

As Blanchot points out, if you ask about the difference between the language of daily use and the language of fiction, a sentence like "the head clerk called" sets off a whole adventure. If someone reads this sentence at work (on a note lying on a desk), Blanchot writes, this same person knows what it is about: the boss is calling and the information presented by the sentence is endless because reality presses in from all directions. Should someone read this sentence at the beginning of a novel, however, the lack of information it provides concerning the fictional world, and also the nature of this fictional world, is striking. In this manner, reading fiction does not awaken the reader's skills for life but, rather, puts her or him in touch with a world that is unknowable. The essence of fiction/poetic prose, Blanchot claims, is this "poverty" in the reader. Fiction can create an experience that is like a discovery – a force that is not bent on relating what is known but that acquires experience from what is unknown (Blanchot, "Language of Fiction," 74–6).

We sense that fiction has symbolic meaning. But what does that mean? The task of a symbol is not to "signify" a specific idea or a specific event. Quite the contrary: a symbolic meaning carries with it a much wider signification, which covers the whole world – human existence in its entirety. The symbol is nothing more than circumstances, Blanchot continues, that it borrows from daily life, circumstances that are beyond our experience. The symbol is therefore its own emptiness; it is an endless distance that it alone can neither signify nor touch upon.

The symbol is, however, not outside time. In other words, it is not abstract but, rather, exists outside of reality in the sense that (1) it confuses itself with *imagined events* and (2) it wants to contain some events as well as *the possibility of the imagination*.

The limit of the symbol, as Blanchot sees it, is *possibility*. That possibility resides inside the symbol itself, not outside it: the symbol is a story sufficient unto itself. In short, the symbol can never realize its potential, but it is precisely this "impossibility of the symbol" that constitutes its essential nature ("Language of Fiction" 79–80). The task of the symbol is to ferry us in our minds over and over again to the "lack" in existence, to a place where we can acquire an experience of the nothingness of existence as a whole. The symbol, Blanchot continues, is always the experience of "nothing," the search for the "negative absolute" that can yield no results. This matters when we inquire about the kind of investigation, and even the creation of experience, that fiction has to offer. This creativity resembles discovery – a force that is intent on expressing what is known but that ends up acquiring an experience of what is *unknown*. This is because those authors who struggle with the experience of death as "unknowable" come face to face with the captivity of the symbol, which they can neither control nor flee.

In this connection Blanchot mentions Kafka and says that far too many interpreters of his works write much too confidently about his intention, about who he was and what he sought in existence and his writings. What Blanchot sees in the works of Kafka is that most of his protagonists are tangled up in the *boundaries* between life and death. In Kafka, there is no actual death to come to, no real ending. If we accept Blanchot's interpretation, we might see that, concerning the possibility of death, Kafka has alighted on a misfortune human beings are unable to overcome: human beings cannot flee from unhappiness because they cannot avoid existence. Life is meant for nothing other than to be lived with the marker of death running through it (Blanchot, "Language of Fiction," 83).

This idea of Blanchot's concerning the circular journey of language, from life to death and back again, is reminiscent of the pursuit of the diarist in Bergsson's narrative, whose thinking is founded on the marker between life and death. The diarist – faced with death in life – confesses his own helplessness to himself through writing. This particular pursuit affects the man's emotional life "as if [he had] in an instant pulled the splinter of death out of his mind and given it an independent existence outside of [himself]" (Bergsson, *Mind's Tormented Love*, 172). He is "less" dead, for a moment, when he writes. But this is also a man who slowly becomes conscious of the part played by death in love and how his writings do not lessen but, to the contrary, quicken his sense of love's imminent death. The search for love therefore takes an unexpected course:

> Maybe life's self-expression, our love of life, our love of ourselves and others, is a constant dying somewhere in our being; the demise of that which we least want to lose, and which we desire to have forever because it is the same with the thought as with matter itself: after it has been imagined, it must also dissipate.
>
> That is why things have happened differently from what I thought in the beginning: which was the conviction that if I made my diary into my confidant, I would be able to give my emotions eternal life in words. My experience has been different. Self-expression and love have had embedded in them a certain kind of death. I think I have not been able to give anything in my life permanent, artistic form or immortal content, and I think I love nothing but the material I put in my journal in order to have it dissipate there. (172–3)

It appears that the diarist finds a place for his passion in writing by acknowledging that passion's mortality. But are we then talking about *possibility*?

Perhaps Blanchot is right, that in fiction, where the authors struggle with the experience of death as "unknowable," the symbol is *buried alive*: that the symbol is in fact self-referential in its signification of death, which is life, which becomes death as soon as it survives ("Language of Fiction" 84). Blanchot discusses the interpretation of those works that make "unknowable" death their subject and comments on the difficulty of that task. He advises people to "plunge the interpretation back into the heart of the story, lose it there and lose it from view, and grasp again the movement of fiction whose details assert only themselves" (83). It is the small particulars that the reader has to experience in order to arrive at the life of the symbol. There is "nothing else to look for," he says, "nothing more to understand."

But what reader in her right mind will accept such a harvest? Is there nothing more to be gained from such fiction, which contains the creative experience? What is "creation"? Blanchot proposes the following:

"Each episode contains a question about itself, and this question is also the profound life of fiction; it is the story, it shows itself face to face, it asserts itself, it converses" ("Language of Fiction" 84).

This proposal brings to mind Bergsson's views on the "participation" of the reader in fiction. In Þóra Kristín Ásgeirsdóttir's interview-book, *Guðbergur Bergsson Metsölubók* (*Guðbergur Bergsson Bestseller*), we find the following passage, uttered by Bergsson to his interviewer: "No one understands fiction. It is not about finding 'beauty' in it, the key, the right image, what the author actually means, or the right interpretation; but, rather, fiction and the work of art are a tool the reader is given to interpret or shape or distinguish" (195). In order to discuss in greater detail the experience of creativity in modern fiction, it is advisable to take a closer look at Blanchot's ideas on the matter.

THE CREATION OF EXPERIENCE IN MODERN LITERATURE

Maurice Blanchot is the twentieth-century literary interpreter who has, most often and most seriously, asked: What is literature and why does it continue to captivate us? These questions have left their mark on literary theory and the humanities not only in France but also in the English-speaking world and elsewhere. The generation of French thinkers that has had the greatest influence on modern theory in later years is the one that seems to have answered Blanchot's call, and it includes people like Jacques Derrida, Michel Foucault, Michel Leiris, Jean-Luc Nancy, and Georges Bataille.[9] It is noteworthy that, in English-speaking countries, Blanchot's influence is first and foremost discernible in the works of the writers of fiction and poetry. Perhaps the reason for this is that, aside from his influential theory of language, as well as the emphasis he places on the *phenomenology of aesthetics*, Blanchot is said to be, most importantly, an existentialist who addresses the finality of things.[10]

It is a generally held view that Blanchot's writings are challenging. Chritchley, for example, likens the exceprience of reading Blanchot to being "drawn from daylight into an experience of the night" (36). But what kind of night? What Critchley perceives is not the experience of night that nourishes and strengthens and prepares a person for heroic exploits the next day but, rather, the experience of the night that is full of dreams and ghosts, the night that nails a person – without an exit – to existence. This is, in other words, "the night that is stronger than death" – a subject that Blanchot also writes about in his fiction, as the following fragment from his novel *Thomas the Obscure* shows: "Just as the man who is hanging himself, after kicking away the stool on which he stood, heading for the final shore, rather than feeling the leap which he is making into the void feels only the rope which holds him, held to the end, held more than ever, bound as he had never been before to the existence he would like to leave" (73).

This situation – of being nailed to existence – is the experience that is brought on by insomnia. The desire that lies behind Blanchot's writings may have its roots in this particular experience, this experience of a death that is stronger than death itself. Writing is not the desire for a beautiful work of art but, rather, the desire for the origins of the work, the wellspring that resides in the night.[11] Blanchot's description of the writer should not come as a surprise; indeed, he talks about "the insomniac of the day" (Critchley 37).

Furthermore, it seems that the experience of reading Blanchot's texts is based in an unquenchable desire for what human understanding cannot fathom. If philosophy is bound to the movements of the *concept*, then Blanchot's works are not philosophy. To read Blanchot is not to read a wholly consistent work. As Critchley suggests, Blanchot's writings are better considered as a scattered work, in a movement of "worklessness," which bears a likeness to the works of the Jena romantics, especially to those of Friedrich Schlegel (1772–1829). As a Blanchot-inspired reading of Jena romanticism points out, Critchley further notes, there is an "alteration or oscillation within romanticism, where the systematic intentions of the Work, the desire for the *Gesamtkunstwerk* – for Schlegel, the great novel of the modern world – are interrupted and disseminated in the Work itself, producing instead incomplete chains of fragments." This is, in fact, what Blanchot identifies in his *The Infinite Conversation*, as the "non-romantic essence of romanticism" (Critchley 38).

If we are to agree with Critchley, the writings of both Schlegel and Blanchot stand outside of philosophy. This kind of writing, or *literature*,

introduces into the Subject a certain impotence and passivity that escapes the movement of comprehension, of philosophy's obsession with meaning: the desire to master death and find fulfilment for human finitude. Writing outside philosophy means ceasing to be fascinated with the circular figure of the Book, the en-*cyclo*-paedia of philosophical science, itself dominated by the figures of unity and totality, which would attempt to master death and complete meaning by letting nothing fall outside of its closure. In writing, one is no longer attracted by the Book, but rather by the energy of exteriority that cannot be reduced to either the exteriority of Law – even the written Torah – or to the *Aufhebung* of the exteriority of Law in Christianity or dialectics: neither the Book of God nor the Book of Man. Writing is the experience of language unworking itself in an irreducible ambiguity that points towards an exteriority that would scatter meaning – a dizzying absence, the space of dying itself. (Critchley 38)

This point is of importance in the discussion of the experience of creation in the works of writers like Bergsson. In works like these, the one who writes is not enraptured by fully finished works but, rather, by the energy that lies in their creation – that which is neither harnessed by the Book of God (the Bible) nor by the Book of Man (law). We are not talking about writings that we may consider irrelevant or in some way free of the demands made by history, culture, and society. The references in Bergsson's *The Mind's Tormented Love* are complex. The distinguishing feature here is, if anything, ambiguity, or the part played by the *unfathomable*, a feature that makes itself felt in the modern relationship between love and death. In his reading of Blanchot's works, Critchley emphasizes the part played by ambiguity and equivocity, not only as they pertain to history and culture but also as they pertain to politics and the economy. Modern humans still belong to the era of the Book but have lost their belief in it (55–6).

What remains is that those works that contain the experience discussed above awaken in the reader a consciousness of the experience of language, when language, in its own ambiguity, fragments its referentiality by pointing to its outer limits. Those outer limits of language are what Critchley calls a "dizzying absence," which is a space wherein death happens. For Critchley, the question is therefore whether "such an exteriority can be tolerated by the human organism, or rather whether there must be a moment of bad faith in the experience of writing in order to protect us from its truth" (38). The question is whether the human organism can withstand that kind of distancing, fragmenting ambiguity. Because, we ask, what is the truth of writings such as those of Kierkegaard, Blanchot, and Bergsson?

The development of Blanchot's own writings may contain a possible answer, for we see in them this kind of movement towards the
outer limits of language itself. As Critchley notes, at some point,
Blanchot's writing reaches a stage where both his fiction and criticism "undergo fragmentation and pass into one another." Critchely
further suggests that "one way to read Blanchot's work would be in
terms of a movement towards a writing that would result in a certain *Aufhebung* of the distinction between fiction and criticism"
(39). Regardless of those debates circulating around the question
whether Blanchot's criticism can be viewed, first and foremost, as
a commentary on his own fiction, Critchley may be right when
suggesting that no one – with the exception of Kafka – is known to
have bridged the gap that tends to exist between fiction and criticism
like Blanchot.[12] This much is certain, and is affirmed by Jacques
Derrida: Blanchot is far ahead of his time and awaits his contemporaries from a great distance. It is also Derrida who points out the
desire of certain critics (who call themselves political) to interpret, or
rather to *judge*, Blanchot, particularly those critics who have not
read his work.[13] In an attempt to explicate Blanchot's writing,
Critchley suggests the road to Jena. This is because Blanchot high-
lights the Jena romantics' central project: *the production of literature
as its own theory*. And in what genre is this production expressed?
The fragment (Critchley 39).

If we consider Blanchot's ideas of modern writing, then the possibilities of literature arise from its impossibility. That is, the possibilities of literature arise from the impossibility of an "aesthetic
consciousness."[14] Blanchot does not explain this. Critchley, however,
suggests that "we might think of aesthetic consciousness as the total
realization of meaning in an artwork" (41). Since the possibilities of
literature are rooted in the impossibility of creating a complete work,
we may understand Blanchot as saying that it is the "impossibility of
literature" that makes for its very possibility.

This idea is not foreign to Guðbergur Bergsson. Again and again
he expresses the idea of the *unfinished* nature of art and the *poten-
tialities* that reside in a work that is not "complete." This feature of
Bergsson's aesthetics is discussed in the following chapters. Bergsson
is also a poet who, in the infancy of his authorial life, wrote in the
spirit of Blanchot's existentialism: "I have lost life / the night has
come and offered me wakefulness."[15] Later, I discuss the issue of
Bergsson's existentialism and how the aesthetics of his works may

respond to the idea that the production of literature is its own theory. Now, however, it may be advisable to look at the essay of Blanchot's that provides a continious passage into the language of literature, its creative experience, and the part played by ambiguity in modern writing.

LITERATURE AND THE RIGHT TO DEATH

Blanchot's "Literature and the Right to Death," written in the mid-twentieth century, is one of his most important works.[16] Here I focus neither on Blanchot's dialogue with Hegel's major work, *Phänomenologie des Geistes* (*Phenomenology of Spirit*), which appeared in 1807, nor with his dialogue with the French twentieth-century philosopher Emmanuel Levinas's *De l'existence á l'existant* (*Existence and Existents*), which appeared in 1947.[17] What matters for *Recesses of the Mind* is that, in "Literature and the Right to Death," Blanchot explores, with striking patience, literature's ambiguity: the question.

In brief outline, we can say that the main idea in Blanchot's essay is that ambiguity in literature is dependent on the premise upon which it is built, which is that the question must be allowed to remain a question. In this matter it is possible to distinguish two opposite "slopes" of ambiguity. If we agree with Critchley's interpretation, there are two slopes of literature possible and two forms of death (57). On the one hand, we talk about that slope of literature that is premised on "refusal" and that tries to express the Subject itself. This slope of literature harbours the need to kill that which necessarily appears in language and thereby becomes understandable. This is the part played by referential narrative, which, because it relates to the way humans organize meaning, expresses things in clear, comprehensible language. On the other hand, there is the slope of literature that carries within it thoughts about things before they are subjected to the "refusal" of language. In this light, we may view literature as an attempt to awaken the reality of things (Critchley 71).

If we look at the first slope of literature (language as refusal), we can say that the words "revolution" and "terror" are key in Blanchot's exploration. If a person calls literature "the reign of terror" it is because the completed ideal of literature is in fact revolution, that moment in history when understanding is negated, when *life endures death and maintains itself in it*. In this way, life can "gain from death

the possibility of speaking and the truth of speech." This, Blanchot
further claims, is the question that seeks to pose itself in literature –
the "question" that is its essence.

But what does literature have in common with those revolutionary moments in history when *life endures death and maintains itself
in it?* Perhaps an answer to this is contained in language. Language,
Blanchot writes, is reassuring at the same time as it is disquieting.
When we speak we control matters, and we do so in a satisfying way.
We in fact control everything, with the exception of that which is
nameless. In the wake of this, we might assume that the disturbance
created by language is rather to be found in the unnamable rather
than in that which is named. Is the ability to name things not com-
forting? This actually happens in a contradictory manner. The disturbance caused by language comes, in fact, from the act of naming.
This is because words *proffer* meaning by *emptying* it from things.
As an example of this, Blanchot names the word "woman": If someone says "this woman," he thereby deprives that woman of her reality; she loses her flesh and blood and becomes *distant*. The word is
the *distance* of existence; the word is her *nothingness*. In other
words, the word is that which *replaces* the thing that has lost its
existence. The licence to speak is a strange one, Blanchot adds:
"When I speak, death is speaking in me" ("Literature and the Right
to Death" 322–3).

Does Bergsson's *The Mind's Tormented Love* show the reign of
terror Blanchot points to, which arouses comfort and distress simultaneously? Let us again consider the fragment of this narrative
wherein the diarist discusses the difference between his friend's flesh
and blood and the words written about him:

> As soon as I took up writing, it was instantly easier to be with
> him in word than in act. Words can only give you what might be
> called the dust from the drumbeat. They do not serve us the
> drum itself, its girth, its weight, nor the palm of the hand that
> pounds hard on the skin, because words are signs for the mem-
> brane with which we satisfy ourselves when we lack what they
> refer to. They warm the mind but are hardly more than compen-
> sation for the fact that one cannot – fortunately – attain the ma-
> terial object or the world. That is simply impossible. If we were
> granted everything without a struggle, language would be lost

and we would grunt instead, ceaselessly drawl and curse the same way animals do, especially the bull.

With words, almost everything is possible but not obtainable. (48–9)

It is with words and in words that humankind touches its wound: we understand that we cannot actually acquire the object and the world. At the same time, we know that, without words, there is no such thing as ourselves, the world, and existence. Such is the human condition.

What is this "right" literature has? In Blanchot's mind, the right of literature is found in the revolutionary freedom of death.[18] If this is correct, death in literature contains a certain *potentiality*. The two slopes of literature and their dual right to death are of major concern in this context. Literature is marked not only by a freedom that opens the way to death both in and with language but also the thought (which has certain boundaries) of things before they are subjected to the "negation" of language. The latter is the attempt to awaken the *reality* of things, and literature is where this happens: "Literature seeks this moment of existence or Being prior to the advent of the Subject and its work of negation."[19]

As Critchley points out about Blanchot's terms, we can discern in the second of literature's slopes (the thoughts about things before they are subjected to language) a fate that Blanchot considers worse than death; that is, the impossibility of death. Confronted with this unknown free and silent existence, the unknown and unknowable "I" is filled with terror when faced with its endlessness. The dual nature of literature comes about in this way due to the dual nature of death. He or she who writes is sundered between these two slopes: "*death as possibility and death as impossibility*" (Critchley 78).

What is the search for the possibilities in literature headed towards, then? If we consider the ideas of Blanchot, the paradox of human expression brings about not only humanity's misfortune but also its hope and mission. Death, he asserts, ends in existence. This is humanity's hope and mission, where the *nothingness* of existence is what creates meaning in the world: it is the nothingness of existence that enables the creation of the world within the human being. This is also the source of humanity's misfortune, where death is borne in humanity and meaning rests in the nothing of existence because of humanity. In order to acquire an understanding of ourselves and our world, we need to refuse ourselves our own existence by making death possible (Blanchot, "Literature and the Right to Death," 330). In spite of an all-embracing mortality, we nonetheless discern in modern literature the *possibility of reality*.

Another phenomenon makes a difference in this context, and it concerns more than the existence and aesthetics of language in modern literature. If Blanchot is right when he writes that the original ambiguity of meaning – which is lodged deep inside every single word and lies in wait for us there as condemnation and as joyance – is in itself the *source* of literature, and that it has *chosen* literature as its own form, then we may suppose that its expression is not a new thing and that literature has been its target long before modern times.

In chapter 3, I discuss historical aspects of the expression of this ambiguity. Next, however, by exploring a few fragments from the history of aesthetics in Iceland, I address how Icelandic culture responds to the above creativity.

Fragments from the History of Aesthetics in Iceland

In *The Mind's Tormented Love*, the diarist protagonist at one point discusses Icelandic logic and how a "capricious mentality" replaces a way of thinking that might be marked by "diversity and questioning" in an isolated nation. The inspiration for these reflections is his observations concerning his friend's homosexuality:

> When I was young, this was called a "sexual mistake," a term that was probably coined out of Icelandic logic and insight rather than out of superstition: arising from a kind of loyal faith in the connection between human sexual love and the love of god, and therefore thought of in the same terms as heresy, which is to have the wrong religion in relation to what is official and considered the right one, therefore making it a mistake. It is impossible to expect anything else from an isolated nation, other than that it create a language that suits its own thinking and understanding, a language that is lacking in nuance, except insofar as it appears in poetry that is tied to nature and the weather, since these two are almost the only thing an isolated nation has as its own, or at least what it confronts every day, thus the people acquire a capricious kind of mentality instead of a diverse, questioning attitude. (Bergsson, Mind's Tormented Love, 163)

These are the reflections of a character in a novel, let us not forget. However, if we consider Bergsson's dialogue with Icelandic culture and society, and how it is interwoven with aspects of European cultural and narrative history, then we see in this textual fragment an attitude that frequently appears in his fiction and essay writing; that is, that there is no shortage of logic and capricious thinking in the country, but diversity of opinion and inquiring minds are rare.

If the opinion of the diarist is not in itself based on "Icelandic logic" and a "capricious mentality," then those who wish to investigate Bergsson's discourse will have reason to pause. It is certainly tempting to do what some readers of his works in Iceland have done, which is not only to attribute these opinions to the author himself but also to spice them with various additions, all according to what happens to be fashionable thinking at that particular moment. Here, I do not do that. To the contrary, I go along with the opinions of his narrator. However, in order to follow such a line of thought, I need to take a look at certain elements of the history of aesthetics in Iceland. In particular, I look at the ideas of a few specific major poets and critics of poetry and Icelandic culture from the romantic era to the present day. I discuss the ideas of Grímur Thomsen, Benedikt Sveinbjarnarson Gröndal, Sigurður Nordal, Sigfús Daðason, and Guðbergur Bergsson. It appears that Bergsson's ideas about Icelandic culture and society are not entirely unique in the history of Icelandic culture, nor are his ideas about Iceland's reaction against an aesthetics that does not fall in with traditional ideas about the nature and vocation of literature.

But first it is necessary to introduce the circumstances. It was in the university town of Jena where the ground was laid for the romantic movement in Germany. Jena is in the former Austro-Germany and lies close to Weimar, the town Goethe made famous, and it may be appropriate to begin right there, especially if we consider a suggestion that has been raised already: that the Jena-romantic inheritance has not entirely disappeared from modern literature.

ROMANTICISM IN JENA AND IN ICELAND

In the fall of 1799, some friends met in Jena and lived together for a time. They were the brothers August Wilhelm and Friedrich Schlegel, their wives Caroline Schlegel and Dorothea Veit-Schlegel, and their friend Ludwig Tieck. Novalis lived not far from them and was a frequent guest. For the most part, this group laid the cornerstone for the romantic movement in Germany, and it did so in a relatively short time. Their journal *Athenäum*, which came out in the years 1798, 1799, and 1800, bears in its pages much of what is important for an understanding of the artistic and philosophical roots of the romantic movement in Germany. This group of friends was also particularly well read and creative: August Wilhelm was a textual scholar, translator, and also wrote on literary history; his brother Friedrich was a poetic theorist and philosopher; Caroline was a writer who staged literary salons; Dorothea did the same; Ludwig Tieck wrote fairy tales; and Novalis was the poet of the group.

If you leaf through *Athenäum*, you find fragments of texts such as: "The spirit is equally mortal, whether it finds itself within a system or without. In the end the spirit has to combine the two";[1] "It is not possible to be a philosopher; it is only possible to become a philosopher. As soon as someone calls himself a philosopher, he stops being one";[2] "What happens in literature never happens or always happens. Otherwise it is not true literature. No one should believe that what happens in literature is real";[3] "The definition of poetry can only be about what poetry should be, not what it was or really is; otherwise it would sound briefly like this: poetry is what people called poetry, sometime, somewhere."[4] These fragments reveal ideas that are characteristic of this group. The same goes for the following quotation:

> Romantic poetry is forward looking and classic. Its ambition is
> not only to combine all disparate types of literatures and bring
> poetry into contact with philosophy and oratory. Soon it will also
> mix together, melt into one another, poetry and prose, ingenuity
> and criticism, art and nature, make poetry alive and social, and
> make life and society poetic, make mischief poetic and fill the
> various forms of art with subject matter of all kinds, soothe them
> and liven them up with waves of humour. Only it can do as the
> epic can: function as the mirror of all the world, put our own
> times into words. But it can also glide in between what is shown
> and what should be shown, free from all palpable and subjective
> concerns, on wings of poetic meditation, able to multiply itself as
> in an endless row of mirrors; yes, that is its actual nature, that it
> is always becoming and it never has become. No theory can ex-
> plain it fully and only the most prophetic critique will dare to
> define its vision. It alone is endless, as it alone is free and admits
> as its first law that the poet's will submits to no law.[5]

These are the moments of history that Simon Critchley discusses in Lecture 2 of his book *Very Little … Almost Nothing*. There he also talks about the trace of romanticism in modern times not by

deconstructing the ideas, theories, and creations of the Jena circle
but, rather, by rethinking the difficulties this group was facing: What
is a meaningful life? What can give life value after religious foundations have been rejected? How to address the crisis of modernity?
Critchley thinks of the continuity of the conviction of this group –
that only art can help people when they are faced with the confusions of modern times, that art and a continuously developing
literature can become a kind of gospel for humanity and culture
(Critchley 100). This dream did not come true. Jena romanticism has
also been called an art movement without art works.

The aesthetic mistakes of the Jena group have been viewed as being connected to their political mistakes, but the demand for the
absolute rule of aesthetics was inextricable from the political scene
of their day. Here, the group's fall was no less hard. The life of
Friedrich Schlegel bears witness to this. In Blanchot's interpretation,
the atheist, the radical, the prophet of the spirit of the free individual
– this man who surprised Goethe by making him feel "less intelligent, less learned and free" – became, a few years later, a "fat philis-
tine" in Vienna. Blanchot further asserts not only that romanticism
came to a dreary end but also that it could not help but do so. In his
opinion, romanticism is "freedom without realization" (*Infinite
Conversation* 352–3).

But how to interpret the contributions of this group? Is it the incredibly creative beginning moments that explain them? Or the
dreary end? Critchley chooses a third option: his suggestion is that
the era of romanticism is not of the past. The current era is still in the
phase the romantics created and left behind, and the experience of
romanticism is – to some degree – an experience in which modern
humanity is still participating. But what does he mean by this?

Critchley perceives a possibility that allows him to introduce and
defend another version of romanticism, a version he calls "unworked
romanticism." The fact, Crtichley writes, "that romanticism does not
work, rather than being a proof of weakness, will be interpreted instead as a sign of its strenght. Its very weakness is its strength" (113).
This version of romanticism does not exclude naiveté. Quite the contrary. It will be "rooted in a self–consciousness of naiveté. That is, an
acute awareness of failure and the limitedness of thought" (ibid.). Such
could be the still present contribution of what Critchley calls "unworked romanticism." I have already mentioned how this acknowledgment concerns both contemporary philosophy and literature and

is more in tune with the times than is the dream of an aesthetic revolution pertaining to life and culture. The acceptance of finitude can also breathe some life into the "relation" between thought and everyday life in modern literature (ibid.).

The group of Icelandic nineteenth-century poets that has been linked with romanticism has in common with the Jena group that it did not create a literary work that became gospel for its culture. It may also be claimed that the aesthetic revolution inspired by the Icelandic poets, like that inspired by the Jena group, came to a sorry end, although in a different way.[6] However, the difficulties the Icelandic group faced were not the same as those the Jena group faced. Nor was the former an actual "group" in the same sense as was the Jena group. The ambitions of this group were diverse, perhaps as diverse as the poets themselves. As is well known, among nineteenth-century Icelandic poets the Fjölnismenn (the men of Fjölnir) came closest to what might be called a group of romanticists. In their journal Fjölnir it is possible to distinguish clear aims in the areas of poetry and beauty. Here, I discuss the ideas of these poets regarding aesthetics, beauty, and literary heritage. However, I place greater emphasis on those ideas that, in the spirit of the Jena group, trace their origins to the philosophy of art and beauty. It is worth investigating these Icelandic poets in light of how they see themselves within their literary tradition. It is this tradition that reveals the special difficulties with which some romantic poets in Iceland were struggling.

If we take into account the ideas of later poets and novelists, such as Sigfús Daðason and Guðbergur Bergsson, it appears that they faced the same predicament as did earlier writers. Do the roots of this conflict perhaps rest in the notion of the importance of the Icelandic literary heritage – a notion that acquired resonance in the nineteenth century and, thanks to the critic Sigurður Nordal, made great headway in the twentieth century?

WHERE EUROPE ENDS AND THE PLANET'S WASTELANDS BEGIN

In the introduction to the first issue of the journal Fjölnir, which came out in 1835, written and published by Tómas Sæmundsson, Jónas Hallgrímsson, Brynjólfur Pétursson, and Konráð Gíslason, we find the following words: "Some think the [sense of beauty] is rather

weak among us Icelanders" (*Fjölnir* 1 [1835]: 12). The unavoidable
problem the nineteenth-century Icelandic poets, all of whom were
fascinated by romanticism, had in common is no doubt their compatriots' "weak sensibility" for beauty. For how do you awaken a
whole nation to thoughts of beauty? In the same introduction these
four men offer their answers to this question. In the spirit of romanticism, the men of *Fjölnir* urge Icelanders to consider their creative
inheritance – their literature. But to what end? "Whoever reads the
Sagas of Icelanders carefully must necessarily acquire a burning passion for his native country, or else he does not understand them
rightly" (*Fjölnir* 1 [1835]: 2).

Although we see here the well known influence of romanticism on
the importance of the idea of a "national trait" as part of one's cultural heritage, it may be said that, in Iceland, the "burning passion
for ... native country" concerns beauty and literature in a specific
sense. The struggle for independence and its relation to literature is
obviously part of this concern. Here, however, we have the appearance of the idea of a correct reading of the Sagas of Icelanders – a
notion that, in itself, cannot be called romantic (as in Jena romanticism) but that could have become embroiled in the discussion of
romanticism and literature in Iceland.

But what is the beauty to which Icelanders are supposed to awak-
en their senses? Is beauty in nineteenth-century Iceland perhaps
overly tied to pragmatic concerns and utilitarian themes? And this at
the same time as beauty is acquiring independent value in other
European countries? What do the men of *Fjölnir* say in their introduction to the first issue of their journal?

Beauty is an objective these men claim they will always have and
will never relinquish. However, the same applies to what is *practical*,
what is *true*, and what is *reasonable*. In their ideas about beauty,
therefore, we can see at work what was later viewed as characteristic
of this group: the tradition of utilitarianism – a tradition that is in
large part based on the inheritance of Enlightenment – blends with
the more romantic notion that beauty is by nature independent and
so propitious that all people should desire it for its own sake.

In Chapter 3 I briefly discuss Ástráður Eysteinsson's ideas on the
Fjölnir group and how they "rewrite" the literary heritage in the
spirit of romantic nationalism and place the beauty of the land on a
pedestal.[7] But what does the next generation of romanticists think of
this same heritage? Just like the men of *Fjölnir*, one might say that

Grímur Thomsen and Benedikt Sveinbjarnarson Gröndal also struggle with the apparent lethargy of Icelanders when it comes to the
notion of beauty. They are also bound to the romantic notion that
nations are obliged to nurture their creative heritage; however, it
seems that their thinking about beauty and literature has greater
aesthetic depth than the provisional, regional, and national understanding would allow. In fact, for these two men, aesthetic consid-
erations are independent of other things. Perhaps Gröndal's ideas
are more revolutionary, if not more "Jena-like," than are those of
Thomsen. This is evidenced in Sigurður Nordal's 1924 essay
"Continuity in Icelandic Literature":

> Medieval Icelandic Literature is still the most prominent of all
> the Nordic countries. Ibsen and Strindberg will become anti-
> quated and fade, like Oehlenschlager and Tégner, but the Sagas
> of Auðunn and Hrafnkell are as fresh now as they were in the
> thirteenth century. It would take a long time for us to bridge the
> gap that would occur, should we lose these works, and they
> would never be fully restored to us.
>
> It is thanks to the continuity of our literature ... that our poets
> have taken so few side roads in the last centuries, and their work
> has come under much less foreign influence than is the case with
> other nations. Much of the romantic literature of Germany and
> Scandinavia is barely readable for modern men, but among
> Icelanders it was Benedikt Gröndal (the Younger) alone who
> allowed that movement to put him off balance to such a degree
> that few of his poems are viable. In this way, a healthy conserva-
> tism has rescued many a mighty talent from getting lost, and this
> is invaluable for a small nation. We cannot afford to have our
> writers sway and bend like straws in the wind of any and every
> literary fashion that blows across the northern seas and, in so do-
> ing, allow their works to be useless for future generations. (36)

Nordal's aim here, as the title of his essay indicates, is to explain
what he calls "the unbroken continuity in our language and literature from the origins of Icelandic settlement to our day," or up to the
third decade of the twentieth century. But are the *Fjölnir* men then
not, in Nordal's estimation, those who preached the correct reading
of the Sagas of Icelanders and thereby obtained what they saw as a
burning passion for the fatherland?

What is seen to most endanger the continuance of the Icelandic literary tradition in the literary output of the poets of the *Fjölnir* group,
in Nordal's mind, is "foreign romanticism." Jónas Hallgrímsson and
Bjarni Thórarensen were influenced by this, Nordal writes. However,
eventually, both find "the Icelandic sources" preferable to foreign romanticism. According to Nordal, the living literature of the nation,
with which these poets were raised, was directly connected "to the
poetry of the ninth and tenth centuries. If anything else were the case,
their poems would have become cold stylizations, pale imitations,
which the nation would not recognize as their own and they would
have served no constructive purpose" (31).

Such comments as those by Sigurður Nordal concerning the destructive influence of romanticism on Icelandic literature were not
unique among scholars in Iceland in the 1930s. There is, for instance,
Einar Ólafur Sveinsson, who, in the essay "Icelandic Literature after
the Reformation," explains why there is little romantic excess in
Icelandic literature: "Iceland is not well suited to cradling sickly
dreams" (143).[8] In the same essay, Sveinsson says: "There is no need
to discuss here the romantic movement in other countries. The only
thing that matters is what concerns Iceland" (142). I will not engage
in a further discussion of Sveinsson's ideas; however, it has been
argued that it is easy to explain his comments on romanticism from
the point of view of his cultural politics, which was distinguished by
a "repulsion for foreign influences." Sveinsson judged Icelandic literature primarily on the basis of its "national value" (Óskarsson,
"What Is Romanticism," 115).

But time goes on, and nowadays scholars discuss romanticism in
Iceland in a less restricted fashion. Þórir Óskarsson's research on
romanticism is evidence of this new attitude.[9] The same can be said
of Svava Jakobsdóttir's research on the poetry of Jónas Hallgrímsson
in her collection of essays entitled *Skyggnst á bak við ský* (*A Glance
behind the Clouds*).[10] In his book *Arfur og umbylting* (*Heritage and
Upheaval*), Sveinn Yngvi Egilsson discusses not only the reign of the
romantic movement in Iceland, and what Nordal calls the "loss of
balance," but also the manifold and creative interactions among the
romantic writings of Benedikt Gröndal, Jónas Hallgrímsson, Grímur
Thomsen, and Gísli Brynjólfsson.

Although times have changed when it comes to discussing romanticism in Iceland, we nonetheless encounter resistant ideas, such as:
"Little remains of the poetry [of Gröndal], who is very romantic on

the one hand, and at the same time a little out of touch with Icelandic reality" (Thorsson, "Benedikt Gröndal," 415). This comment is to be found in a book entitled *Þjóðskáldin* (*The National Poets*), which offers a selection of the literature of the nineteenth century. Here we meet the notion, long-held in Iceland, that literature should answer the call of a given reality in a specific way. But is that in the spirit of romanticism? Is what the poet says, that Iceland is where Europe ends and the planet's wastelands begin, perhaps true?[11]

GRÍMUR THOMSEN: AN ATTEMPT ON ISOLATION

Grímur Thomsen's ideas on poetics are wide-ranging. His literary essays, which first appeared in Danish in the 1850s, bear witness to this.[12] For some reason these essays, which Þórir Óskarsson calls "the most ambitious literary scholarship of the nineteenth century," never became a model for other Icelanders ("What Is Romanticism?" 112). Could they have been too foreign in their aesthetics?

At one point, Sigurður Nordal expresses his views on Thomsen's style and presentation. In an essay on Thomsen's master's degree (which was on Byron and which he wrote at the University of Copenhagen), Nordal maintains that the dialogue form suited him better than the essay form, "for he was sometimes ponderous, abstruse, and even unclear, as if the fog of German philosophy, which he has wallowed in, covered over his words." Nordal further asserts that, if Thomsen had wanted to, he could have lectured on English literature at the University of Copenhagen. Then he would most likely have "slowly come to a style and presentation in the Anglo-Saxon taste and spirit, which was much more suitable to the nature of an Icelander than the romantic philosophy of the Germans" (Nordal, "Master's Thesis of Grímur Thomsen," 155).

Here we discern certain aesthetic provisions. But what was Thomsen himself thinking? As is mentioned in the translator's foreword to Thomsen's essay collection, *Íslenskar bókmenntir og heimsskoðun* (*Icelandic Literature and World View*), Thomsen's essays were not written for Icelandic readers but, rather, to create an interest among Nordic people in Icelandic literature. In particular, they were written to make it known to Nordic writers that they have a common heritage and to encourage them to write in that tradition. Sveinn Yngvi Egilsson discusses this in his book *Arfur og umbylting* (*Heritage and Upheaval*) and points out how, in his essays, Thomsen

promotes the literature of his own people. He was patriotic; however, his ambition reached across not just Iceland but the whole of
the Nordic world (Egilsson, *Arfur og umbylting*, 121). In the spirit
of the writing style of the times in which Thomsen wrote, the purpose of his essays was to show his contemporaries the development
and validity of medieval literature. As Sveinn Yngvi Egilsson maintains, however, what is just as important as the medieval literature is
the influence of the aesthetics of the German philosopher G.W.F.
Hegel (113–24). Hegel's tripartite differentiation of art into romantic, symbolic, and classical, according to its form and subject matter,
is clearly evident in Thomsen's writings on literature.

In "Sérkenni islenzurz bc'kmenntz" [The Character of Icelandic
Literature], Thomsen discusses the special features of Icelandic literature by comparing its subject matter and form to what is found
in ancient Greek literature. Just as Nietzsche would do later (he was
only just born when Thomsen was publishing his essays), Thomsen
inquires knowledgeably into the notion of beauty as it appears in
relation to religion and philosophy. Later, in *The Birth of Tragedy*,
Nietzsche compares ancient Greek and Christian cultures, but
Thomsen writes on the difference between medieval Icelandic and
ancient Greek literature. His attitude towards his own literary heritage is, in brief, not tied to any form of nationalism. Nor does he go
on about the beauty of Iceland. It is possible to see here the notion
that the literary heritage of Iceland is important but in a more literary context than we find in the introduction to *Fjölnir*.

What Thomsen sees in Icelandic literature are proud feelings of
freedom and independence, which have their counterparts in romanticism: "Nordic literature is not, therefore, in any way rooted in classical literature; quite the contrary, it can in truth be called heathen
romanticism" ("Character of Icelandic Literature" 85). Thomsen
further asserts that a belief in the individual's power and importance
is a mainstay of medieval Nordic people. For this reason, the Nordic
person suffers alone and in silence, and never wavers. The suffering
endured in this image of humanity is therefore silent; it is a "stoic
suffering." And it is this view of life that informs "the entirety of the
Nordic man's activity and life" (67).

Such an introverted way of being is, in Thomsen's view, proof of
the spiritual nature of our ancestors: those who sensed the incompleteness of the word. What differentiates the Nordic spirit from the
Greek spirit is, therefore, not only the Nordic's passion for quiet

fortitude (or a still, smouldering anger) but also a certain unflinching and overriding will, which Thomsen calls *kyrrleiksástríða* (passion for tranquility). The main characteristic of Nordic passion is, in Thomsen's view, self-restraint: "Nothing is wasted of that precious passion, and instead of squandering it with words and expressions, [to the Nordic] words are much more likely to be irritants" (61). Nordic passion is not always silent, though. And here Thomsen points to an obvious feature of the Sagas of Icelanders – the obligation to exact revenge. This is the "shadow side of passion," Thomsen says, "which even we Christian men must admit has artistic merit when looked at apart from moral law." Yes, this "shadow side" acquires a more positive sheen when we remember that "blood revenge was an obligation in the society of our forefathers" (61–2).

But what about beauty? What are Thomsen's ideas on that subject? According to him, the belief system of Nordic people did not lead to coarseness and immorality. Quite the contrary: it created an exaggerated self-restraint and modesty. In light of this, Thomsen comments that self-restraint, modesty, and dignity, along with elegance of movement and a mental excellence that knows how to express itself, combine to form a beautiful image of humanity in medieval Icelandic literature: "The Sagas of Icelanders also invariably emphasize this and most often tie it to physical beauty and personal gracefulness, and the same sagas are not deficient in courageous and strong heroes with greater muscle mass than is necessary for true beauty, but these personages' excellence consists in dignified and proud manly behaviour" (69). In this connection, Thomsen also mentions the admiration Nordic people had for "beautiful dress, shining amour, bright and elegant weapons ... [as well as] cleanliness and sportsmanship" (69–70). It is here, Thomsen proposes, that ideas about the "beauty of the individual nature" have their roots.

The worship of beauty, Thomsen says, never became as prominent in the Nordic countries as it did in Greece: "This the depth of the Nordic spirit prevented, as well as the hard and barren nature" (70). The depth of the Nordic spirit and the hard and barren nature of the North turned our ancestors' minds inward, Thomsen continues, trained them to be forbearing and to withstand suffering, while the Greeks were blessed with a mild and gentle nature and, thus, were more in tune with beauty and with themselves. Nordic people, on the other hand, learned from the chill sky and barren, stony ground to "acquire control over nature and simultaneously over themselves" (70).

But what are the criteria of beauty, in Thomsen's mind? What is beauty? It appears that his ideas on beauty have a broad base:

> The Nordic spirit is severe and lofty when it comes to serious-
> ness, but boorish when it comes to amusement. It is comprehen-
> sive and therefore branches out to both sides of the Greek notion
> of beauty and harmony. There is no need to answer the question
> here whether and to what degree this is the most elevated idea of
> beauty, or whether it is not possible to find another, even higher,
> notion, wherein a moral sensibility might sunder this harmony
> but, thereby, clarify beauty. One thing can be maintained, which
> is that literature, where there is a continuous emphasis on psych-
> ological characteristics, more or less de-emphasizes strict markers
> of artistic requirement; that is, if those psychological characteris-
> tics are of an abnormal nature. As is the case with Shakespeare,
> such literature breaks down the walls of criticism. (77)

I take up this thread later. For now, however, I want to point out that, in his discussion of newer Icelandic literature, Thomsen is sympathetic towards the need for isolation. He claims that, although it is clear that there had been a decline in new Icelandic literature, and that for some time there has been an ominous deterioration of the language, there are exemplary writers who, through their superb devotion, have enabled the medieval Icelandic spirit to thrive in new literary garb. And he holds that modern culture can easily be expressed in the words of Old Norse. We may thank the geography of the country for this and also the custom of teaching children to read Icelandic literature at a young age and, thereby, to take in the medieval spirit with their mother's milk. Thus, Thomsen sees modern Icelandic literature as a continuation of medieval and, as such, deserving of the attention of other Nordic people. As for the new Icelandic poetry (and here Thomsen mentions Eggert Ólafsson and Jónas Hallgrímsson):

> It is to some degree modern in construction because of the need
> to relate to new social requirements, wherein the poetic soul has
> had to dwell, rather too long, within the conflict between medieval
> and modern times. The new German degeneracy, even the echoes
> of Herweg and Heine, has found its way to the distant and iso-
> lated island nation, although admittedly only as a fleeting, poetic

temperament. But this is only a passing phenomenon, because nothing is more incompatible than the expression of suffering in the neurotic sullenness of modern times and the powerful sorrow of the Nordic mind. (81)

As we can see from this text, unlike what we find in the writings of the *Fjölnir* group, the emphasis is not on the love of country. Still, Thomsen is not very impressed with "newer" streams of romanticism, and, in fact, we see here a similar disposition towards modern literature as that expressed by Sigurður Nordal in "Continuity in Icelandic Literature."

Thomsen's essay "On the Character of the Old Northern Poetry" is no less noteworthy for what it says about Thomsen's own philosophy. It begins with a critique of the philosophy of religion and the aesthetics of Hegel: "It is remarkable that Hegel, who said that the idea of a philosopher required that he knew everything, and who pretended himself 'to know everything,' neither makes any mention of the Northern mythology in his *Philosophy of Religion*, nor of Northern poetry in his *Æsthetics*" ("On the Character of the Old Northern Poetry" 45). Despite the fact that the poetry of the North has no place in Hegel's "scientific classification of poetry," Thomsen continues, the German philosopher describes all its properties in an essay on romantic poetry. According to Thomsen, these properties are "the energetic overbearing will" and the "deep reserved mind" ("On the Character of the Old Northern Poetry" 45).

When discussing romantic literature, it is, in Thomsen's estimation, not possible to miss the fact that it is grounded in something other than, but of equal importance to, a Christian foundation. According to Thomsen, you would have to search long and hard to find a Christian spirit in *Macbeth* and *Richard III* – and it is certain that Shakespeare was rather more of a Northern poet than he was a Christian when he conceived of and developed the characters in his plays. Hamlet, for example, is "much more a product of Northern reserve, with all its passion and taciturnity, with all its eloquence, than of a Christian's struggling self–reflection" (46).

I assess Thomsen's interpretation of the character of Hamlet shortly, but what does he say about beauty in this essay? Here is a fragment in which he draws together his ideas on beauty in Greek and Roman poetry, on the one hand, and in Old Nordic poetry, on the other:

Greek and Roman poetry is regular and harmonious; Northern
poetry is elevated and dissonant. In the former, spirit and form
keep pace with one another; in the latter, the spirit constantly
outruns and overrides the form. In the former, the tragic as well
as the comic elements keep within the limits of beauty; in the latter, sorrow is deepened into humour, and the comic becomes gro-
tesque. The Greek utters his passion in its fullness, he does not
even fear to express himself by inarticulate interjections. The
Northern character grows more silent as his passion increases;
being too well aware of the insufficiency of speech to exhaust his
passion or the inadequateness of the form to express the spirit,
he disdains to give vent to it. (49–50)

If it is possible at this juncture to distinguish the connection between
beauty and literature in Thomsen's thinking, we may see that his
ideas are broader and deeper than the burning passion for Iceland
that is supposed to be ignited by a reading of the sagas. The context
for Thomsen's ideas is in fact immensely vast, and it is far from being
an exaggeration to say that his essays are the most ambitious of their
kind in nineteenth-century Icelandic literary scholarship. At the
same time, however, certain difficult questions arise. We may, for
example, doubt the validity of Thomsen's theory of the silent
Northern character, who becomes more silent as his passion intensi-
fies; who senses acutely how the spirit cannot take any adequate
form; who understands the incompatibility of passion and suffering
so well that he finds it inappropriate to talk about it. We might also
ask about Thomsen's theories of the beauty of Northern literature
and how he uses this as a model for a literature that dispenses with
strict rules of artistic composition and is, as is the work of
Shakespeare, so beautiful that it causes "the walls of criticism to
fall." It was in fact Hamlet, was it not, who not only expressed his
discordant feelings but also philosophized excessively on the subject
of the eternal irrationality of existence.

Is it perhaps the desire for isolation, in spite of the multifarious
and far-from-Icelandic context, we see in Thomsen's ideas?

We find similar modes of thinking in Sigurður Nordal's *Íslenzk
menning* (*Icelandic Culture*), wherein he defends Icelandic literature
when it confronts "foreign" criticism. The scholar Henrik Schück
has, Nordal says, compared the descriptions of the hero in Homer
and in Nordic literature. And what does he find? The heroes of the

Iliad are, admittedly, braver, more beautiful, and wiser than ordinary mortals, but they are "always human" and are not embarrassed by their own emotions. The heroes of the sagas of the Icelanders would have found such shows of emotion contemptible. The Northern hero, in Schück's estimation, is crude and not presentable to civilized society. In the spirit of Grímur Thomsen, Sigurður Nordal maintains that this foreign scholar mistook "control of emotion for lack of feeling, but the very control of the emotions is the essence of culture" (Nordal, *Icelandic Culture*, 135).[13]

In the context of how the characters' emotional lives are shaped, but not exhausted, by a certain religious sentiment, the challenge of the saga heritage makes itself felt. Seen from the perspective of medieval European literature and culture, this sentiment appears to co-exist with, rather than fully belong to, a newly Christianized Europe. As is beautifully interpreted by Grímur Thomsen, the challenge originates in a literary/religious/philosophical tradition that cannot be viewed as a legitimate offspring of the Greco-Roman heritage. Therefore, the question of belonging arises in relation to European culture at large, as does the question of belonging in and of itself. Such is the richness of this passage provided by medieval Icelandic literature – a passage that seems to be remarkably unexplored. Can we perhaps blame this on a secular age?[14]

There are, of course, examples of exploration on this fantastic front. Guðbergur Bergsson's book of poetry, *Flateyjar–Freyr* (*Flatey–Freyr*) (1978), offers a glimpse into the fertile, yet scarcely recognized, region of European literary/religious/philosophical heritage, and that – as tends to be the case with this novelist and poet – in relation to the remains of the cultural heritage of the West in modern materialistic times. Another piece of literature comes to mind in this context. It was published in 1952, not long after the Second World War. Here, I am referring to Halldór Laxness's epic novel *Gerpla* (*The Happy Warriors*). While rewriting medieval heritage, Laxness does not offer a spare satire of everything medieval and remote. If anything, he seems to aim at the very heart of Western narrative tradition and history-making. When on errands in foreign lands, and seen from the perspective of the Greco-Roman heritage, the Icelandic hero and the Icelandic poet cannot shake off their displacement. However, in what could be termed Laxness's masterpiece, the saga characters are not held captive by the Northern tradition and do not come across as elements of the *obscure* on the edge of Europe.

Instead, while serving their foreign king with the requisite blind devotion, they become full-blown participants on the horrific battle-
fields of the newly civilized Christian Europe. Laxness's self-inflicted
conversion to Catholicism may have served him well in this demanding task, not to mention his close encounter with, and (for a while)
admiration of, Stalin's ideology.

For now, I will not belabour this issue further. We are, however,
left with the question of whether the view expressed by Nordal
might open a way into the history of Icelandic literature or whether
it isolates it so much, makes it so unique, that no Continental thought
can come near it. A related question is: how much influence do these
kinds of discourses have on the reception of modern literature as it
appears in Iceland?

What does Benedikt Sveinbjarnarson Gröndal have to say?

BENEDIKT SVEINBJARNARSON GRÖNDAL:
POETRY HAS NO FATHERLAND

A renowned Icelander and the author of many well-known novels
once said that the Icelandic nation was too complacent to know how
to make use of the "giant intellect" of Benedikt Sveinbjarnarson
Gröndal: "And when he sang, nothing but false notes echoed from
his harp among these pitiable people" (Laxness, "Úr drögum til
Gröndals stúdíu" [Sketches of Gröndal]). These words have an even
louder ring when we think of the exceptional contribution Gröndal
made to aesthetics in Iceland. As Matthías Viðar Sæmundsson points
out, Gröndal's aesthetics seriously reassess the attitude towards art
and the value of literature in Iceland's prolonged Age of Enlightenment; in his poetry, a huge stride is made towards modern perspectives (Sæmundsson, *Íslensk bókmenntasaga* [*A History of Icelandic
Literature*], 569). The essay by Gröndal under discussion here,
"Nokkrir greinir um skáldskap" (Some Fragments Concerning the
Poetic) from the year 1853, has been called "the first complete and
the most detailed discussion of aesthetics in Icelandic" (Óskarsson,
Undarleg tákn á tímans bárum [*Strange Signs in Time*], 108). In this
essay, Gröndal attempts to provide an overview of the various art
forms and to answer questions such as: What is beauty? What is art?
What is their nature and basis?

As is the case with Grímur Thomsen, Gröndal is fervently connected to the ideas of many eighteenth- and nineteenth-century

aestheticians and poets: men like Lessing, Kant, Hegel, Goethe, and
Schiller. But it is not only the new and "foreign" ideas that Gröndal
admires. His connection with the past is equally strong, whether it is
to ancient Greek or to medieval Northern thought and art. But what
are his ideas about beauty? What is his position towards ancient
Icelandic literature and its beauty? And what are his ideas concerning literature's whereabouts?

I first look at Gröndal's ideas concerning the great beauty of artistic and natural creation. On one side we see the "great beauty of
creation" when the "laws of nature rule" (61);[15] on the other side,
we see the beauty of creation when "fate intervenes in the course of
a man's life with mortifying power" (62). In a discussion of the former aspect, Gröndal mentions things like thunderstorms and asks
why we fear them. Could it be that all this "incredible visual play of
nature appears somewhat shocking to the human spirit" (ibid.)? And
wherein lies the beauty of the lion, if not in its fearsomeness? The
same can be said of the inclement sea, for "is its beauty not due to its
destructiveness?" (ibid.). As far as the terrible beauty of creation
when, with mortifying power, fate intervenes in a person's life,
Gröndal says that the power of fate makes us into "savage beasts
and oppresses us with torturous distress" (ibid.). We find it amusing
to read war stories, but "is this enjoyment not due to the winding
road mankind takes through ruin and perdition?" (ibid.).

With these comments in mind, we may read Gröndal's arguments
on medieval Icelandic literature and its beauty. He claims that *Gísli's
Saga* is only beautiful because there we see "a great hero undergoing
a desperate struggle with the grim and severe workings of fate" (62).
Gröndal's notions of beauty in the Sagas of Icelanders run parallel to
his ideas on the true nature of creation. In this matter he is undoubt-
edly radical, both theoretically and aesthetically. And his is a radicalism that builds more on romanticism than on the idea of the
magnificence of a literary heritage:

What we call national literature is best found in the nation that
gave rise to it; that is natural. The richer the individual artist's
feeling is for universally held spiritual needs – such needs surely
do exist – the less likely he is to bother about which national culture is being presented by his work; he only cares if the subject
matter and the form cohere. Poetry has no fatherland, except the
land of the human spirit, and its laws are eternal freedom. The

subject matter of a work therefore need not pertain to anything
national but, rather, something aesthetic. We see this in certain
poems, for example, which are so excellent that they find room
everywhere, and no one asks what century or what culture they
come from. This is because they are poetic and are therefore
raised above the limited framework of their time and place. That
is how it is with the poetry of Homer. But to elevate one's mind
to those higher levels requires a great deal of learning and high
intelligence. We should not criticize someone for not taking up
"national" subjects in his poetry, because that is wrong-headed.
It does us no good to make ourselves so isolated that we must
necessarily avoid others; no one will benefit from that, and, in
fact, this produces stagnation. (65–6)

Gröndal is certainly conscious of the difficulty national traits pose in
Icelandic literature, and, in one of his footnotes, he discusses the difference between Germany and Britain, on the one hand, and Iceland,
on the other. In a discussion of the "un-national" works of Shakespeare
and Goethe he says that these two poets have not been criticized for
being unpatriotic in their own countries; however, he adds, "our nation has not arrived at the level of thinking required for us to understand these works: in order for us to really understand them, we must
acquire the necessary learning, which is seldom a reality for the general public of any nation (and we do not even have a 'public')" (71).[16]

If we consider the ideas of Sigurður Nordal referred to above, the
Icelandic nation had not arrived at this perspective in the first half of
the twentieth century. Gröndal's rather modern idea that creativity
and poetry have no fatherland, other than the home of the spirit, does
not get a sympathetic ear from Nordal, one of the most influential
cultural prophets of Iceland in the twentieth century.[17] Gröndal runs
afoul of both Nordal and Thomsen when it comes to the comparison
between the value of medieval literature and the value of modern
literature. On this subject he says: "The beautiful Old Norse [is]
sonorous and noble," whereas language "as it is now" is more flexible
and adaptable, milder, but not as melodious and dignified. And
Gröndal refers to the ideas of Tégner (who is one of the poets Sigurður
Nordal consigns to the literary grave) in the following passage:

If we wish to find poets who can describe the force and power of
our emotions, passions and failings, then we must look to medieval times. But if we are seeking a skilfully rendered insight into

the human heart and wish to peer into its innermost secret caverns; if we wish to understand the recesses of the mind of crime, passion, hatred; then we must turn to the poets of our age. These three things – the time of history, the language spoken, and those who are living then – are all intricately connected. (66)

It appears that Gröndal's ideas on beauty and the roots and nature of creativity are guided more by a romantic perspective, in the spirit of the Jena group, than by the law of inertia that is found in the idea of the greatness of the Icelandic literary heritage. Not only is Gröndal current when it comes to the literary movements of the latter part of the nineteenth century, but he also shows the way towards one of the dominant literary themes of the latter half of the twentieth century: of all the manifold ideas concerning fiction and poetry that appeared in the twentieth century, we might say the idea of the connection between time, language, and the human being has been dominant – an idea that is particularly concerned with beauty (as in "Our time, our life – that is our beauty").[18] This is also the case in Iceland, even though the followers of this perspective still meet with some resistance.

The perspective outlined above, which is based on the idea of the three aspects of the aesthetic – namely, time, language, and the human being – is in opposition to deeply rooted traditional ideas about Icelandic literature. The latter combine the land, the nation, and the language with a historical woof, and little is spoken of either the subject of time or the human being. The law of lethargy (or inertia) that, for understandable reasons, is embedded in the traditional view of the importance of the Icelandic literary heritage may no longer be the dominant one in discussions of literature in twenty–first century Iceland. However, this traditional notion has undeniably left its mark, and, in a way, continues to shape the character of Icelandic aesthetics. If a few romantics have had to tolerate harsh criticism, then the discussion – or do we call it a battle? – is no less fierce when it comes to modern literature. This reality is evidenced by a famous twentieth-century essay, "In Defence of Poetry," by Sigfús Daðason, a poet and a critic. I now turn to a discussion of this piece.

SIGFÚS DAÐASON: "IN DEFENCE OF POETRY"

In the year 1952, the journal *Tímarit Máls og menningar* (*Journal of Language and Culture*) published the essay "Til varnar skáldskapnum" (In Defence of Poetry) by Sigfús Daðason. The stated aim of its author was to try to minimize the distance between the public and modern poetry, not by trying to create a general theory of poetry that would suit everyone but, rather, by confessing his helplessness before such a task. The essay is a defence of modern poetry in Iceland in the middle of the twentieth century as well as a meditation on, and critique of, generally held ideas concerning poetry and its reception in Iceland. Icelandic literature was, in the estimation of many of the critics Daðason gainsays, unattached to the development of European literature. It was said that "Iceland existed in its own time." In this context, Daðason writes: "'Iceland lives in its own time' does not have to mean the same thing as 'Iceland is always backwards,' but of course the latter statement can always be considered true."[19] And Iceland certainly has its own time if we ask where the country might be placed within what Daðason calls the adventurous conquests of European poetry in the first half of the twentieth century. What is even more surprising for Daðason is why some Icelandic critics and poets – the very people who should be bridging the gap between the past and modern times in art and in public perception – not only let themselves be confused by what might be called the "time warp" in poetic subjects but even defend it. Daðason divides his essay into four parts. In the first three sections he discusses: (1) the contention that "modern poetry is a profanation of the Icelandic poetic tradition"; (2) the question "of what concern is this to us?"; and (3) the proposition that modern art "won't fool us." In the fourth and final section, Daðason asks: "What is poetry?" and attempts to determine whether modern poems are poetry. Daðason, in fact, asks his readers' pardon for this upstart essay-act of his and claims to be a follower of the rule that poets should write poems, not essays about poetry. He also reminds the readers of just how slippery this subject is, arguing that the nature of poetry is such that it cannot be explained once and for all and proposing that perhaps it is only possible to speak of poetry in the form of negation.

In the first part of the essay Daðason confronts the view that "modern poetry is a desecration of Icelandic poetic tradition," and here he discusses the difficulties young Icelandic poets have in grappling with this tradition. The essence of Daðason's argument is this: "When the form has stagnated, there must always be a revolution, or else there will be death." Not all critics and poets in the mid-twentieth century entertained this aesthetic view. Daðason points to the commentary of Dr Björn Sigfússon in *Tímarit Máls og menningar* from the year 1951, in which the following lines appear:

> Alliteration, with or without alliterative sound, and some sort of traditional inflection, which alliteration helps maintain, will be a necessity for the Icelandic poetic ear in the next centuries. Poems that are not alliterative are remembered by no one, except as song lyrics, and very few of them are song-worthy. Poems that no friend of poetry cares to recall and take pleasure in memorizing are stillborn, and it helps them not a whit that they are loaded with "symbolism" and first-rate degenerate imagery. (Sigfússon cited in Daðason, "Defence of Poetry," 27)

According to Daðason, however, we write poems for living people and not for some sort of abstract concept like the "Icelandic ear for poetry." In this context, he writes, the following views of Dr Sigfússon – views that are most likely widely held in Iceland in the middle of the twentieth century – should be noticed: poems that people do not learn by heart are bad, and it must be concluded from this that poems are better if people recall them in their minds. Daðason criticizes this view and proposes another, which is that poetry is an event in the mind of the reader. For this reasoning he refers to the French poet and aesthetician Paul la Cour: "The poet baptizes you for an entrance into his mental world. That world will no longer get away from you. From that moment on, you are an accomplice" (Daðason, "Defence of Poetry," 29).

But what about the critic and scholar Sigurður Nordal? Does Daðason have a friend in him, aesthetically, in the middle of the twentieth century? The problems in, or posed by, modern Icelandic poetry, Daðason says, can hardly be discussed in an honest way without involving the views of Professor Sigurður Nordal. Here Daðason takes up Nordal's famous 1924 essay discussed above, "Continuity in Icelandic Literature." As Daðason points out, it was later that Nordal was to take up a broader and seemingly more just position towards Icelandic poetic history, especially towards the Eddas and the court poetry, than he does in this essay. Daðason points in particular to a fragment that gives the reader an insight into Nordal's notion of Icelandic literature, which is that it is a "treasure" that poets need to "preserve." But in this fragment, Daðason maintains, which can also be seen as "some sort of

exhortation and command to Icelandic poets," Nordal's conserva-
tism reaches a high point:

> The twentieth century is much wealthier spiritually than the
> tenth century; it can see further and penetrate deeper, both in the
> material and the spiritual realms. But the spiritual culture is often
> wanting in restraint and control. It is like a great river that cre-
> ates no waterfalls because it disperses itself out among the plains
> and marshes. Icelanders should fetch for themselves a portion of
> this wealth; let it bend to the bounds of their tongue and diction,
> tumble in the gorges of the bardic quatrains, so that all the force
> of their content is allowed fulfilment. (Nordal, "Continuity in
> Icelandic Literature," 37)[20]

Sigurður Nordal's ideas on the continuity of Icelandic poetry are,
however, less conservative when it comes to modern poetics. In fact,
Daðason discusses Nordal's conviction that resistance to change will
never contribute to the creation of great literature.

If we consider Daðason's interpretation, then it is apparent that
Nordal was conscious of the danger that comes with literary isolation. However, in comparison with Nordal, Daðason's position towards the same danger is more clear: he warns young poets in
Iceland against the "preservationist point of view" if it does not contain any new creativity. At the same time, he argues that what is
needed for "a second golden age" in literature in Iceland is an active
connection with the rest of the world. "Icelandic literature," Daðason
maintains, "cannot be a secluded thing in the corner of the world but
must be a fully qualified member, with responsibilities and obligations, of the culture of the whole world" ("Defence of Poetry" 33).

It is clear that, in the middle of the twentieth century, young poets
in Iceland had certain difficulties. As Daðason points out, the
Icelandic poetic tradition was a challenging, unsolved problem. Still,
he hoped that no one would be in doubt regarding what should be
done if there was a choice to be made between the old poetic forms
and poetry itself. Not only does this involve a precise aesthetic concept, but it also contains timeless wisdom for those who wish to
make poetry their life's work. The question, in fact, is whether passion for the old forms of poetry (which could also be called the will
to seclusion, as is mentioned in the above discussion of the inertia
that comes with an exaggerated idea of the importance of one's

literary heritage) becomes more important than the love of poetry
itself. If the answer is yes, then this love of old forms and the desire
for seclusion will, aesthetically speaking, inspire a new time warp.

In the second part of "In Defence of Poetry," Daðason discusses
the view of those critics who ask what modern poetry has to do with
Icelanders. In other words, he deals with those critics who choose
modern poetry as their subject but who lack knowledge and understanding of (as well as interest in) it. Here we may see a long-standing
problem, for if there are "chatterboxes" in Iceland, they not infre-
quently chatter about progressive literature. Daðason also struggles
with a viewpoint that has taken on various guises since the mid-
twentieth century: the belief that a work of art should be in the service of humanity's progressive efforts. In this regard he refers to
what Bjarni Benediktsson has to say about a poem by Eluard in a
review that appeared in *Þjóðviljinn* (*The Nation's Call*) in 1949.
Here Benediktsson asks: "For whom is this poetry intended?"

Here we discern how the critical reception of modern poetry in
Iceland splits into two types: those who attend to the form and those
who attend to the content. We should not forget that, in the mid-
twentieth century, the struggle with the everyday in art was a serious
subject, and this conflict was not necessarily the same in Iceland as it
was in Continental Europe. But instead of being tempted to speculate about the actual difference between the way in which historical
events like the First World War were experienced in Iceland and in
the rest of the world, Daðason argues against the narrow (and
narrow-minded) understanding of "actuality" in art and literature in
his country. And he reminds critics of modernism that, if art has lost
its lustre, it is because it has responsibilities to see to – that is, to
show us that we are human and to compel us to refuse to live only
half a life. This demand of Daðason's has more to do with a love of,
and respect for, the possibilities of art in a disillusioned world than
it does with the progressivism that was preached in *Þjóðviljinn* (a
leftist newspaper) shortly before 1950.

In the third part of "In Defence of Poetry," Daðason discusses
the view that "they [i.e., poets] will not fool us." Among other things,
he says:

One of the saddest things about the ongoing discussion of modern poetry is the many-headed unwillingness that often seems, in
a strange way, to have sprung out of both an inferiority complex

and a fear that sometimes comes close to hatred. When we look
more closely, we recognize this phenomenon. It is a fear of the
unknown, a fear of the new, a longing to keep things as they are,
in the habitual patterns men have accidentally fallen into. (38)

Daðason also discusses here the unfortunate tendency of some to get
on their high horse with regard to cultural topics by vilifying real
experimentalism in art. In the mid-twentieth century, it was possible
to read in the newspapers grand judgments of modern art on the
part of "right-thinking" people. As an example of this, Daðason cites
Eiður Bergmann's 1951 article in Þjóðviljinn, in which Bergmann
criticizes abstract art: "It is sprung from boredom, an unclear understanding of a crazy environment and a complete lack of understanding of, even repulsion for, those necessary and practical activities
that wait everywhere to be taken up. Paintings like 'Inner Landscape'
must appear to normal people as if they were an attempt to ridicule
healthy rationality."[21]

Here we see a disposition that probably moulded the ideas of
Icelandic people regarding the possibilities of art, both before and
after the times of Soviet criticism – disgust with what lies within
humanity. This disgust is part and parcel of a problem Daðason
rightly points to and that, to this day, remains unresolved: the lack
of space (i.e., the absence of the appropriate circumstances) for more
varied taste in art. With regard to art, around the middle of the
twentieth century Western societies had, as Daðason points out, already taken a step in the direction of consumerism. In his view, nowhere are people worse off in this regard than in Iceland, where, for
the most part, the young receive their arts education in movie houses
that show little other than "the dregs from the plate of American
cinema production" (40). It is the job of the arts, he says, to "help in
the formation of taste" (ibid.).

Daðason notes yet another contradiction that illuminates the different sense of time and history held by those who make poetry their
life work (poets and critics) and those who do not. In pointing to this
contradiction he makes an oblique reference to the law of inertia
(see above). Those in Iceland who are opposed to modern art talk
about how "obscure" it is, and this is how they explain away modern forms. But Daðason urges people not to withdraw from the task
of reading modern poetry, regardless of any possible reward:

You can do nothing else, inheritors of Icelandic literature. Icelandic literature is full to the brim of these obscure poems. But what treasures he acquires who has the wherewithal to break through, for example, the "Völundarkviða" [or] the poems of Grímur Thomsen. I think Icelandic readers who know our literature below the mere surface are in fact better able to understand modern poems than are foreigners, because of these characteristics of our own poetry. (41)

Here it is worthwhile to stop and ask: aesthetically speaking, is it a shallow knowledge of their own literary heritage that functions as a preventive to Icelandic readers? As Daðason reminds us, it is one thing to claim possession of aesthetic treasures in the form of poetry but quite another to "own" them (in the sense of having read them). Nations that do not bother to break through their own heritage are perhaps those who claim possession of their literature rather than reading it. Nations that do not read literature but are endlessly yammering on about its importance can become historically lost (again, aesthetically speaking). Works of art are, as Daðason points out, a cooperative venture between those who create and those who respond. Or, to put it another way, the responder/reader participates in the creative act. Even Jónas Hallgrímsson, Daðason says, is not all that meets the eye.

In the closing section of his essay, Daðason discusses the following questions: (1) what is poetry? and (2) is modern verse poetry? He writes: "I don't know what the nature of poetry is. Sometimes I feel like I know what its nature and its function are not" (41). Contrary to what some Icelanders believed around 1950, rhyme and rhythm are not the primary indicators of a poem. The aim and ambition of modern poets, Daðason proposes, has nothing to do with the secure but limited precedent set by the past. In fact, Daðason talks about how modern poets have attempted to remove the gap between truth and expression, between life and art. However, "since this can never be quite accomplished, they have tried to make the distance between as small as possible"(44). But what, then, is modern poetry? A direct expression of real experience, a barely muffled cry? According to Daðason, it is "a distrust of form, a distrust of language, a distrust of words, the demand that the poet has lived every word before it is set on paper: that is the way the modern poet works" (45).

In the middle of the twentieth century, this view was much polemi-
cized in Reykjavík.[22] Shortly before Daðason published "In Defence
of Poetry" in *Tímarit Máls og menningar*, there was, for example, a
student convention at which the poet Tómas Guðmundsson stepped
up to the lectern and reminded "modern poets" of the fact that what
was called modern poetry in Iceland was no longer modern in the
rest of the world. In a footnote, Daðason mentions that, if the way it
was reported in the newspapers was correct, he could see no reason
to take this convention seriously as "most speakers had nothing to
say and had no interest in anything but being clever." He is not concerned with wit when he speaks to his readers as follows:

> I mentioned the view at the outset that "Iceland lives in its own
> time," equally so in literature as in other areas. Yes, we can per-
> haps say that we are always a little behind. But I think a gene-
> ration of poets that has not paid much attention to what is
> happening in the poetry of other nations can hardly criticize the
> next generation for being backward. If the following generation
> is behind the times, then it may be precisely because the genera-
> tion before did not get any further. We invariably take over
> where the previous generation left off! (46)

MORE ON SIGURÐUR NORDAL AND
THE PECULIAR ICELANDIC DECLINE

What is it that, aesthetically speaking, sometimes confuses the sense
of time in Iceland's poets and critics? Is it the love of the stagnant
poetic forms, the surface knowledge of the literary heritage, or the
desire for isolation? Do all of these elements play a part in the en-
tropy that seems to have rooted itself in the idea of the greatness of
the nation's literary heritage? As the fragments of the history of aesthetics discussed above show, we ought to be able to see a connection here. Instead of possessing a dynamic passion for literature, its
freedom and the possibilities inherent in the creative act (which the
romantic thinker Friedrich Schlegel claimed could unite all hearts
and maintain within them the longing for life), this overly complacent nation appears to have fallen asleep at its post.

Sigurður Nordal is conscious of the danger that comes with excessive isolation. Certainly, as he says in his article on the continuity of
Icelandic literature, there is a danger in the willingness to open up

"our language and knowledge to any and all foreign drifters." But, he adds, it is no less hazardous "to wish to turn the land into a national barn, where no foreign ray of light is able to shine in, and where there is nattering and chattering about the Eddas and the Sagas for ages on end" (Nordal, "Continuity of Icelandic Literature," 35). In order to take the golden middle way between foreign influence and Icelandic culture, Icelanders need to have, above all else, "a great deal of knowledge and the right understanding of the history of our literature, from beginning to end, and especially of the literature of later centuries" (ibid.). He also talks about the passion for literature, which is a uniting force that did not just appear by chance, and says that we did not maintain our passion because we were asleep and isolated:

> It would not be far-fetched to claim that Icelanders are the most literary nation in the world – not in the sense that they have created the greatest literary works of all time, although they have achieved a great deal in that direction – but rather because no other nation has all in all given as much of its powers, so much of its passion and loyalty, to literature, and no other nation has turned to literature to the same degree for its comfort and strength. (34)

Turning back to Guðbergur Bergsson, the character Tómas Jónsson in Bergsson's novel *Tómas Jónsson Bestseller* has equally lofty notions regarding Iceland's worthiness among nations. His interpretation of the context for literature in the capital city, is, however, radically different from Nordal's: "I looked for a new antiquarian book seller, and a few years ago I had combed all the antique book dealers in the city, full to the brim of this particular Icelandic phlegmatic torpidity and self-love, that slow form of decline that sucks the energy out of what is supposed to be Iceland's 'leadership role in the world'" (94). This is the same character who asserts that "the only dangerous epidemic that assails this town is lethargy" (34).[23] These are the words of a character in a novel, we must not forget that. But what are the ideas of the author himself on literature? And what does he say about the attitude towards creativity in his country?

In the interview book *Guðbergur Bergsson Bestseller*, Bergsson at one point discusses his novel *Tómas Jónsson Bestseller,* modernism in literature, the trace of romanticism in contemporary literature, and his own view of aesthetics:

The book is two things at once: an act of "modernism" and a
satire of it as well. For me, so-called modernism in literature is a
great example of the freedom we have in this century. For within
modernism, the individual, the novelist, is allowed to do anything
as far as subject matter, style, and treatment of language are concerned, not to mention character creation or the deconstruction
of character in his novels. The same can be said for poetry.

Never in the history of the arts has the romantic disposition of
the individual for the self been as unconstrained and free as it is
in modernism. But at the same time, this freedom invites ridicule.
You may have noticed that a free man is also rather comic. He
often acts strangely. We laugh when things run out of bounds,
and freedom encourages this. An unfree man is in chains. I think
I have seen and known that condition.

Tómas Jónsson Bestseller is based on this observation or perspective of aesthetics. (Ásgeirsdóttir, *Guðbergur Bergsson Bestseller*, 115)

In the same book, Bergsson reacts to readers' responses to *Tómas
Jónsson Bestseller* in his own country. Here we see his ideas on technique, method, and unity:

After I started to translate South American literature, it was
claimed that I had created in my works a village similar to
Marquez's Macondo, only my village was Grindavík. Thus I was
supposed to have acquired my methods from him [Marquez]. It
served me little to point out that his novel *One Hundred Years of
Solitude* appeared several years after my novel *Tómas Jónsson
Bestseller*, and that you are influenced by what has appeared
before you and not what appears after you. We make our judgments based on what we see at home, and since *One Hundred
Years of Solitude* appeared in Icelandic after *Tómas*, people
thought they were right. That is how confused we are about
literature here on the "literary isle" itself. I hope Scandinavians
never hear about this; otherwise the same thing would happen to
the "well-read savage" here as happened to the god who failed.

But I think Icelandic readers did not have to go to South
America to find a model or a similar technique in novel writing.
This is also one of the many characteristics of the Sagas of
Icelanders: in them the same names come up again and again,
subject matter and events are woven together with the same

places and people's names. The method is Icelandic even though it is similar to what traditionally transpires in classical tragedy: to unite events, places, and times in the web of fate. (117)

In my final chapter I discuss the novel *Tómas Jónsson Bestseller* in greater detail, but the texts being referred to here can be read not only as the fruit of a subtle thinking about creativity and aesthetics but also as a continuing response to a rather narrow understanding in Iceland of what literature is or could become. As in the writings of both Benedikt Gröndal and Sigfús Daðason, here we see an Icelandic poet airing his ideas about literature and aesthetics in the context of the movements in the world at large; and he does so not by rejecting features of Icelandic literature and culture but, rather, by making a creative connection with them. In other words, Bergsson is conscious of the time warp that envelopes Icelandic aesthetics. In one of his essays he discusses Icelanders' sense of colour and time, and how both of these are tied to the natural light and the position of the country on the globe, and what effect this has had on them when looked at from the vantage point of classical European culture:

> The act of avoiding the colourfulness of nature is a flight into the colours of wishfulness and into the timelessness of dreams. That timelessness can be alluring, if it is demarcated in a poem, but it is disagreeable and turns into a time warp if it is forced onto reality, onto daily life and the attitude of the nation and its people, onto what is actual. Most aspects of our daily life are affected by this anachronism concerning time, which gives the aura of a clumsy and ill-made work of art that someone has cobbled together because his sense of time is off-kilter.
>
> We are on the other hand very fond of light and bright colours, which remind us of the spiritual or poetic character of the "endless" summer nights. It is because of the outer brightness and because of the position of the country on the globe that both our sense of colour and time in Iceland is confused when seen from the vantage point of classical European culture. (Bergsson, "'Time' in the Work of Art," 162–3)

In order to arrive at a better understanding of this idea of the Icelandic sense of time, how it influences life and art, and how it can be considered confused, I now turn to Bergsson's essay "Hugmyndir um fegurð" (Ideas on Beauty). Here we find many of Bergsson's ideas on beauty not only as they concern the sense of beauty in Iceland but also beauty itself, what it could be and from where it might originate.

GUÐBERGUR BERGSSON: "IDEAS ON BEAUTY"

As is the case with other writings on aesthetics in Iceland (i.e., the essays of Grímur Thomsen and Benedikt Gröndal), Bergsson's writings have been given scant attention. Perhaps the reason is that he, like a few other poets and writers, is not working in an aesthetic context that is specifically Icelandic. His writings can hardly support the attitude he says reigns in his country and that is forced not only upon the arts but also upon the daily life of the nation as a whole. In "Ideas on Beauty," Bergsson discusses this attitude. He discusses the perception of beauty, both in art and human behaviour, and how, in Iceland, little attention has been given to this subject. He also discusses the relationship between the sense of beauty and cruelty, the ethics of cruelty, and how the ethics of beauty may serve coercive purposes – a subject he claims often to address in his works (117). At the close of his esssay we read a parable from contemporary Iceland, in which the subject (according to the author) is a wide-ranging aesthetic experience.

Literary heritage comes up in this context, and this involves the particular time sensibility of Icelandic aesthetics: Icelanders of today do not concern themselves with beauty as a specific subject, either in the arts or in their behaviour. Normally, Bergsson continues, Icelanders are content with the connections they make between beauty and the land and, especially, their country of origin: "The Icelandic understanding of beauty is no more colourful than what we appear to have inherited over the ages from the *Njálssaga*, in which Gunnar is described as saying he thinks the mountainside is beautiful" (111). But how does Bergsson come to this conclusion? If we consider the way in which the saga hero Gunnar from Hlíðarendi distinguishes beauty, it becomes "fairly obvious what the impression beauty makes on the inner life of the person amounts to: a love that shackles" (ibid.). The outer world affects the inner world: beauty chains the human being to the country that is his/her home. This condition, Bergsson says, is something Icelanders have not been able to get over, either in art or in life: however much their standard of living has changed, their sense of beauty remains tied to landscape and loyalty.

But how does Bergsson think about beauty? He says that he does not know with any certainty what it means when someone says "this is beautiful." On the other hand, he says that there is no way of perceiving beauty without "the involvement of some form of comparison and contrast" (111). This is perhaps why beauty is challenging. For what is the comparison and what is the parallel? If he is right about Icelanders' sense of beauty, then we can see the local comparison as well as the parallel: Gunnar is their man and the outer landscape is what tethers their inner life. The passion that is awakened by beauty is thus bound by material things. This long-standing condition raises insistent questions not only about art and the function of art but also about ideas concerning behaviour and view of life. Beauty is no small matter when we think of the impact it makes on life and art. What is it that the "tethered Icelanders" are missing in this matter? According to Bergsson: "In most aspects of life, we do not take an aesthetic position towards anything, even though we are all philosophers of aesthetics and enjoyers of pleasure and beauty from morning till noon – also at night, for dreams are not simply the confusions of the soul thrusting forward but, rather, the aesthetic life of the senses displaying itself" (112). This is about not just Icelanders but everyone: we are all *philosophers of aesthetics*. But what does this mean?

In "Ideas on Beauty" Bergsson addresses aesthetics in the history of Western culture generally. He first discusses the aesthetics of the ugly and how it is much more complex than the aesthetics of the beautiful, perhaps because "beautiful ugliness, or, rather, 'what is beautifully ugly,' in man's demeanour and in his acts is much more common than the other" (112). Beautiful ugliness is most common in art, Bergsson says, "and it is there on purpose. No work of art is completely beautiful" (ibid.). He writes that he is mainly discussing the invention of the ugly in the aesthetics of the nineteenth century and, especially, the twentieth century. The worship of ugliness has invariably been tied to progressivism in the arts, but we are now at a stage in history when progressive movements from the beginning of the twentieth century are acknowledged, taken for granted, and have, in many ways, become classical themselves, creating their own traditions. And so they may bow to themselves, worship themselves, and then die off – or refuse to admit to their own demise.[24] Now we are at a point where artists have "understood the problems they face if they are to sail the ship of new ideas and new styles into the next century in an artful way – a way that has a future in a world where everything concerning the earth and man has become known" (113).

Continuing, Bergsson talks about the time of history up to the Renaissance in Italy and how it was thought that noticing the ugly meant that one had acquired a Christian perspective on beauty. He also discusses the theological attitude towards beauty and how the teachings of the medieval Church were waning and how painters began to see the body of Christ and the human being from the point of view of beauty, which, in some ways, is related to the advertising technology of current times: "Everything concerning the Christian faith was turned into a commodity" (114).

As far as religion goes, Bergsson asks whether the arts and the need for art spring from a need for religion, and whether what lurks in the artist is actually the spirit of god. And he responds: "No one knows the answer to that" (115). What he does claim to know is that, in the artist, there is a secret memory that hovers in the mind like a persistent murmur. Some people, he contends,

> might call it the need for faith. I do not know. Whatever this murmur might be, it is not directed at some specific God by the means of prayer, or to a certain political power, even though it is possible to manipulate this power and use if for purposes of propaganda. Perhaps the talent for creating art is really a hunting instinct, where the artist captures unclear ideas and slays them in his works. Every artist must recognize how he chases after ideas. Either overtly or covertly, he tries to entrap them and redress them in recognizable garb, which is usually dependent on the spirit of the times and changes accordingly. Upheaval in the arts and the forms they take are dependent on the times and the prevailing aesthetic perspective, even though the ideas themselves and their content remain more or less constant while the style changes. Both of these are to some degree in a hide-and-seek game with the sense of beauty, so that in each case the appropriate style allows the perception of the idea and its content to come through. (115)

It is not the subject matter that changes, but the way in which it is clothed. However, there is another matter Bergsson mentions, which is the fact that taste is ever changeable. Fortunately, we can change our tastes; if we could not, "life and the world would become an unendurable torment" (115). But why do we need to be changing our tastes all the time?

This question concerns both the issue of human happiness and the possibilities of art. Bergsson puts it this way: "Happiness in life is derived to a large degree from our knack for self-deception concerning things connected with beauty, flattery, beautiful words, beautiful people, and, of course, also from the ability we have of duping ourselves in the hope that something new might happen in our dreams of how to enjoy the variety of life" (116). In our time, however, he points out that people flee from the variety of life. Now it is fashionable to unite all diversity and attempt to make certain forms fit all people – forms "that are supposed to be good for all, few in number, and easy to learn and to understand" (116). Our times are hazardous due to what Bergsson calls "mechanical memory." The automatic, mechanical, and habitual memory is raised above all else – above the need to revolt and to face the uncertain, and this makes it "harder and harder to convince ourselves that new things happen" (116). When we consider the ever-changing tastes of people, this mechanical element of the mind creates a problem. The ability to pull back from an opinion is not only a good idea but also, if any change is to take place, a necessity. In this connection, Bergsson discusses the position of the artist. If an artist is inconsistent in his aesthetic views or in his work, it might be because of what Bergsson calls "creative inconsistency," which stands in opposition to what he calls "disheartening inconsistency":

> Disheartening inconsistency occurs when a man shows utter confusion and has no control over his thoughts for psychological reasons. An artist who is in the grip of this ... form of confusion does not possess the control that is required to hold up the silver star of which Nietzsche spoke. An artist who is endowed with creative inconsistency is able to raise the silver star in his works, moulded in the smithy out of the darkness of chaos and the burning waters. (116)

Perhaps this is what might be called admitting to being human without falling for the temptation of popular, but contrived, consistency. Clearly, the fluctuating sense of beauty we have makes its mark not only on our behaviour but also on our art. This aesthetic perspective is therefore concerned with chaos – not thoughtlessly so, but as a deeply grounded acknowledgment.

This matter is important in a discussion of Bergsson's aesthetics and is treated in the chapters that follow. It helps explain Bergsson's position on the connection between the sense of beauty and cruelty – a matter he considers to be one of the most important in the subject of aesthetics. These two things (beauty and cruelty, or the beautiful and the ugly) often go together, he says, both in daily life and in our celebrations, but they are "most noticeable in matters political, social, and religious, and in the raising of children" (117). But how?

In all these areas, Bergsson claims, ethics and the sense of beauty are closely related. What we have here is an ethics "that considers itself to have the right to be cruel, and even to take the life of another in the name of a specific aesthetics" (117). Most evil deeds are nothing other than "a consequence of his sense of beauty, of his aesthetic sense" (ibid.), and, in this connection, Bergsson mentions homophobia, religious extremism, and a lack of compassion for others. We see cruel deeds throughout human behaviour, especially "with regard to sexual behaviour" (ibid.). But to what kind of aesthetics is he referring? He is talking about Christian aesthetics, which, he claims, "is directed at the idea of improving the world and humankind and of beautifying the spirit of man, by good or ill. This kind of ethical aesthetics is of course attended by violence, which is easy to resort to because a large portion of humankind is blind to some area of its own behaviour, if looked at from a Christian point of view" (ibid.).

As a result, and in the spirit of Benedikt Gröndal, Bergsson sums up another kind of terror and beauty, one that is not tied to "the dark deeds of man" but, rather, to those of nature. He relates a short story about nature's terrifying majesty and two very different kinds of preference. The story is set in the beginning of the nineteenth century. In a mail carriage riding through an uninhabited, forested area are the British painter Turner and a middle-aged aristocratic woman. Suddenly it grows dark, there is thunder and lightning, and the rain pours down. The passengers try to avoid the downpour by pulling the covering over themselves more tightly. Turner all of a sudden excused himself, "rose up, opened the window, and stuck his head out. There he stood in an awkward position and glared at the stormy weather" (119). The companions in the carriage do not understand his behaviour, and the lady gets the idea of asking him what he has been looking at, since "she herself thought the goings on of the weather were terrible." The man answers: "I have seen greater beauty than my eyes have ever before beheld" (ibid).

As it appears from this story, the woman is "a noblewoman, an enjoyer of art and beauty," and one year later she goes to an art show in London and sees a certain beautiful, well-known painting. Even though she cannot quite fully take in the subject matter, she decides to buy the work, arranges to meet the painter, and, upon seeing him, recognizes him.

According to Bergsson – whatever the answers may be to questions like "Where was the beauty located in this instance: in nature itself, in the woman, or in Turner's talent? In his eyes or in hers? Or was it only in that part of his aesthetic sensibility that he could use to change the subject by the use of colours and tools?" – it is obvious from this example that the painter has sought inspiration from the events of nature, not from the place in the landscape where he happens to live. The painting, moreover, is of course not of nature itself because art and nature are each subject to different laws. In the story it is most important that Turner has painted "an inner vision rather than what he actually witnessed." And here is the explanation: "He did not say: 'Beautiful is the storm, the blazing and ruffled clouds, and out of the postal carriage I will not venture.' Instead, he went and created an abstract, classical, and artistic image of nature." (120).

This would be a fine ending to an essay on beauty. The author has given the reader a chance to think about the perception of beauty, beauty's power in life as well as in art, how it is connected to human happiness because of the necessity of illusion, how it is connected to aesthetics, how aesthetics is connected to cruelty, and how it is possible to talk about the ethics of cruelty and the difference between the "dark deeds" of humanity and those of nature. Last but not least, Bergsson gives the reader a chance to think about what people are missing if they pay too scant attention to their own sense of beauty and, instead, hold fast to the idea of beauty that comes as a consequence of the tethers that chain them to their native home. But the essay does not end there. The story of the British painter and the aristocratic woman (which is about creativity based on experience) also raises another question in the author's mind: what is beauty? This question, Bergsson insists, is so important that he must turn to a more down-to-earth example than that provided by the painter Turner, thus giving the aesthetics of the everyday unhindered space. And what is the "example"? It is the youth Jói, who cannot be bothered to stay at home on Saturday night and watch television or read books and, instead, goes out in search of "amusement and a drink" (120).

The story goes as follows. Jói goes to a dance, gets drunk, gets infatuated with a woman who falls for his adulation, and they sleep together. Jói wakes up the next morning and is repulsed by the woman (who, the evening before, reminded him of his mother and his aunt) and demands that she leave. The woman "does not at all like Jói's new-found taste" and doubts his forthrightness, for how can she be old and ugly now when just a few hours earlier she was "the loveliest girl in the world?" Jói blames it on drink and rationalizes his infallible good taste and his good sense of "feminine beauty." Then they end up fighting (the woman calls Jói a mommy's boy and he answers by giving her a black eye), and Jói's mother throws the woman, who was "ruining her son with her ugly behaviour," out of the house. Jói is sure he has done the "right and beautiful thing" by rejecting the woman. Alcohol is to blame for what he calls a "misunderstanding," and when he promises never to taste liquor again, his mother tells him that that is a "beautiful vow": "She goes to the store to buy him a new computer game. She is sure that she can keep her son with her longer and that, if she does this, he will remain good. The story ends and Jói re-establishes his good taste, his confidence, and his manhood" (121).

The meaning of this parable is not immediately obvious. The interpreter will have to be careful because, just like human beings themselves, a parable on aesthetic experience is far from clear-cut. The story also awakens some related questions, not least of which are those concerning the never-satiated hunger of the physical urges and the constant conflicts they cause in people's lives. The story of Jói, his mother, and the fluctuatingly lovely woman might possibly be read as a parable for modern Iceland. But it is not tied to any specific time or place. In the mind of the author, it is in fact an example of normal behaviour, even though people usually move from admiration to repulsion more slowly. This change of preference also has its parallel in "marriage, friendship, relating to paintings and art and our taste in books and music. Few people know what is happening and rarely ever bother to worry about it, and so they endlessly fall into the same trap. That is how people go forward; either they allow themselves to be deceived or else they deceive themselves" (121).

What is beauty, then? The essay does not end with an answer but with the following question:

But is the sense of beauty actually our inner desires making themselves felt? And when our various needs are fulfilled, each one in turn, are we then satisfied and have we been satiated mentally and physically? And do we then despise what before we had thought beautiful – so much so, even, that we are repulsed after we have been satisfied, and we forcefully push away from us what we before embraced because of the beauty we saw there, which was only beautiful in the eyes of a changeable sense of taste, brought on by the hunger of our yearnings? (121)

I do not know whether the sense of beauty is disguised desire. But it is easy to see how the question is based on a dense aesthetic perspective. Like the aesthetic ideas of Gröndal and Daðason (and, to a certain degree, Thomsen), Bergsson's ideas are not shackled to the landscape and nation. We can interpret his written works in light of the fact that he is involved with certain key themes in the history of humankind and the narrative history of the West. Now we must turn to another friend of the great hunt: Saint Augustine, author of the *Confessions*.

The Human Image during the Formative Phases of Christianity and in the Era of the Dizzying Void

In *Repetition*, Kierkegaard (or "Constantin") discusses the significance of Job in the Old Testament and says that we cannot find a more powerful human image, for everything about Job is so human it borders on poetry. Constantin also asserts that nowhere else in the world has the passion of anguish been better expressed (204). Another nineteenth-century philosopher discussed here claims that people, events, and speeches in the Old Testament are drawn with such mighty strokes that the figures in Greek and Indian literature cannot compare to them: "We stand in horror and awe before this monstrous vestige of what humanity once was, and then reflect sadly on old Asia and its protruding little peninsula of Europe that desperately wants (over and against Asia) to stand for the 'progress of humanity'" (Nietzsche, *Beyond Good and Evil*, 48). Those who are not distressed or astonished when encountering these ruins, Nietzsche says comfortingly, are dull, tame house-pets "and understand only house-pets' needs (like educated people today, including the Christians of 'educated' Christianity). The taste for the Old Testament is a touchstone for the 'great' and the 'small'" (ibid.).

The above literary interpretations will become relevant in the discussion below concerning Augustine's *Confessions* and Bergsson's novel *The Mouse That Skulks*. Augustine's depiction of himself in the world has in it something of what Kierkegaard calls the passion for anguish. In the *Confessions*, Augustine's passion for God is at such a high level of intensity that critics like Nietzsche balk: "It has a certain oriental ecstasy, as when an undeserving slave has been pardoned or promoted – in Augustine, for example, who is offensively lacking any nobility of demeanor and desire" (*Beyond Good and Evil* 47). I discuss Nietzsche's ideas in greater detail later and show how his theologically charged passion bears the marks of excess, albeit in a different way than Augustine's. Perhaps it is Augustine's excesses that awaken the house-pets of the early twenty-first century and encourage them to take another look at the history of ideas as it relates to the image of humanity in twentieth-century literature. Clearly, with his depiction of himself, Augustine, in a unique way, touches on the interface between life and writing, or the sense of fiction incurring in narratives of human life.

In this chapter I discuss this interface, as well as the double-edged power that is let loose, and how the image of humanity in the writings of a saint from the fourth century AD relates to the image of humanity in Bergsson's writings, even though the circumstances of their thinking are radically different.

THE VOICE OF AUGUSTINE

Within the tradition of hagiography and autobiography, Augustine is considered to be one of the fathers of Western literary culture. He is also thought to reveal more about the self than any of his contemporaries in that he combines, in a unique way, the talent for interpretation, reflective reading, self-searching, and first-person narrative. Augustine's voice is simply unique in the Western tradition of thought and writing. According to Edmund Husserl,[1] there is no voice in autobiography remotely like it. Charles Taylor points to a radical element in Augustine's thinking and how he "shifts the focus from the field of objects known to the activity of knowing" (130). Karl Jaspers reiterates this view in his discussion of the singularity of Augustine and how he can be considered a predecessor of thinkers like Kierkegaard and Nietzsche: "All comparisons between the thinking of these men show the depth of feeling in Augustine; his ability to acquire experience of the most extreme kind; the power of his personality and his 'modernity.'"[2] Jaspers says that this way of thinking not only allows the reader to participate in his subject but also to gain insight into the development of various trains of thought (*Grossen Philosophen* 375). In interpreting Augustine's unique writings, Hannah Arendt takes an additional step in this existential approach. According to her, he assisted in the birth of two empires, the "Roman Empire reborn in the Catholic Church" and the "empire of the inner life" (Arendt 123).[3]

In short, Augustine's *Confessions* has left its mark.[4] "Too much
and not enough is owned by Augustine," says Robert Smith in relation to twentieth-century thinking on autobiographical writing and
the nature of literature (46). I will not elaborate upon that argument.
A more pertinent matter for purposes of the present discussion is an
idea he raises that has its roots in Derrida and that concerns the
nature of autobiographical narratives. It involves how the border
between life and writing (the spirit and the letter) becomes, in such
writings, less important than the more pressing question of force.
This force could "never be filtered – or *only* be filtered – by philoso-
phies of the subject" (Smith 7). It is, in other words, necessary to
approach this force in a philosophical way, although such an approach is limiting. This is an important paradox – that philosophy is
both needed and limiting – and it is relevant not only to the
Confessions but also to the writings of Guðbergur Bergsson.

Smith offers an interpretation of sin in Augustine's *Confessions*
and the relationship between literature, faith, and philosophy. He
may be right when he says that, just as with Augustine's childhood
pranks (the chapter in which Augustine confesses to having stolen
pears in a neighbour's garden is a famous one) and his later sexual
escapades, so with Augustine's literary interests: these obsessions/in-
terests hinder the spiritual sanity he would like to derive from adher-
ing to God's ways. In fact, it could be asserted that, after baptism, the
rejection of sexual pleasures is a greater trial for Augustine than is
the rejection of the enjoyment he has from reading literature. As can
be read in the first two books of the *Confessions*, it is much harder
to reason with the flesh than to find great fault with literature. While
the flesh is restless, whether asleep or awake, it is still possible for
Augustine, as a mature man on his way towards God, to analyze
where literary works go wrong. He sees clearly how, with its deceptive webs, literature confuses the spirit: instead of loving God, the
reader chases the wayward emotions conjured by fictional characters. However, as Smith points out, this is not a simple matter. The
experience of these separate things (the theft of the pear, the pursuit
of sexual pleasure, the reading of literature) are the experiences
Augustine wants to single out in his *Confessions*. The telling of the
narrative is supposed to bear the burden of the sin so that he himself
can be relieved from its tortures and become a whole man: "Religious
confessions seek the exchange of that diabolic other for a Godly one,
literature for Scripture, the devil of a father for the good one, the one

that will regulate literality as law rather than as error, lifting the spirit up for sure, rounding off its identity, not leaving it to languish, having finished with the suffering" (Smith 47). At the same time, contrary to Augustine's will, the narrative acquires literary value. For in order to be able to reject sin, Augustine must confess it. Thereby, sin becomes a narrative, and instead of contributing to the completion of the confessor here and now it can be shared forever (46).

In order to hone in on the narration of the image of humanity in Augustine's *Confessions*, we need to turn the discussion towards the excesses of his religious passion. Here we need to look not only at the boundaries between life and writing (spirit and the letter) and the resulting contradiction but also at the paradoxical boundary between the search for identity and the rejection of the self. When those boundaries are dealt with as intensely as they are in Augustine's *Confessions*, we can see they are running up against the poetic impulse. The uniqueness of the *Confessions* may therefore reside in those paradoxical boundaries that Kierkegaard sees in the passionate and tragic struggle in which Job engages with God, so that which is *human* is simultaneously *poetic*. As is the case with the three narrators discussed in the previous chapter, so with Augustine: the power of his imagination sets alight the poetics of the inner life and, thereby, the slow dissolution of that inner life as it confronts reality.

Another matter of importance in this connection is that the boundary between faith and aesthetics is not quite clear in works like Augustine's *Confessions*. On first view, the aesthetic possibilities of the confessional mode may seem quite removed from the traditional Christian form of the confession. It is possible to view the Christian confession as more closely connected to the autobiographical than to the poetic, to view Christian confession as a more worldly (and therefore more true) story of a person's life than a work of the imagination (S. Einarsson 346). Nonetheless, the confession of faith itself does have a poetic basis: it is at once a person's material autobiography and God's window onto the world; it is the world that "translated the ancient, holy scriptures so they became new again" (S. Einarsson 348–9). It is therefore as useless to inquire into the aesthetic possibilities of the confessional form apart from its connection to its Christian meaning as it is to inquire into the Christian confession apart from its connection with the role of poetry and a philosophy of life. Jesus himself (in his interpretation of the human condition) did not sneeze at the power of the imagination.[5]

THE SELF CAUGHT BETWEEN SEARCH AND DENIAL

In the *Confessions* we see how sin – in the mind of Augustine – is rooted in the quest for pleasure, beauty, and truth when these are apart from God. In this situation, human beings find in themselves and in others only suffering, disorder, and confusion.[6] In Book II of the *Confessions*, Augustine admits that God watches over his creation and that he would sooner kill us than have us destroy his work. By remembering his past and himself in the spirit of God's creation, Augustine's search and desire are directed towards the origins of his being: the Creator (Arendt 6). But in order to arrive at the origins of his being, Augustine needs to turn his gaze away from the knowable world and towards the events of the mind, away from public and communal knowledge and towards his inner self (Taylor 130). It is in fact this cognitive movement from the outer world to the inner life of the mind to which the *Confessions* bears witness. With the mind's ability to reflect, Augustine is able to acquire experience of himself; in his mind he is able to sense his own nearness, but only with the assistance of God. In this light, we may discover the flickering margins between the search for self and the denial of self, and how Augustine's expression of the experiences of his inner life become irresistible to him. In the sorrowful quest for pleasure, beauty, and truth, Augustine glimpses the faint inner flicker that lights up the space in which he can become present to himself. It was Augustine who "introduced the inwardness of radical reflexivity and bequeathed it to the Western tradition of thought" (Taylor 131).

Augustine's theory concerning the sacredness of the inner life, and how his heart and mind owe everything to God, has left deep marks on Western culture.[7] Hannah Arendt finds that he goes beyond the Christian ideocosm in his description of himself in the world, but in this context she points out the influence of neoplatonism in his thinking and how it becomes possible to speak of its "revenge" after he has adopted Christian beliefs. Unlike other Christian fathers, such as Luther, the choice between philosophical self-reflection and the obedience of religious faith is alien to Augustine (Arendt 6). He is himself the seed of the ambiguity in which his thoughts thrive; in his own mind, the realm of the spirit and the realm of God are in struggle with each other. He searches for himself via a radical route of denial and "in terms of the ideal of autarchy and self-sufficiency, he cannot but arrive at an ideal of absolute isolation and independence of the individual from everything 'outside' this self over which the self has no power. And this 'outside' includes not only my 'neighbors' but also my own body. This is an alienation from the world, which is much more radical than anything requested or even possible in orthodox Christianity" (Arendt 40–1). The uniqueness of the *Confessions* may rest in a self-searching that ends in a man's complete alienation and freedom from all that lies outside himself, even his own body. But, if the search has expelled the man from the world, where, then, does his self reside? In the narration?

Another interpreter of the *Confessions*, Brian Stock, notes among the unique qualities of these volumes something that he claims is unusual for all ancient narratives: how the self is realized in narration. According to him, in that moment when Augustine's story is *born* into the world ("enters the world") in words intended for other readers (until then the narration is hovering between the margins of mind and world), the *confession becomes narration* and readers reformulate it into a subjective confession (Stock 16). Does the uniqueness of the *Confessions* then possibly lie in a self that can only be realized in narration?

Here we may see a relation between the views of Smith and those of Stock. The latter goes a step further, however, by taking a few steps backwards and arguing that this quality of self-realization through narration is built on Augustine's conviction that words and images play a fundamental role in mediating an understanding of reality (Stock 1). But what is this reality?

If Augustine's heart and mind are subordinated to God's realm, it is the same for other interpreters of Christianity: we are all separate, Augustine believes. Between us there is an unbridgeable chasm. We arrive into the world abandoned by God, and like shipwrecked people in a foreign land, our participation in life is a pilgrimage of the flesh. We are in exile from our *native land*, which we perceive but cannot touch. Only through reading can we for a moment *fill ourselves* with others; it is only in the company of ideas that any connections can be made.[8] Stock further argues that Augustine also believed that reading and writing were among the burdens that fell onto the shoulders of Adam and Eve in the garden. Before the Fall, there was no need to resort to such a cumbersome method of communication: God expressed His will extemporaneously, with or without words. After the pair showed both haughtiness and curiosity, God ceased communicating directly to them (16).

In this context, interpreters of the *Confessions* could dwell on the concept of sin in language; how language in Christianity stands between myself and that which I am addressing as a harbinger of death – an idea that has grown with great speed in the last two centuries and given interpreters occasion to call Adam the first serial killer (Critchley 62).[9] But those are the words neither of Augustine nor of Stock. What matters in this connection is that, near the end of the fourth century AD, Augustine's ideas were built on Christian thinking. As witnessed by his radical denial, Augustine goes a step further than his contemporaries in his interpretation and expression of the reality of the inner life. For this reason, it is appropriate to take a closer look at Augustine's findings concerning the society of ideas and what light they throw on the reality of the inner life.

As has been pointed out, Augustine lays a theoretical foundation for Western reading culture. But if reading is thought of – in the spirit of Augustine – as a way to self-understanding, then a certain problem comes to the fore, which Augustine also saw and explained. The knowledge that is borne of reading cannot, in fact, be separated from human perception, and it is bound to time, place, and circumstance. In the presence of texts such as the Bible, the reader may, however, approach a "higher" understanding without the need to alter his or her perceptions. In this light, we may see reading as the final step in a "mental ascent": in the reader's journey from the outer world to the inner life, reading brings about not only an awakening from the deception of the senses but also a rite of imitation (Stock 1).

Here we are not talking about a spiritual resurrection generated by reading the Bible but, rather, the awakening of a perception of the deceptive nature of the senses and how such knowledge is connected to Augustine's complete denial as he excludes himself from the world in his search for self. These features are connected directly to his excesses, to which we now turn.

AUGUSTINE'S EXTREMES

Augustine's excesses might be, if anything, a greater hindrance to him than were the infractions of pear-thieving, sexual dalliances, and literature that Smith notes above. These excesses derive from the thinking to which Augustine became habituated before his baptism and that produced a renunciation similar to that discussed by Ludwig Wittgenstein: "As I have said many times, philosophy does not support any sort of renunciation on my part. I do not forbid myself to say something, but rather, I consider certain verbal combinations to be meaningless. On the other hand, philosophy requires repudiation; not the renunciation of the mind, but rather of the emotions."[10]

Wittgenstein's interpretation of the repudiation of philosophy is perhaps better suited to a discussion of the nature of Augustine's radical renunciation than, for example, are the ideas of Jostein Gaarder. In Gaarder's book *Vita Brevis* (which, on the cover, is referred to as "an erotic tragedy"), an opposing view of Augustine's renunciation is developed. Gaarder speaks of Floria, the woman who bore Augustine's child and his lover of many years, and maintains – in her name – that first it is necessary *to live* and only then *to philosophize* (Gaarder 185). One may doubt that this view is Augustine's.

What matters is that, in the *Confessions*, the question is not *whether* a line will be drawn between life and thoughts about life but, rather, in what manner a human being *lives* his/her thoughts about his/her possibilities in life. Such is the excess of Augustine, the inner excess that asserts itself in the doomed intensity of Constantin in *Repetition*, the diary writer in Bergsson's story, and the narrator in Blanchot's *Death Sentence*. In the *Confessions*, Augustine not only parts with the possibility of love for woman and child but adopts complete isolation from everything that lies outside the self and the body.

But Augustine is a man of flesh and blood, and there is, of course, a difference of degree between the *Confessions* and works such as *Repetition*, *The Mind's Tormented Love*, and *Death Sentence*. In the *Confessions* we may occasionally glimpse dramatic moments that may have had a deep impact on Augustine's repudiation of life and the excesses of his thoughts. Perhaps the fear of death and the angst he faces in his life constitute the emotions that propel him forward, but in the *Confessions*, when his best friend is taken to the grave, he says: "'Grief darkened my heart' (Lam. 5:17). Everything on which I set my gaze was death" (*Confessions* IV, iv, 9). A deceased friend is more real, more alive, than everything else he sees, and Augustine is conscious of how his mind becomes death's harbinger. At the same time, this death becomes a reminder to him of life, and what follows is a serious struggle in the labyrinth of love, where Augustine condemns himself for his lack of knowledge: "What madness not to understand how to love human beings with awareness of the human condition! How stupid man is to be unable to restrain feelings in

suffering the human lot!" (IV, vii, 12). As is the case for the other
narrators whose stories are discussed here, Augustine knows no
moderation. Such is the repudiation that cannot be viewed as ordinary in the history of confessional works. This kind of self-denial does
not make it easier for Augustine to discover the origin of his own
being, God himself, which he longs to find – perhaps because humanity is not only a riddle to himself but also to God: "Man is a vast
deep, whose hairs you, Lord, have numbered, and in you none can
be lost (Matt. 10: 30). Yet it is easier to count his hairs than the passions and emotions of his heart" (IV, xiv, 22).

THE THIRST FOR KNOWLEDGE
AND THE CHRISTIAN ETHOS

As we have seen, Augustine's thinking is marked by neoplatonism,
and we detect its revenge in its influence on his examination of himself in the world. The motivating force in his life before baptism –
namely, the thirst for knowledge – becomes, after his adoption of the
Christian faith, a dangerous temptation: "Beside the lust of the flesh
which inheres in the delight given by all pleasures of the senses (those
who are enslaved to it perish by putting themselves far from you),
there exists in the soul, through the medium of the same bodily
senses, a cupidity which does not take delight in carnal pleasure but
in perceptions acquired through the flesh" (*Confessions* X, xxxv, 54).

Awakened to consciousness of the shackles of original sin,
Augustine is reminded of the serious temptation that his thirst for
knowledge represents – what he refers to as this worthless pursuit
that masquerades under the name of science and knowledge. When
our consciousness stoops to our desire for knowledge, in Augustine's
judgment, and when this knowledge is built on our visual senses, a
serious problem arises: "Pleasure pursues beautiful objects – what is
agreeable to look at, to hear, to smell, to taste, to touch. But curiosity
pursues the contraries of these delights with the motive of seeing
what the experiences are like, not with a wish to undergo discom-
fort, but out of a lust for experimenting and knowing" (X, xxxv, 55).
Even our faith in God is not exempt from this temptation, Augustine
continues. We are testing God when we demand miracles and other
signs – not in the hope of being saved but, rather, because of our love
of experience. Are we at a crossroad here? In the words of Charles
Taylor: "We might say that where for Plato the eye already has the

capacity to see, for Augustine it has *lost* this capacity. This must be restored by grace. And what grace does is to open the inward man to God, which makes us able to see that the eye's vaunted power is really God's" (139).

In this manner Augustine attempts to diminish the effects of the mind's temptations. He also wants to find pleasure, beauty, and truth that are apart from sin. However, this struggle also shows his sincere passion for the experiences of the mind, and it is in his descriptions of the life of the mind that the aforesaid temptation manages to shake not only his possibilities in life but also the laws of God: "To satisfy this diseased craving, outrageous sights are staged in public shows. The same motive is at work when people study the operations of nature which lie beyond our grasp, when there is no advantage in knowing and the investigators simply desire knowledge for their own sake" (X, xxxv, 55). Obviously, in their search for God, human beings cannot make use of this *unrestrained power*. However, Augustine needs to resort to every possible recourse in his struggle with temptation; he claims that the secrets of human nature have nothing to do with our lives and that knowledge of those secrets has no worth. Still, again and again, he feels as though he is lost and "frequently becoming stuck in the snares" that surround him "on every side" (X, xxxv, 55). Only God's laws can save him, as Augustine also confesses in Book X, many years after he has adopted the Christian faith. The question, however, is whether God can always protect humanity from the death that resides in the inner life and from the imagination that fulfills the unhealthy curiosity as vigorously as though it were a theatrical production.

Perhaps Augustine's *Confessions* contains the grave thought that we acquire the ability to live only by repudiating existence and being "on show" as a *narration* in human form. Humanity's full abilities (if they can be called abilities) cannot be reached in any other way because what are they if not the reality of imperfection? Is this perhaps why Augustine has been called the first modern man?

The power Augustine unleashes with his *Confessions* rests on the boundaries between life and writing. The description of sin acquires literary value, quite against Augustine's own will: instead of leading to the completion of the confessor in the here and now, the narration of his imperfection becomes an eternal exchange. Perhaps all the possibilities it holds are to be found in the paradox that is said to reside in the very power that is let loose by Augustine, the power that will never be unlocked through philosophical explorations of the self but that no other approach can really address. Is the human image only capable of being expressed on the margins of life and death, where paradox itself reigns? Which is to say, on the borders of *literature*?

Augustine lived during the developmental era of Christianity, and his text bears the marks of its time. In terms of the inner life, he steps out of neoplatonism into Christianity. Another and no less intriguing question is, therefore, whether this kind of examination of human nature could take place in another era, such as our own – a dizzying void brimming with the splendour of science and technology. Does this power that Augustine uncovers in his *Confessions* perhaps make a second appearance in Western narratology in the writings of certain later philosophers and, occasionally, novelists and poets?

A HOUSE AT THE OCEAN, FULL OF GOD'S DISRUPTIVE DEPARTURE: *THE MOUSE THAT SKULKS*

As is discussed in the first chapter, modern humanity still belongs to the era of the Book, even though it may have lost its faith in it. In that chapter I also discussed Blanchot's idea that the modern era is characterized by humanity's profound experience of its ambiguous lot. Few Icelandic authors delve into this experience of modernity as deeply as does Guðbergur Bergsson. His novel *The Mind's Tormented Love* bears witness to this. It is safe to say that the same goes for most of his other works.

In 1961 Bergsson's first books appeared – the poetry collection *Repeated Words* and the novel *The Mouse That Skulks*. When considering the themes of Bergsson's writings, we see already in these first works what direction they take. In the poetry collection, he presents himself as belonging to the world of repeated words – words that at once assert the idea of god, that proclaim god to be the author of life, and that at the same time demand freedom from that assertion in favour of a creative image of humanity. Consider the poem "The Fastening":

Give me a red sun
and a yellow paper moon
to glue onto a blue background.
And seven stars.

I make from the clay
of earth
two human beings,
burn their palms together,
and fasten them.

But I do not reign over like
god.
Give me a red sun,
clay and a yellow paper moon.
(*Repeated Words* 9)[11]

While this poem is engaged in pitting humanity the creator against God the author and ruler of everything, we can see this argument even more clearly in *The Mouse That Skulks*.[12] Bergsson is said to be finding his way in this first novel, and reviewers have claimed that never before in Iceland has a "better beginner's novel" appeared.[13] Here the author can be seen to wrestle with the declining state of faith (i.e., the Lutheran faith) in postwar Icelandic society by describing the surroundings and inner life of a boy who becomes the victim of existence itself once his mother's power over him has been shattered. Sprung from an open, naked landscape (which is reminiscent of a seaside village in southwestern Iceland), a barrenness of life and a cultural reality only literature can describe, the boy senses both his limits and his desires in the face of a dizzying task: to live.

The story takes place during the course of one summer. The boy lives with his domineering mother (his sailor father is deceased). In the upper storey of the house lives a woman who is also a widow. The boy's grandfather, who is a sailor, lives nearby with his second wife, whom the boy calls "grandma." The relationship between this man and his daughter is strained. The same goes for the relationship between the daughter and her father's wife. The boy, however, finds a refuge in his grandfather's hovel. On the surface not much happens – so little, in fact, that one reviewer of this book writes: "Instead of such an even reading pace, there could have been the occasional sprint" (G. Sveinsson 237). But not everything is as it seems. One of the neighbours becomes seriously ill, and his struggle with death not only captivates the boy's mind and occasions his uncontrollable inner tumults but may also be the cause of the sense of doom that hangs over the society.[14]

The boy never tells his mother what he is thinking: "Just like her, I didn't make a habit of exposing my feelings, like those other people whom she talked about with such contempt. I definitely did not want to be like them" (*Mouse* 16). The same boy, however, later becomes a storyteller, and here we see his objective: "In this story I am going to try to describe the changes that took place in my life, as accurately, clearly and conscientiously and objectively as I can. These changes occurred, as far as I can tell, at the close of the winter, although their roots are no doubt much deeper" (12). The narrative therefore straddles the genres of the novel and the autobiography. Those markings are significant for Bergsson's aesthetics and are discussed in greater detail in the following chapters, in particular in the context of his fictional autobiography. As far as those changes that the narrator wishes to describe, and their roots, we see that the mixed genre plays a part. What are those roots, anyway? Are they perhaps so deep that they remind the reader of the human passion and suffering we find in the Old Testament?

As noted above, Kierkegaard and Nietzsche, around and after the middle of the nineteenth century, wrote passionately about the status of and possibilities for the human image in Western literature. The Old Testament is important in this respect. Now we are in a very different era, and speaking of a passionate struggle with life, long after god has stopped listening to humanity's sufferings, perhaps signifies a dead aesthetic. But what if human nature cannot be measured by genetics or financial profits? Bergsson has this to say on the subject:

> Let us allow man and nature to keep some of their secrets, and let us withdraw from the often silly need to arrive at conclusions in the name of reason and science, and to look after our comfort and pleasure, and to make a parade of scientific accomplishments, as is the rule now, when scientists claim that only they are able to offer the world a true, living narrative, and create men and animals out of their surreal web – as it is called in literature – if they alter the genetic makeup of things. They seem to be self-declared dictators of everything, until they are given some sort of quota in this matter and some equalization is imposed on their all-encompassing greed. ("Man in Nature" 74)

He also says, in the same essay:

> In all that man sets out to do, he has to remember that his nature consists of these four things: nearness, distance, height, and

depth. He should in particular take care to protect the distance in himself. The same goes for nature and man's relationship with it. Because if man and nature are both without distance, they will suffer from suffocating nearness. The fact of living in a place and in a country or world where distance has been conquered is to have arrived at closure, and at a meaningless end of the world. If natural distance is obliterated, the human nature of man will also be gone. He can never again be electrified. (87)

This author's thinking (both in poetry and in other writings) is responding to certain realities of modern humanity at the same time that it is in step with the narrative tradition and the history of ideas in the Western world. This is borne out by the boy's roots in *The Mouse That Skulks*. Here I am not saying that the novel's heterocosm is directly aimed at the development that has occurred in the West concerning science and technology and the concomitant growing greed of the last two to three centuries. But if humanity is still interested in human nature, we may read *The Mouse That Skulks* as a kind of reminder of the importance of distance, whether for an individual or a nation.

THE MIND'S CURIOSITY IN A DIZZYING VOID

The changes the boy in Bergsson's *The Mouse That Skulks* goes through concern both his environment and his inner life. The house in which he lives with his mother and the woman Guðrún (who lives in the upstairs apartment) is situated where a village had been located before the great fishing company arose on the peninsula and everything was moved. Even the church has been moved, and when that happens, the boy's mother says to the reverend: "We keep death and the graves but you take from us the church and god to a place where work thrives but faith does not" (*Mouse* 11). Nothing is left in the village except the house in which the boy lives, the house in which his grandfather and his second wife live, and the house in which the sick man, Einar, lives with his wife and grandson.

At first glance, nothing much takes place here. It seems that the great changes that have occurred have completely obliterated the old village. There are still stories to tell about people's relationships, though, as the low, conflicted murmurs of the boy's mother and her father indicate: the mother will not hear of her boy's going out to sea, while the grandfather would like him to. The mother's religious practices are also of some interest. After the church was moved, she bought a radio, and, on Sundays, she spreads the altar cloth over a table and arranges the chairs in front of it: "Mother decided it would be best for us to form our own little congregation for god; two pious women and an innocent boy, just like in the early days of Christianity, and she talked to grandpa about it on the gravel road between the houses. Grandpa wouldn't listen to her eccentricities and just scoffed at them" (11).

The other neighbours attend one of the services, but Magga, Einar's wife, thought something was missing from the ceremonial ambience as they congretated "in front of a radio on a kitchen table" (11). Not many guests come and go from the boy's house. Nor is he allowed to participate in the work of the household. The only tasks he is given are to run to the store for his mother or to go for fish for his grandfather. His mother believes that he was meant for something other than hard work, that he should "study" (12). If Guðrún, who lives in the apartment above, didn't sometimes come downstairs, sit at the kitchen table by the window (when there was no religious service), have a cup of coffee, tell people's fortunes from the grounds left in the cup, and sit gossiping with his mother about Einar's illness and hallucinations, then the boy's life would be completely uneventful.

But the conversations between Guðrún and the boy's mother not only keep his mind alive, they also fan the flames of his uncontrollable imagination. The discussions of Einar's illness are entangled in dreams of everything between heaven and earth, on the margins of the understandable and the tangible, between thought and reality, life and death. Finally, the boy awakens, like Augustine, to the consciousness of death in life. The effects are equally dramatic, although they take a different form: in the wake of the fear of death, the boy decides to focus his attention and his faith on "the earth and all its material things" (12). However, at the same time, he admits to still thinking "of the discussions between [his] mother and Guðrún as a natural way to approach life, perhaps not as it is, but rather as it could be in all its mystery in the words of those who must suffer through it and who have no recourse against its hardships other than to speak of it quietly in the kitchen, usually after it gets dark" (ibíd.). Such is the existential struggle in a place where nothing but death and the grave await.

There are important elements at work here concerning the novel's relation to the history of Western ideas. As with Augustine, Bergsson attempts to describe the human condition from a Christian perspective. The environment in which these ideas are expressed is, however, completely different from the environment in which Augustine expressed his ideas. The disruptive absence of god has a deep impact not only on the modern poet's existential struggle but also on the idea of life without resolution, or what, in the first chapter, is termed the finitude of life. Thoughts regarding humanity and its possibilities have not lost their impact in Bergsson's novel. What is different is that, while Augustine turns to God, the narrator of *The Mouse That Skulks* turns to the world and all its material things.

The mother's mind and faith oscillate between heaven and earth. She thinks a great deal about her son's future career and can think of nothing more praiseworthy than that he become a doctor and be able to save "the lives of his peers with his surgical knife" (16). It would be "all one" to her, however, if he were to "choose the priesthood and set out on that path" (16). Her ideas are adventurous:

"If it should happen that you took the road of service to god, then the most obvious thing to do would be to go for the missionary career," she said with hope in her eyes. "That is a more important and more difficult job, and therefore it suits those who are emotionally and physically qualified."

When I heard that, I dared look up at her dress. "If my child were to become a missionary, I could imagine nothing more admirable," I overheard her say one day to Guðrún. "Then you will have to let him go to Africa," Guðrún said. "I don't care at all where he goes so long as he finds his way in the end," mother answered. (17)

The way he eventually finds in the end is not necessarily the way his mother had imagined. It is the road neither of the reverend nor the missionary. The mother is herself only half-Lutheran in spirit. She had been a devout reader of inspirational literature, but after the church was moved, she lost interest in "spiritual affairs and life after death" (15) and turned to other kinds of reading, in which the focus is on "the body and reasons for its demise" (ibid.). After the discussion of the career of the missionary, however, she takes up a subscription to the *Missionary Newsletter*. The boy drinks it up, pores over the exciting pictures, and decides he wants to be a missionary. He wants to "travel to the furthest most mysterious countries and observe unknown continents, and I knew," he says, "that if I became a missionary I would someday see what is beyond the horizon and my most cherished dreams would be answered" (17). What is the road the boy eventually chooses, then? He who, in his struggle with life and its treachery, is planning to focus his mind and faith on that which is tangible and material, the earth and its objects?

Early on in the novel the boy admits to the sin of eavesdropping on his mother and Guðrún as they discuss Einar's illness: "I knew full well it was bad to eavesdrop but I was curious to know what they were saying, so my interest outweighed any notions of good and bad or right and wrong. My desire was all-consuming" (*Mouse* 19). This "sin" – wanting to know things – clearly has deep ideological and literary roots. Here, in fact, we see the most serious temptation: the desire for knowledge. The boy, like Augustine, is reminded of this grave temptation, this search and longing for the pleasures of discovery. But unlike Augustine, who earnestly tries to turn his back to an equally dangerous desire after he accepts Christianity (with the help of his mother, the truly Christian Monika), the boy in Bergsson's novel allows himself to imagine all possible things in order to test them in his mind. Accepted ideas concerning good and bad or right and wrong are dismissed, and it is this all-consuming inner desire that disturbs the laws of life – if not the laws of god, who has departed the village of Tangi, then the laws of humanity.

This inner transformation is centred on the boy's relationship with his mother, and it starts to unfold on a certain Sunday, when she accused him of theft. After a protracted illness, the boy acquires a strong urge for coffee. His mother and Guðrún are outside on the lawn, listening to a radio broadcast of a church service. While they are there, he seizes the opportunity to drink up one cup after another, adding water to the coffee pot in between cups. Sweating profusely, he grimly eyes some sausages he has retrieved from the cupboard. He contents himself with licking them, wraps them up again in their paper, puts them back in the cupboard, and throws himself on his bed just before the women come inside.[15] But his mother sees the cup that was not on the table when she went outside, and she sees that the coffee pot is in the wrong place, as is the copper kettle. The boy denies having drunk any coffee and says that his grandfather came in and drank from the cup. His mother knows better:

"The coffee pot is on the range and I never leave it there," she said. "And the copper kettle was on the table by the window, where it never is. Do you think I am such a mean housekeeper that I don't remember exactly where I leave things?"

I wanted to confess the crime, but since I hadn't done that immediately, and had instead started to lie and argue, I knew there was no way to change my mind and confess. Either one had to admit it willingly or else keep up the lie and stand or fall with it. I was not yet hard-nosed enough, and I was near tears when mother said:

"So this is my son's disposition. Well, well. I would not have believed that my child was a thief and a thug." (151–2)

What looms up before us are not only the excesses of a weakened Lutheranism – the boy who had a future as a mentally and physically capable missionary is now, in his mother's eyes, a thief and a thug – but also the fall of Lutheranism itself, this system of thought wherein everything had its place, just like in the household of a "great mother." The moment of parting has arrived. Or should we perhaps call it a rite of passage in a dizzying void? It is the mother who says:

"It is best for your life that you turn around and face the facts. You cannot get around people by sneaking away. That is my experience, at least," she added after a brief pause.

The gravity in her voice was such that I thought everything inside me would come tumbling down. I thought I recognized this grave tone from something that had happened while father was still alive, and at that time I was petrified.

"In parting I'll say to you that if you want to follow your grandfather instead of your mother's advice, then it is best if you move to his place," she said. "Then you can go on drinking all the poison you want and lying and cheating." I covered my head with my hands and thought she was going to hit me. I curled myself up, but she didn't hit me. She patted me gently and stood in front of my bed for a while. Then she left saying she would remember this.

All of a sudden I could tell how the smell of cooking sausages filled the house and I buried my face in the pillow with my mouth watering. (153)

PERCEIVING THE WOUND OF EXISTENCE

The events in this boy's story occur at a time when the value of religion (i.e., Lutheranism) in the reality of postwar Icelandic society is falling: everything has disappeared except death and the grave. And the inner life? The boy not only stops sleeping in his mother's bed, but it is as though, after his mother's power over him has shattered, he becomes prey to existence.

This feeling grips him somewhat before his "crime." The coffee theft is not the turning point for the boy, any more than is the pear theft for Augustine. Like Augustine, the boy cannot overcome the temptation of the mind – the thirst for knowledge. All related ideas about good and bad and right and wrong crumble, and this all-consuming inner desire shakes the laws of his life. He stands alone against the vast expanses in himself and in others, in life and in death. Down by the sea, where he always had the most fun, he feels these distances more acutely than elsewhere. At the same time, he begins to withdraw from those who are closest to him: "When I sensed this distance I was filled with grief. I felt alone and lost. No one knew about this except me. Many things were piling up inside me. Mother could not sense this, even though she could sense most things weeks before and she said I was sick. It was true, she could see the sickness in me" (*Mouse* 92). As the story progresses, however, the mother stops being able to tell when the boy is sick. He continues:

> Her mind was on Einar. He had come between us with his own illnesses. His illnesses and I, although completely unrelated, were somehow inexorably connected.
>
> When I thought about this I was overcome with grief and cried violently in the grass. I cried in the seaweed. I cried in the sand, as if I were searching for a consolation that is impossible to find, either in nature or in other people, because one is no longer a child and therefore one is unconsoled. (92)

Various writers attempt to explore, or even create, an experience that literature can reveal. This creative process is similar to a discovery that does not aim to describe that which is known but to experience that which is *unknown*. Already in his first novel it seems that Bergsson, like Kafka, has discovered humanity's fate in the face of death: the human being cannot flee from unhappiness because she/he cannot depart from existence. The purpose of life is nothing other than to live it to the end, with death as the demarcation point.

That is the nature of the perception at work – it is an interchange with existence, an experimental perception that takes shape in the creative imagination that resides on the outskirts of Europe. In the end, what is found is neither the path of god nor the path of humanity but, rather, a path that resides on the margins of heaven and earth, thought and reality, life and death. Unlike the exploitation of humanity and nature under the banner of modern science and technology, creativity of this kind thrives on human qualities and results in a passionate struggle that still might concern the living:

> When the north wind ruffled the sea in the sunshine, which scattered upon it a silver-gleaming veneer, I thought I knew that someday I would myself become like that expanse, and soon I would be like the stark white clouds on the horizon, those billows I once thought were the mountains of foreign lands; that I would become like them: a vastness in the great vastness.
>
> Once when I was small and had wandered late in the day along the seashore singing "Now the cold deep seas are shining in the sunset," I suddenly felt that what came next was the right thing, that *this is how it should be every evening*, and I felt in my heart for the first time that something was beautiful, because it lived both inside me and in nature. The feeling was so achingly sore – to find beauty in my thoughts and in the surrounding world – that I started crying. Father was still alive. At that very moment the boats sailed out of Vör, all of them together, to lay the nets for the night. This happened just before the end of the season, and the white, yellow and red boats sailed in a long row in the direction of the white clouds, which were almost like these clouds, and it was almost evening. Even though I sing the same song in the same place now, in order to get that same feeling again, the beauty is gone. Only the searing pain in my heart remained, and that did not come from the beauty but from reality itself. (93)

But what about this beauty the boy has felt – the beauty that resides both in people and in nature, which becomes an aching feeling? What is this beauty, and how can it be approached?

Participation in Beauty

In discussing beauty in Bergsson's writing it would be useful to explore the notions the ancient Greek philosopher Plotinus (CE 205–70) had on the subject. Plotinus's longing for beauty is bound up with his search for an *authentic existence.* The same holds true for Augustine. If we consider the existential possibilities of human beings in modern times, we might assume that the issue is not the search for an authentic life in the spirit of Plotinus and Augustine but, rather, a recognition and pondering of the authentic existence in the spirit of twentieth-century existentialist philosophy. In fact, one might suppose that the ideas of Plotinus concerning beauty and existence are altogether irrelevant to contemporary discussions on the subject, that those ideas are remnants of forgotten times in Western philosophical and literary history. But this may not be the case; it would seem that modern authors are not altogether free of the inquiry that occupied Plotinus. So long as the modern writer makes the idea of the human being's possibilities in life his/her subject – in so doing touching on ideas of the possibilities of existence itself – then that subject is in line with, and related to, classical concerns about humanity and beauty, or how *beauty comes to exist through human participation.*

Of all Icelandic poets and novelists, Guðbergur Bergsson is the one who has written most about the relation between humanity and beauty. He has also written a great deal on the way Icelanders in particular experience beauty, whether in life or in art. Certain aspects of those writings are discussed below; in particular, the 1996 essay "Ideas on Beauty"; the novel *The Heart Still Dwells in Its Cave* (1982); and the short story "The Man Who Suffered a Misfortune" from the collection *Man Is a Camera* (1988). If we take notice of Bergsson's ideas, as well as the search undertaken by his characters, then we see that the subject of beauty is as much a theme in his work as is the search for an authentic existence in the work of the neoplatonists.

Bergsson's writings on this theme are not only a part of his dialogue with Icelandic culture and history but also a part of his dialogue with the history of ideas and existentialism. The aesthetics found in Bergsson's fiction and poetry have elicited some interesting responses from writers and critics in Iceland. Here, we might ask whether it is (still) thought better for an Icelandic writer to limit him/herself to a somewhat segregated idea of the Icelandic heritage or to take part in the larger context of ideas – not to mention in the aesthetic possibilities of the modern era in general. In the wake of this question, there is another, which is whether there is in Iceland some sort of national consensus on the subject of beauty, spirit, and emotion, and whether that is why writings that are more concerned with the ambiguity of beauty than with making vast generalizations on what beauty is or should be are viewed with scepticism. Perhaps the notion of beauty in Iceland is still concerned with outer beauty and the responses it elicits, as has been noted earlier. In any case, Bergsson's writings, along with the various critical responses to them, not only throw light on certain superstitions concerning Icelandic cultural inheritance, traditional mannerisms, and creativity but also awaken the consciousness of readers to a persistent, and far from uniquely Icelandic, way of dealing with and participating in beauty.

PARTICIPATION IN BEAUTY

Plotinus would not diclose anything about his parentage or origins. It remains uncertain, but he is thought to have been born in Egypt and to have moved to Rome in his middle years. There he managed a school and wanted to raise a city in the Roman Empire that would be built in the spirit of Plato's *Republic*. He is famous for his *Enneads*, a collection of essays in six parts, each of which contains nine essays. The essay "Beauty" is one of these.

If we consider the influence of Plotinus's ideas on Western philosophy and literature, we encounter some famous names. Among the Christian Platonists we find Augustine and Boetheus (ca. 480–524), and in the introduction to his Icelandic translation of "Beauty,"

Eyjólfur Kjalar Emilsson discusses the influence of Plotinus on the
neoplatonism found among the fathers of Christianity as well as
among later thinkers and poets. Plotinus's "Beauty" and "On
Subjective Beauty" are, in short, thought to have affected the development of Western ideas concerning "the nature of beauty and its
place in existence."[1]

"You must close the eyes and call instead upon another vision
which is to be waked within you, a vision, a birth-right to all, which
few turn to use," writes Plotinus in "Beauty" (71). I do not discuss
this essay here but, rather, the ninth essay in the fifth *Ennead*, "The
Intellectual-Principle, the Ideas, and the Authentic Existence." Here
Plotinus discusses beauty as it comes to be through the participation
of humanity; how the lives of all people are, from birth, bound more
to the realm of the senses than to the intellect; and how people respond to their need for beauty. The inner movement that causes
Plotinus to conclude that beauty is created by human participation is
the *movement from pleasure to distaste (or disgust)*, the fact that *the
same material can at once create pleasure and distaste*. What he takes
from this is the idea that beauty, in and of itself, is a borrowed thing.

Again, we are not dealing with a grandiloquent subject but, rather,
a well-known and oft-repeated event out of humanity's daily life. As
we can see from inquiries into humanity's tastes, the sense of beauty
is uncertain and oscillating. It is as though what gives me pleasure
for the moment is doomed to cause me disgust later.[2] This same
movement is also seen in the fine arts as they suffer the same fate as
humanity: what is in today will be forgotten and buried tomorrow.
The same goes for ideas – for religions, mythologies, and all major
theories. Our lives are, from beginning to end, bound up with the
material world and the resounding repetitions it creates with its endless movement from pleasure to distaste. In this way beauty is borrowed, again and again. But how do people who long for an authentic
existence endure such a state of affairs?

Plotinus answers by saying that people struggle alternately with
the sweet and the sour fruits of their senses, the good and the bad,
and they feel fortunate when they acquire the former, attempting to
bar the door to the latter. Human beings are just like heavy birds
that have become too used to life on the ground: in spite of the wings
nature gave them, they cannot fly. Nor, Plotinus adds, is it enough to
merely seek what is noble and pleasurable. People will despair and
slip back into the very situation from which they were trying to

extricate themselves. But how, Plotinus asks, does humanity arrive at beauty itself, "delighted in the place of reality"?

> It is to be reached by those who, born with the nature of the lover, are also authentically philosophic by inherent temper; in pain of love towards beauty but not held by material loveliness, taking refuge in things such as virtue, knowledge, institutions, law and custom, and thence, rising still a step, reaching to the source of this loveliness of the soul, thence to whatever be above that again, until the uttermost is reached: the First, the principle whose beauty is self-springing. This attained, there is an end to the pain inassuageable before. ("Intellectual-Principle" 499)

Such is Plotinus's search for an authentic existence. Reality is, in his mind, a specific idea of life that exists outside the pressures and sufferings of the material world of forms. I do not discuss Plotinus's ideas any further here but, rather, turn to some other experiences of beauty, which, in the spirit of Plotinus, reflect upon the movement from pleasure to distaste, the connection between humanity and borrowed beauty, and whether or not it is possible to find beauty that is free of the treachery of the senses.

Augustine's *Confessions* deals with questions such as these. In it we may read of a profound participation; but, like Plotinus, Augustine goes where he deems he and his reality belong. Here the longing for beauty takes up residence in the unclear consciousness of the deceptive senses, and, from a Platonic perspective, it is hardly possible to go any further in the direction of beauty. But from the vantage point of Christianity, the dogma that teaches acceptance of humanity's responsibilities in matters of the passions, Augustine may love the experiences of the mind too much. When it comes to one of the most important commandments in Christianity, Augustine is on dangerous ground: how is he to love his neighbour as he loves himself if he arrives at his reality only by acknowledging humanity's self-deception? Unlike Plotinus, however, Augustine does not get a chance to live out the life of the mind alone. The reason for this is original sin; that knife in the mind, continuously sharpened, in sleep as in wakefulness. This is the root of the suffering of Augustine, which will remain unrelieved until he feels his heart and mind are entirely given over to God. For Augustine, the quest for beauty becomes a holy quest, and, while Plotinus's ideas have deeply influenced

Western culture, the thunder of Augustine's notions of the holiness of the inner life has been equally powerful.

In what follows, I discuss in greater detail this manifold web of Platonic and Christian ideas as it manifests itself in the description of the experience of the inner life. As has been noted already, both Kierkegaard and Nietzsche are ideational descendants of Augustine. Karl Jaspers thinks that all three of them write with blood; that they live what they think (*Die Grossen Philosophen* 374–5). But why go over this old ground again?

In the introduction to his translation of "Beauty," Eyjólfur Kjalar Emilsson raises the suspicion that many who are alive today might find the notions of Plotinus rather eccentric. I agree with that assessment, but with a caveat. The interests of a man like Plotinus (who did not become famous for focusing on his body, his parents, his family ancestry, or his country) no doubt go against the grain of today's zeitgeist. At the start of the twenty-first century, it is imperative to admire the beauty of the body; the relationship to one's parents is a much-treated subject; a person's family ancestry is a matter of great interest; and one's country, seen from the vantage point of modern history, is still capable of stimulating the expression of dark deeds. A question such as "How can I find beauty that is free and unattached to the deceptions of the senses?" may seem out of the ordinary today, whether it be entertained during aerobics, a discussion with a therapist, or in front of the mass graves of ethnic groups.

But Rome in the third century AD is not simply a figment of Plotinus's imagination. In this context it is possible to ask whether Plotinus's longing for beauty is not something inherent in all people in that, when beauty is thought of, its eternal difficulties and its relation to life and thought become apparent. Humanity's life does not provide answers to questions such as: How am I to find beauty that is free of the deception of the senses? If we were to remove ourselves from the movement from pleasure to distaste, what would remain for us, whose lives are necessarily bound to the life of matter? But a narrative of humanity's inner reality – a reality that no one can see but that everyone can experience – will have little to say if questions such as these are never asked.

As was the case centuries ago, there are people who inquire into the relationship between us and beauty, into how imperfect we are in this respect, and into how beauty that is created through our participation cannot be greater than can we ourselves. In Western cultures of the present day, we see such thinking appear in literature and poetry. Such thoughts about beauty lead to thoughts about life as a whole, as was the case for Plotinus and Augustine. However, in the present day, the idea of beauty does not revolve around the notion of a life that is free of the deceptions of the material and its repetitions. To the contrary, we can claim that, today, thinking about the connection between humanity and beauty is centred in the material itself – the eternally thirsting body. And what are the possibilities?

A PARABLE FROM MODERN ICELAND
WITH A EUROPEAN TWIST

In a land where landscape is almost everything, and man's life rather impoverished, courage is required if one wishes to see something other than the natural environment the weather has created. (Bergsson, "The Echo, the Ferocity, the Mildness," 134)

In "Ideas on Beauty," Bergsson discusses the perception of beauty in the arts as well as in human behaviour and notes how little people in Iceland have thought about this subject. He also writes about the connection between the perception of beauty and cruelty, the ethics of cruelty, and how the ethics of beauty can serve the interests of violence. Towards the end of this essay we may read the contemporary Icelandic parable of Jói. Here the subject (according to the author) is an aesthetic experience of a wider sort. In the aforementioned parable we are reminded of how the questions concerning the relationship between humanity and beauty are awakened in the context of contemporary Western welfare society.

Aside from the question of the conflict of interest between the various human instincts, the parable raises questions such as "what is the nature of the perception of beauty"? The reader can also inquire into the roots of this aesthetic experience: Do these roots lie in the fact that humanity's life is governed more by the senses than by the intelligence? Or do they lie in a peculiar tradition requiring a person to trust the heathen god of wine to impart the gift of beauty? It is Jói's hangover that arouses him to consciousness of his behaviour towards his life and the lives of others, and this leads him to acquire what is called a "new sense of beauty." In light of this, it may seem that concepts like beauty and responsibility are easily come by or that the relationship between the perception of beauty and thoughts of the emotions are completely unrelated to Jói and his circumstances.

This parable about aesthetic experience, and its wider context, is not easily explained. The story of Jói, his mother, and the unattractive woman cannot be said to be bound to a specific time and place. We have yet to get an answer to the final questions of Bergsson's essay, which concern whether the perception of beauty masquerades as the preference of the senses and whether beauty is "only our inner desires making themselves felt." On the other hand, when we begin to explore this movement from pleasure to distaste, something unmistakable emerges. Instead of going straight back into the same trap again and again, thus maintaining the same patterns and self-deceptions, we gain insight into the reality of the inner life, into the elusive connection between the emotions and the perception of beauty.

Bergsson is engaged in such an inquiry; however, unlike Plotinus, he is not looking for a life that is free of the deceptions of the physical and the repetitions it engenders. Instead, he is inquiring into the potential of the reality that is decisively bound up with materiality – namely, with the body. Thought does not, in and of itself, overcome the repetitions of life's deceptions. Although the sense of beauty may possibly be masquerading as the desire of the senses, and although beauty may be "only our inner desires making themselves felt," more is required. Still, it is as though the sense of beauty were able to lessen the hold of deceptive influences by means of a possible defamiliarization.

This realization is important if one does not wish to be the victim of traditional notions and simply to believe in a preconceived idea of beauty. The fact is that, in Western intellectual history, some of the most influential theories have been those that pertain to beauty. Here I am not referring only to the endeavours of aesthetics proper or to ideas originating from the fine arts in general but also to more specious theories, such as the ethics of Christian aesthetics, national socialism, and ideas about Icelandic culture. When it comes to the potential of imaginative literature, we might require what Sigfús Daðason (in another, yet similar, context) calls a "radical" author: "When truly new works of literature emerge, men invariably focus on that which is new in them and pit it against what was known before. Later it might be discovered, however, that these radical authors nonetheless had some roots in past times, and their courage consisted of harvesting that inheritance rather better than those others who travelled the better known paths and who *wanted* to 'write classical works'" (Daðason, "Expression of Negativity," 424).

Here Daðason is referring to Bergsson's novel *Tómas Jónsson Bestseller*, which I discuss later. What is important in this context, however, is that, in Bergsson's works, we read not only about Jói's metamorphosis and the tradition that lies behind the freedom of the more melodramatic perception of beauty but also about the particular sensibility concerning beauty in Iceland. We "appear to have inherited [this] over the ages from the *Njálssaga*," this sensibility that is above all based on outer beauty and the impression that the form of beauty has on us – a sensibility that "we have seldom managed to get over ... in our art and in our way of life, regardless of how much our society and culture have changed." In fact, "our understanding of beauty is tied to the landscape and to our sense of loyalty" ("Ideas on Beauty" 111). In Bergsson's works we also find a response to the ethics of Christian aesthetic thinking – this doctrinaire assault on humanity's emotions and spirit in the name of beauty. We also find deeply rooted questions concerning the possibilities inherent in this aesthetics – possibilities that respond to the paradoxes of modern times, which stem from our being without faith in the Book. As truly new as these questions may seem, they do have a lineage – just as does the particular perception of beauty experienced by Icelanders.

But do artistic people on the "saga island" need a radical author? When, one might ask, have Icelanders not considered the subject of beauty and its place in existence to be high-minded? Among the descendants of Ingólfur Arnarson and his entourage, the inner life has not been considered as heroic as, for example, the assumed virtues of efficiency and industriousness.

Some of the ideas Icelanders hold concerning beauty have already been alluded to in connection with fragments from the history of Icelandic aesthetics. However, my focus is not limited to the question of how Icelanders perceive beauty. What I want to elucidate is the connection between humanity and beauty in the context of certain indubitable, although nameless, inner human circumstances. As has been discussed, it is difficult to describe the movement from pleasure to distaste. Human beings need to hold on to a certain form of pretence in order to overcome the deceptions of the senses. In poetic writing, however, we are able to penetrate such issues, even though this will not necessarily help us in real life. Bergsson himself has written on this subject:

Lambs can live by the natural requirements of the full-grown
sheep; children by the laws of their parents; but I think that even
god's help would not be enough to save a reader who intended to
live his daily life by the guidance of art and poetic writing, because the aesthetics involved and the ethics displayed in written
texts are deceptive for daily life, and there is no way to equate
the daily behaviour of a man who operates in society and the
morality of a personage in the aesthetics of words, sentences, or
novelistic constructions. ("Can Literature be Helpful?" 445)[3]

When we consider, in particular, the possibilities of the emotions, we
see that the creation of a character in literature can elucidate how
this relates to the human condition. According to Blanchot, drama
occurs in the madness that follows from people deciding to live out
their relations in order to test their potential, their truth. And what is
revealed? Whoever chooses this pursuit can only reluctantly repeat
the words of Benjamin Constant (1767–1830), the author of the
novel *Adolphe*: "True feelings have never created anything but misfortune for myself and others." Thus, truth creates misfortune in the
same way that clarity creates misfortune (Blanchot, "*Adolphe*," 240).

The madness here referred to is similar to the madness that besets
the journal writer in *The Mind's Tormented Love*, Constantin in
Repetition, and the narrator in Blanchot's *Death Sentence*. This type
of madness can also be seen as an attempt on the part of the characters to map out their inner possibilities and thereby acquire a feeling
for their emotional breathing space while, at the same time, gaining
an understanding of the boundaries within which they live. As has
been seen, the space these characters experience is, in part, historically determined. They are situated in the Bible, whether or not they
believe in it. In this context one may mention another kind of space
– that which one finds in the characters of the Sagas of Icelanders. I
have already discussed the different interpretations of the inner life of
the saga characters. However that may be, their emotional space is
bound by the ideological world to which they themselves belong.[4]

I now turn to the fiction of Guðbergur Bergsson. Here, the particular madness with which we are dealing is called upon to *test reality*, as is testified to by the characters in many of his works. However,
before looking at this theme in *The Heart Still Dwells in Its Cave*
and the short story "The Man Who Suffered a Misfortune," it is necessary to inquire into the modern-day circumstances of these

creations. Ever since Plotinus searched the mind for an authentic existence, god has reigned and died in the inner life. And now what?

GODLESS PARTICIPATION

Shortly after the publication of Bergsson's novel *The Search for the Beautiful Land* in 1985, the author's interview with Tómas R. Einarsson appeared. In this interview Bergsson says: "The book is the final stage of the imagination. It is there that the imagination dies, in a certain way – the individual's imagination. Then it is quite possible that society's imagination takes over, who knows? But the work of art is the final stage of the imaginative process, not the beginning."[5] Difficult questions are likely to arise here regarding whether the creation of a work of literature still involves the participation of the reader. What, for example, does Bergsson mean by the death of the imagination? And who is this "individual" if not the reader? Are we perhaps confined to watching performances from on high? Is that the author's wish? Hardly, if we go by the following statement taken from the same interview:

> Icelandic readers ... want to get themselves into some sort of
> mental high. They want art to be some kind of intoxicant. The
> need for an altered state is rather intense, but I don't think auth-
> ors should provide for this need. I think authors should rather
> lead people to self-recognition. If people want to be in an altered
> state, they can go to church, or into politics, or take drugs, alco-
> hol and such. It is a much greater and purer form of intoxication
> than what art has to offer with all its intellect.

Here we see at work both the sociological and the aesthetic approach the author takes to the art form he practises. If he is to be believed, then there is a tendency in Iceland to search for a form of inebriation (whether it be provided by religion, politics, drugs, or alcohol). There also seems to be some confusion concerning the inebriation provided by intoxication, on the one hand, and art, on the other. However that may be, Bergsson does not wish to lead the reader into any form of mental high and, in fact, states that art does not bear any comparison with intoxicants. The singularity of literature is its intellectual quality, which, as is the case with humanity's intellect in general, is demanding but not reliable. When it comes to

the subject of beauty emerging only with the intervention of humanity, the willfulness described here is important. When intellect and
beauty meet, the reader's imagination must be as involved as the
author's. But to what end, if the imagination should die?

Perhaps critics are slow to appreciate this particular difficulty. We
may say it is a double-edged problem because it involves both the
reader's participation in Bergsson's works and the identification of the
aesthetics found there being based on a form of reader-contribution.[6]
Bergsson is not only conscious of the role of the reader but also expects her/his active participation. In this context, we may mention the
textual fragment alluded to in *Guðbergur Bergsson Bestseller*, in
which Bergsson discusses how no one understands a work of literature; how it is not about finding beauty in a work, or "the key, the
right perspective, what the author actually means, or the right understanding – literature and art are, rather, tools that the reader is given
to interpret or to shape and distinguish" (195).

It seems as though, for Bergsson, reading is nothing other than a
creative act. The author's position towards the reader's role is significant, especially in the context of discussing the possible participation
of modern people in beauty and the ideas that lie behind it. In modern
times, the voice of beauty may speak in a low volume and is perhaps
barely audible to the most conscious souls (which is how Zarathustra
perceived it on his mountain).[7] In fact, Bergsson does not scratch the
reader unless he himself is bleeding as well. And, with regard to the
ideas expressed in the works we are discussing here, can we not consider them to be more in tune with the reaction of the soul and the
emotions to nihilism itself rather than with nihilism's *messenger*?[8] In
comparison to the golden era of the message (a golden era that may
have lasted a while longer in Icelandic literature than in other litera-
tures), this kind of participation (i.e., of the reader with the book)
may appear raw, even ironic, and hard to bear. But is there not something to be said for a participation bereft of (divine) providence?

It appears that one of the distinguishing features of Bergsson's
writing, aside from its suspicion of any interpretation that seeks
shelter from established teachings and theories, is the faith it shows
in the importance of the imagination for human perception. Human
life is still confined to the necessities and needs of the senses. And
even though one has – in a seemingly godless universe – little more
than uncertainty and doubt, naked participation cannot be dismissed. The circumstances for such thinking are understandably

disappointing.[9] However, the human project remains the same as ever, and, in modern nihilistic times, it becomes more challenging. For how is one to approach something like the love of self, of life, and of others in a serious manner if there is no certain truth to be found in a person's life? What is to become of love in the midst of a barren vastness?

It may be that this experience of the *barrenesque* quality of our inner life is a major feature of our times, an experience that could also be defined by the slippery concept of nihilism. Contrary to what some believe, nihilism is not always to be understood as an irresponsible negativity. Quite the contrary, nihilism awakens people to a consciousness of the responsibility each and every one of us has when confronting that which we have called true and right.[10]

It seems that the aesthetics of Bergsson's works emerges from concerns that relate to both life and art. It is also a response to how the relationship between humanity and beauty has been considered in the past. It is, in other words, possible to discover some of the roots of Bergsson's aesthetics in the longing for beauty in ancient Greece and the creative struggle in the wake of Christian teaching. Although Bergsson freely admits to the deception of the material and to the repetitiveness of life's illusions, we see how the connection between humanity and beauty is as unresolved now as it was in the time of Plotinus. Given this, we may refer to the theme involved here as a subject of continuous creativity.

Now we turn to Bergsson's characters, to the meeting ground of the emotions in godless participation, to see how, in the narrative of a modern novelist engaged with possible realities of the inner life, the desire for beauty becomes a reflection of beauty.

THE HEART STILL DWELLS IN ITS CAVE

The soil and nature, the animals and the colour of the sky, give man peace. But he, by nature, is restless and deceitful. (*Heart* 172)

If the attempt to create Plato's Republic was more successful in Plotinus's *Enneads* than it was in the Roman Empire, then the story may have repeated itself, much later and on a different level. I am referring to what may be termed the "Republic of the Kiosk" in the far north, which is the setting for Bergsson's *The Heart Still Dwells in Its Cave*. There, characters appear as flickering souls, reminiscent

of the shadowy images of what we cannot know. Though some of
the characters could not care less about these things, others are more
thoughtful, as if on the brink of a need for faith. In this narrative, we
follow a divorced man, shrouded in the darkness of earth, land, and
human life, and roam aimlessly about in the lives of vodka-and-coke
drinkers, on the vague boundaries between heathendom and
Christianity. And what do we perceive?

For twenty-four hours, a psychologist searches through the laby-
rinths of both mind and city for some version of truth about himself,
his relationships, and what has made him what he is. The story begins at noon, and the protagonist, who has just moved (for the seventh time in less than a year) into a rented room, has put his things in
a pile on the floor. After a conversation with the woman from whom
he is renting, he heads off to the Reykjavík city centre, restless and
missing his former wife Dóra (who is a sociologist) and his daugh-
ters. At Hlemmur (a town square) he meets up with them. After a
failed attempt to interact with them, he drinks up his courage and,
later in the evening, makes another attempt to "conquer" Dóra. She
calls the police, the man is thrown in jail, and, at or about midnight,
he is sitting in a cell as a result of a misunderstanding, thinking:

> "God, you devil, you know as well as I do myself and the banks
> too, that I never keep any money in a secret account. Both you
> and Dóra, you misunderstand me drastically, if you really think
> – unless you are both lying – that I steal from my own paycheck
> and spend it on women. Where do you find any whores here?
> When would I get a chance to spend a single penny on a prosti-
> tute? If a man rented a room for such things, it would quickly be
> discovered in a small town like this, where everyone is spying on
> everyone else. There are limits to infidelity here because of the
> small size of the city, even though the need and desire for such
> acts are greater here in this narrow mouse-hole world than in
> any metropolis. I hardly waste more money than, for example,
> Gunni does on alcohol and tobacco. God, you also know that as
> soon as I get drunk I start to mess with Dóra, but that's some-
> thing I can't help and it doesn't mean anything. You are both
> blithering idiots, she and you, if you think I am hiding anything
> from you."

After this speech the man felt better, but he had become hot at
this mental exertion, and he grimaced again and thought: "No,

this kind of prayer goes nowhere. This is cowardly behaviour and god would be a complete fool if he took me seriously."

After this the man's misery was complete; he could not confess to anyone what was on his mind, both because his mind was full of monstrosities that were in continual motion and ceaselessly changing, and also because he didn't really believe in anything. The man stared powerless and diminished into the blue, at the barren walls; he couldn't talk to god and fill the emptiness around him, and he couldn't find the words to describe his misery because the words became false and unnatural and untrue. All the learned prayers to god are predetermined and have been created by others, in minds that are different from his, and in times long past that have no bearing on his own time, and yet they often demand to be presented in an organized way, even if it is done without any underlying belief. But the man knew from experience that when despair grips the mind and people feel the need for god, all patterns disentangle and the true prayer becomes complete and utter nonsense. That is why it is necessary for the confused person to momentarily search out the creator and the organizer of his life, so he can get a grip on the churnings that are going on in his brain, which he presents to him in their directionless and confused state. At such a time his weltering thoughts most resemble a mess of strands from a heap of yarn skeins that he does not know how to wind into balls, and, in the end, his mind can find no end to its quivering. That is exactly why the person who, not with a prayer in the usual sense, but with nonsense alone, is more real and honest than one who prays in a deliberate way, with a calm mind, who is, in fact, a person of ingratiating greed, demanding gifts of god without giving anything himself in return, except maybe vain words and useless promises. (87–8)

Even though this occurs at another time in the history of civilization, and the ideas about the boundaries of god and the devil are completely different from those in the Bible, the portrayal of inner suffering here resembles the despair of Job: the happy days of family life are over and there is nothing left in this man's life but the illusions that attend his departure. He stands helpless against the meaninglessness that looms before him, and who but the organizer of life could be responsible for such an imperfect creation? But times have changed, and though people have been able to turn to god in the past, this protagonist is in grave doubt about any possibility for a real connection: emptiness is all around, his misery is complete, and within there is "nothing but monstrosity" in "continuous flux and ceaseless change."

While facing the slim chanches of divine intervention, the man would still like to believe in Christianity's hypnotic effect: "'Thank god that my inner self has disappeared and flown away,' he said in a low and heavy voice" (90). However, what remains is an earlier idea: the notion of the soul and its never-ending roaming, who may acquire it, and how one is to live with others in the shadow of its meanderings. Added to this is the inexorable perception of nothingness and inner horror, which is continuously mutating and involves the man's sense of his own materiality.

But what, then, is the heart?

What makes the reader conscious of the complexity of Bergsson's story is this strange staging of the protagonist's search. In the republic of the *Heart* – which is shaped by the living conditions within the "Republic of the Kiosk" – the divorced man is the reader's guide not only along the anguished avenues of modern life and their fierce conflicts of interest (which tear apart the best of households in the late capitalist era) but also along the ambiguous border between Greek and Christian cultures.[11] This kind of "staging" is not uncharacteristic of Bergsson's entire oeuvre.

When the story appeared in the beginning of the 1980s, there was much public discussion about the relationship between the sexes, women's liberation, and women's literature. Special attention was paid to the relevance of the novel, in particular as it relates to the possibilities of the emotions and the coexistence of the genders. A review by Þorvaldur Kristinsson that appeared in that era, "These Are Our Times," comes to mind. In it Kristinsson says the married couple in Bergsson's story belong to a set of people who are expected to be able to sort out their difficulties. The man is a psychologist and his former wife Dóra is a sociologist. Instead of problem solving, however, what awaits the reader is endless meandering in a state of anguish and paranoia. This does not, however, mean that there is total confusion: the man is not a "complete idiot," as some readers claimed shortly after the novel appeared. Nor is this kind of attitude confined to the 1980s. As is discussed below, Bergsson's exploration of the enigmatic nature of humanity, of human emotions, and of human beings' fluctuating sexual orientation, self-destructive tendencies, and need for art causes aversion in those readers who require a prefabricated stance rather than a creative search.

In this context, it is important to remember, when discussing the picture this novel gives of its time and place, that we cannot expect the author to present us with a preconceived idea of reality, such as that which gives us our preferred vision of the role of women. On the contrary, the story challenges such expectations, as Ástráður Eysteinsson points out. Eysteinsson also notes that the women's movement, like all movements, whether in politics or literature or elsewhere, has diverse qualities. The discussion itself no doubt contributes to a healthy uncertainty in people's thinking, he says. It is quite another matter "when it appears that the women's movement or women's literature have gone off on a tangent and started to propose some sort of unquenchable 'truth,' then it is time to take another look at that truth and challenge it" (Eysteinsson, "To Give in the Imperative," 127). In Eysteinsson's opinion, that is what Bergsson is doing in *The Heart Still Dwells in Its Cave.*

When discussing the contemporary theme of this novel, it is important to note that we are dealing with a modernist work. As is mentioned by Þorvaldur Kristinsson in his review, the protagonist's roaming (or searching) takes place on the boundary between dream and reality: "Here introspection is foregrounded, through the use of the man's emotions, dreams, and imagination – but with constant references to outer reality – and the reader is presented with his anguish and dissolution." In short, "the depiction of anguish is too nuanced to be thought of as irony and pedantry" (Kristinsson, "These Are Our Times," 337). It is not only bourgeois feminism that the novel critiques for being somewhat shallow but also family life in an era of property ownership, power struggles, greed, and rampant consumerism. However black the author's worldview may seem, his fictional world does not revolve only around itself. Bergsson does not intend us to "be content with misery," Kristinsson says. I would agree with this assessment. The question is, however, what are the creative possibilities inherent in such a fictional world?

Let us turn to the protagonist's struggle and the underlying aesthetic positioning. As often happens in modernist works, the human being is "alone and alienated from others, without perspective over or understanding of [his or her] life" (Kristinsson 339). In this condition we continually question our own potential. In reference to this matter, it is well to remember a factor that has affected not only the

story presently under discussion but all of Bergsson's oeuvre: the
creative struggle with language, with what has been called the aesthetics of language, and which Bergsson himself describes in one of
his essays. Here, we are reminded of the ethics of aesthetics in
Bergsson's writing and of his thoughts concerning the boundaries
between life and art:

> A self-respecting author does not think of his needs or his duties;
> he is propelled forward like an electric charge, drawn by the eth-
> ical problems of the words themselves, after literature has van-
> ished from the pure stream of thought and arrived in the world
> of letters and words. He is so independent on account of this
> electricity, which is brought about by the rubbing of his aesthetic
> sensibility against the social order, that he is able to let ugly
> words into his poetry, in among the greatest beauty. In fact, that
> is the morally right thing to do, artistically speaking, in his view,
> even though it would be thought immoral and even tasteless to
> use such words in similar contexts in daily life. ("Is Literature
> the Way" 449)

AWAY FROM THE PROBLEM OF BEAUTY
AND INTO THE SHADOW OF THE SELF

"It begins gracefully for me, as usual," (12) says the protagnist at the
outset of The Heart Still Dwells in Its Cave, as he stands and senses
the physical proximity of the woman who rents him the room behind the closed door. In spite of his supposed failure in marriage, the
man sets off on his journey. As with the diarist in The Mind's
Tormented Love, this man continually questions his own potential
in the face of creativity and death. Is what his mother says to him
perhaps true? That "to ask is to want to know and to destroy"?
(Heart 122)

I will not trace the entire story of this man but simply go with him
on his visit to Big Jói, a regular fellow down the street and a former
co-worker. At around midnight, after having been twice in prison, he
has now come to Jói's place to party. Big Jói lives with his friend
Little Jói, a woman, and a child. And what do we see?

> Now the man looked vacantly at the woman who lay curled up
> next to his friend Big Jói, and his friend Little Jói lay prone next

to the woman, dressed in his cotton underpants. In the same instant the child began to play his idiotic game. He sprayed coke onto his mother's bum. The man was unable to form any thoughts about what he was seeing. Little Jói curled his feet up and the woman did the same after the boy had sprayed under her dress, which was open up to the thighs, and the man watched disinterestedly, with a vacant stare, at the fat breasts that spilled out between her knees, soaked in coke-drink.

"What a heap of flesh," the man thought to himself, and in his mind there flashed a picture of a stomach out of a newly slaughtered, sick sheep that has been thrown onto the rubbish heap. There the sheep stomachs lay bloody and unclean and split open in among the paper refuse, shards of newspapers, and books and empty bottles. (144)

On the sofa are sitting a man, woman, and child, something one is supposed to look at but not count among the beautiful things of the world. Big Jói advises his friend:

Hey, you are not optimistic enough, my boy. Look around you and rest your eyes on the beauty and stop looking mournful with that grime in your eyes. Everything we see is the pure beauty of nature and life. But the sofa there isn't part of it; don't count that. (145)

And, somewhat later, the friend emphasizes his warning:

"Worlds rise and fall like waves of the tides. That is why you should hold on carefully to your inner seas. But man should protect his unquenchable faith and optimism, however the weather at sea may throw him about. Don't let – and listen carefully – the mind's raptures deceive the eye. That sofa there is a historical necessity. See what you see, and not what you think."

Jói dried his mouth with his flat palm and added:

"Now I'm chattering on, but the mind should be far-reaching and recognize only that which is directly in view, instead of constantly interpreting and adding to reality with its imagination. You educated people are always in danger of this. No, do as the new man does, the humanity of the future, who has already grown to maturity in the lands of the rising sun in the East." (145)

On the sofa is that "historical necessity," even though it is there in an exaggerated form, for here we find free individuals in a free country. Not only is the call of Plotinus – "you must close the eyes and call instead upon another vision which is to be waked within you, a vision, a birth-right to all, which few turn to use" ("Beauty" 71) – far removed from good fun, according to Big Jói, it is better not to awaken the inner vision. The idea of the relation between human beings and beauty gets no play in a tradition that puts its trust in the heathen god of wine. But the man is not allowed to enjoy this traditional form of entertainment for long. Even though he tries his best to follow the mores of the times, whether out of historical or habitual necessity, he is not successful at maintaining the illusions that allow other people to go on, to live. But what, then, is left for him?

After the debaucheries of the night, as he sits weary in a taxicab (which reminds him of a hearse) on his way from Big Jói's back to his room, with a prim, quiet, and cold woman at his side, it is as if he decides to live out his thoughts. In order to do this, he needs to put reality to the test, and, at that moment, something interesting occurs:

> The driver did not move his head; the man leaned forward in the front seat and told him where to drive. Then he was overwhelmed by a sense of calm and peace from the silent, cold woman. At first the man expected her to steal her hand over the seat towards him in the darkness, so the driver would not see, and her hand would be cold to the touch, but he would warm her hand with his own cold hand; and at that moment he figured that two cold hands would make a thorough warmth. But the woman did not budge and kept her hands to herself, which seemed to be resting in her lap. (*Heart* 152–3)

The man is not sure of the nature of the woman's "existence," and he wonders whether this could be the one and true Dóra. The woman in the back seat, though, is wearing a green hat, and the man knows that Dóra never wears a hat since, in her view, to do so was a sign of "the aristocracy." Who is she, then? Or, rather, where is the man going?

> Now the man remembered that the woman with the green hat had made a strong impression on him before. She pushed herself through a crowd and there was a feather in her hat. But that

woman was fictional, and the man wiped the sweat off his face, dubious that, out of a book and with his own memory, he could have made real this woman's existence, until she not only stood before him as a vision but sat beside him in the flesh. "I am going to test reality," the man thought. "Is the one who sits beside me an illusion or for real?" He hesitated for a long time and enjoyed the thought that he was living in reality and in a dream simultaneously. "I exist between day and dream," he thought and tried to remember where that line of poetry came from. His excitement grew. (153)

The man becomes so animated that he thinks: "I am going to make love to you" (ibid.). And he does – not by looking at her but by "enjoying her nearness" (ibid.).

The man becomes fully aware – in the middle of the confusion – of how enchanting this desire is. Instead of just running in and fetching the shaving gear from his room and then going off with the woman who exists on the border of day and dream, she whom he nonetheless wishes, in his heart of hearts, could be the real Dóra, he finds a moment's need to stop and talk honestly with the woman who rents him his quarters, as if to ascertain what his possibilities in life might be. He "longed to be able to say to her clearly and articulately how men actually were, at least how he himself was, and what kind of terrible beast he was, and then add at the end that the difficulties women faced were very similar to those faced by men" (154). His need to speak dissipates, however, and he runs in circles outside, again looking for the waiting taxicab, which is nowhere to be seen. Worse for wear, he stumbles back inside. There he is met by the "rented stage" of his present life. But reality in the Republic of the Kiosk is not all that meets the eye:

After a few hours' passing, day would come and the cave would open, and one would be able to see people moving about, far inside, like living shadows whose original image and mental activity lay hidden and buried in another era, on another stage, far back in ancient times, and that would be why they moved about lonely, confused and worn. Dawn was looming. (160)

It appears as if the man's search finally brings him home to his own shadow. Maybe that is why, after failed attempts to sleep with her, he allows himself the luxury of saying to the woman: "Never look for consolation in mankind when you need it; look for it in the plant world instead" (173). Her response, which is in perfect keeping with the nature and circumstance of both of them, is this:

> The woman jumped up and leaned forward on her elbows and stared directly into the man's eyes.
> "Do you want to be my daddy for a while?"
> The man could feel how an air of imbecility filled the room, soupy and slimy. The air suddenly turned into thin gruel and the man repeated:
> "Yeah – yeah." (173)

But where does he go if he is to get on with life and withdraw from the problem of beauty? Now he knows that he and the imagined Dóra could never come together except in the mind; he would have to combine the image of the real Dóra and the Dóra of his imagination. He feels that "an image of a person is different from the real person, because people disappoint one another, and the image does not" (174). He remembers a picture of Dóra that lies in the heap of stuff in the bedroom, tears himself away from the woman, gets into his own room with some difficulty, grabs the picture out of the rubble, and smashes the glass. The woman, hurt by this, takes a shard of glass off the picture and "mumble[s] under her breath that both she and the glass [are] transparent and sharp-edged" (175). Then she helps the man die: "'All right,' she whispered. 'We will cut time loose. Go, flow away, because life is cut off from its terrors'" (176).

Perhaps this reality is created in what we might call the interface of beauty and death. It is in circumstances such as these that the creation of character sheds light on humanity's struggle with the deceptions of the senses and the need for illusions. We not only see the author's focus on the relation between humanity and beauty but also how this relation is just as unresolved in our day as it was in ancient times. There is, however, a marked difference between ancient times and modern times. God has both reigned and died in the inner life since Plotinus set out to search for an authentic existence. In our time, not only are we caught up in our own unmediated participation in existence, but this participation is an expression of the material world that allows it to take place. We are unable to approach the human heart without thrusting our way through the crowds and the piles of debris we are unable to avoid except through death. And the man in Bergsson's novel cannot come near his own heart without first feeling his way through the emptiness that resides inside himself.

Now we will take a closer look at Bergsson's notion of creativity by discussing his short story "The Man Who Suffered a Misfortune."

ON INTIMATE TERMS WITH REALITY

In "The Man Who Suffered a Misfortune" we read of another nameless, confused, and helpless modern man who, like the protagonist in *The Heart Still Dwells in Its Cave*, puzzles over things, not least of which is his relationship with his wife. Unlike the psychologist, this man is not divorced but lives with his wife and experiments with his emotions inside the walls of his home. His thinking and his search take him away from his home life, however, and the question the story addresses is: where does he go and what experiences does he encounter?

The story begins with the words: "When the man had become certain that his wife was unfaithful to him, he stopped performing his usual tasks. Then he completely stopped going to work" ("Man Who Suffered" 39). What follows is a peculiar description of an unusual sequence of events, told by a man who is no "specialist." He claims to be an ordinary man with all his talents in his hands, and he considers any talk of emotions to be a "complicated affair." Perhaps that is why he trusts his tactile sensations when he becomes suspicious of his wife's faithfulness. He cannot, in his mind, see a definite alteration in her behaviour, but he claims to be able to *perceive* the changes in her when he touches her body. The conclusion proves to be deeply troubling to the man: his wife's change "was only evident in the little things that are so secret that they can only be intuited, so one's state of mind becomes skewed and things start piling up" (40). Just like the psychologist, he is alone and helpless in his trouble; however, unlike the latter, he does not compare himself and his experiences to past eras in world history. He perceives what is.

Maybe the changes he is concerned about are all inside himself. If that is so, they probably have to do with fluctuations in sexual orientation and are therefore a sign of his own unfaithfulness, emotionally speaking, towards himself and his wife. After having rummaged about in his wife's cosmetics in the bathroom while searching for proof of

her infidelity, and painting his lips with lipstick while he is at it, he
looks in the mirror. His "nerves seemed to collapse" (40) when he sees
himself. He gets the feeling that he is "unclean and outcast"; he feels
as if he has broken "ancient rules," and, instead of being filled with a
sense of "happiness" or "release," he gets the urge to "beat his wife
senseless, as if he could that way be cleansed of the disgusting image
of himself in the mirror and reclaim his masculinity" (40). The "out-
ing" in the bathroom may seem obvious, as is the attendant description of the "nervous collapse" after the breaking of "ancient rules." As
a result, it is possible to conclude that the man's misfortune consists
of a suppression of his sexual orientation and that his true nature is
bursting to the surface in a violent way. But if this is the case, then the
man's fluctuating sexuality may also highlight an existential crisis.

Of course, the man's rage takes tangible form in a dramatic connection to the satisfying of his sexual urges. One morning he makes
love to his wife and then proceeds directly to his sister's, who lives
nearby, and he confesses to her his suspicion of his wife's infidelity.
She tries to talk sense into him, tells him that his marriage is not
"over, either spiritually or physically," and that love is one thing and
physical need is another. She also says that the progress of love invariably leads to "a mistake" (44). The man, "speechless and confused," says he does not want to understand that kind of argument.
After a lot of argumentative back-and-forth in the kitchen, the sister's husband enters in his underwear and begins swearing and
shouting about, among other things, the educated class. The sister
says to him: "I can stand your drivel even less than the whining of
my brother ... the mutterings coming from him remind me of the
atmosphere at home, but your continuous claptrap reminds me of
the tiresomeness of marriage, and it's affecting me" (44). It is not her
husband who responds violently to these words but her brother.

In this story we see an argument concerning love and marriage
that is very similar to those that we find in Bergsson's other fictional
works. As with the characters in his other works, this man is helpless
against the force of his own emotions. Still, he does not put a stop to
his inner journey. It is not only he himself who is lacking the mental
balance to resolve things but also the system, the society in which he
lives (see quotation below). After his attack on his sister, he lets himself be put in jail. After a year of hard labour, he is pardoned. He
then commits another crime in order to be incarcerated again, and
this time he is removed from his life for some time:

He had now remained unbothered by the world for several years, while neither the psychologists, the sociologists, nor the criminologists could decide whether he was insane and should be in a mental institution or just a plain criminal. The only thing those specialists knew for sure was that he had committed more crimes, and that made him a serial criminal, and since there were no institutions for such people, the result was that he would remain in the working prison. But they also thought that if he did his work regularly and did not take too many sick days, then he could be considered reformed and of normal health, both mentally and physically. (45)

I am not interested in the specialists' conclusion but, rather, in what happens to this man.

It seems as though the man chooses to be "free in order to be not free and alone" (45). This is a paradox: in prison he is free to search his inner self and to wander the labyrinth of his emotions. He thinks it is an "odd absurdity" that it is inside the prison that he feels "free for the first time" and that it is there that he enjoys an "inner freedom" (46). In these circumstances he sets off to discover his inner reality. And what does he find?

Perhaps the man's difficulty consists of living in his own skin and having all the sensations to which he is subject without being able to find himself; he exists in a condition that is both untenable and unnamable. In prison he understands that it is easier to remember a photograph of his wife than it is to remember her in real life. How could he have loved the woman if, in his mind, she is only a photograph? How can a picture of a person be more real to the memory than the actual, living person? This is the question he asks himself and his cellmate. His cellmate tells him that the picture is easier to deal with than are real people. The man agrees, but wants to take it further. He goes into his cell, closes the door, and wonders: is the memory not more sensitive than film? Is the memory not made of feelings? At this thought he knocks his "head against the wall" and wonders "how it is that such thoughts are taking place inside him, he who has simply worked at his job with his hands all the while until his wife was unfaithful to him" (47).

But when he has been pardoned and released, "his vision of things goes awry." After having been "free to be not free and alone," he is faced with "distance and endlessness" – phenomena that awaken an existential dizziness. As a result, he not only becomes "unsteady on his feet" but everything around him becomes "strange and foreign and extraordinarily uncertain; and the outlines of the landscape look monstrous" (48). He has returned to life. He does, nonetheless, find his way back home to his wife and, in their ensuing conversation, the misfortune he suffered resurfaces:

> "Don't say anything," the woman asked of him. "I want to talk uninterrupted."
>
> He said nothing. In fact, he was speechless with surprise, and disappointment covered over his eyes in a strange way.
>
> "I have been faithful to you while you were in prison," the woman said. "As soon as you were given a long sentence, my body decided that it should be true to you, and that it should also be in prison."
>
> ... The man closed his eyes. He listened to how the woman kept talking in an even monotone, while she continued to watch the picture on the television. He tried to recover his image of her in his mind, but that picture was nowhere to be found, neither in a photograph nor in the face of the woman herself, even though he was seated next to them both.
>
> Suddenly it seemed as if he had received a blow from a fist, the same blow his sister received before. He automatically covered his mouth and felt like vomiting.
>
> "What's this?" The woman asked. "Are you getting sick?"
>
> "No," he answered weakly.
>
> "What then?" She asked surprised.
>
> "It's just reality," he answered and stood up. "It hit me like a misfortune." (48–9)

With these responses, the protagonist stirs up the reader's feelings regarding the "strange emptiness" that hovers over the godless and helpless image of modern humanity. At the same time, this story gives rise to suspicions regarding the ambiguities and limitations of modern science as it attempts to demarcate this miraculous creation: the human being.

As he shows in *The Heart Still Dwells in Its Cave*, Bergsson's criticisms concerning the possible limits of science and technology are not confined to irony or ridicule. What we discern in his fiction is, on the one hand, deep thinking about the powerlessness of humanity with regard to itself, others, and life, and, on the other hand, doubts about the approach science and specialized fields take towards the same. Although thoughts of human powerlessness may involve an admission that human beings are engaged in a struggle with life, it seems as though science and its related fields have a tendency to neutralize that struggle through endless compartmentalization and the classification of illnesses. One of the questions a reading of Bergsson raises is, therefore: is art necessary for modern human beings?

Blanchot may be right when he says that our era is an era of restlessness, distance, and exile – an era that is bereft of gods. In his mind, art does not replace religion. But in our times, art can be recognized because it contains in itself the proximity of unrest (Blanchot, "Kafka and the Work's Demand," 83).

THE INESCAPABLE CONTRADICTION

Even though the place of beauty, in the context discussed here, is not obvious, it does seem as though Plotinus's search is not altogether over. So long as novelists reflect on the possibilities of existence, it follows that thoughts of beauty are not only unavoidable but actually elucidate the inescapable connection between humanity and beauty, or how beauty is created through the participation of humanity.

But what is the creation of contemporary aesthetics? Here I propose that, in narratives of inner reality, this place no one sees but that all experience, nothing much occurs that is not inevitably connected with the relation between humanity and beauty. But of course, what occurs is not necessarily comprehended. When we ask about the possibilities of the emotions in contemporary literature, the creation of character can throw light on the way in which modern humanity participates in beauty. Literature can also show specific aspects of the human condition – aspects that are experienced in the mind when a decision has been made to live out relationships in order to explore their possibilities. These are often referred to as a form of madness, and we could say that the characters in Bergsson's stories are cases in point.

As is to be expected, writing of this nature elicits mixed responses. In order to approach these works, as well as the responses to them, we need to examine not only the tradition out of which Bergsson's aesthetics comes but also the circumstances of its creation. In addition to the confusion and chaos that the subject matter itself (humanity's inner life and its participation in beauty) inevitably brings about, it seems as though death is haranguing the inner life. Instead of its being impossible to perceive a bridge between aesthetics and nihilism, we glimpse not only some creative possibilities but also the effect of responsibility.

Life, Bergsson said at one point, is just a harsh necessity. And literature? "Literature for me is much the same as life: if a man could choose some other venue for his senses or his being other than life, he would choose that and repudiate life ... That is why I say that, fortunately for my emotions, I feel as though I am both dead and alive" (*Guðbergur Bergsson Bestseller* 70).

The discussion of the ethics of Bergsson's aesthetics is not thereby exhausted. I have already mentioned that nihilism – in the context of the particular form of aesthetics at issue here – is far from being simply an irresponsible negation; rather, it awakens people to a consciousness of *each and everyone's responsibility* towards that which we call *true and right*. This point is important to the existentialist nature of the ethics of Bergsson's aesthetics. In this context it is possible to come to grips with one of the main features of his writing: a persistent lack of faith in a view of life that finds resolution in dogmatic theories. This lack of faith is directed not only at the theories Icelanders offer regarding the relationship between humanity and beauty, both in life and in art, but also at academic and scientific theories in general. Kierkegaard and Nietzsche are pertinent here, for they, like Bergsson, persistently ask about the human being's possibilities in life, moving beyond the dogma of powerful theories. More will be said on this matter in coming chapters.

In light of this discussion, it is hard to disagree with Vilhjálmur Árnason's idea of the difference between the ethics of aesthetics, on the one hand, and logical/discursive ethics, on the other. The former concerns the question of what constitutes a good and desirable life, while the latter concerns the classification and critique of right and wrong when reasoning about social mores and rules. As Árnason claims, the practice of art (and religion) is very different from the pursuit of a scholarly science such as ethics ("In a Red Light" 229). The contribution of the ethics of aesthetics that can be discovered in literature is also relevant in this context. As discussed, we can see that the ethics of aesthetics in Bergsson's writing does not revolve around the good and desirable life; rather, his writing calls forth a special kind of participation in the question of what constitutes a creative or a destructive way of life. Such are the possibilites of the imagination, not only in relation to existence but also in relation to the text.

This distinction is particularly relevant to one of the main features of Bergsson's aesthetics, which is the artful and existential re-evaluation of life and of those who live it. The circumstances in which Bergsson's characters end up are, more often than not, moments of existential profundity. In such cases, the logic of ethics has limited potential, or, as Árnason phrases it: "As far as experience can be articulated, it acquires meaning in narrative for the reader only if he or she has had similar things to deal with. That is why individuals who are experiencing peak moments are likely to find resonance in the symbolic language of religion and art, which invariably are combined in music" ("What Is Ethics Capable Of?" 167).

Moments of existential profundity awaken us not only to our participation in beauty but also to the freedom of our individual responsibility. However our responsibilities play out in life, in literature we are able to explore them and ask questions about subjects such as the possibilities of the emotions. Regarding the complex relationship between beauty and life and the potential of aesthetics to deal with such topics, Bergsson comments:

> But aesthetics, beauty, to enjoy life, is, among other things, to see objects, people, and the world and then be able to transform everything into feelings that are visible and tangible, regardless of whether the emotion is comfortable or uncomfortable for the artist or for others. Only he who is alone dares to admit this – not only by the creation of his works of art, but also in a certain way in existence. ("Spirit That Reigned in Súm" 108–9)

Now we turn to the part played by existentialism in Bergsson's fiction and attempt to discover whether his aesthetics answer – however indirectly – the call of Kierkegaard's philosophy of religion.

When Paradoxes Are Allowed to Unfold

The kind of aesthetics discussed here are not designed to deny inconsistencies, either in life or in art. We might say this form of aesthetics awakens our consciousness to a reality in which paradoxes are allowed to unfold. The way in which modern novelists participate in beauty raises persistent questions with regard to the inner life. In this chapter I continue to explore the possibilities of emotion, particularly those related to love and faith. I am not especially concerned with the conditions that Icelandic culture and society might place on the inner life. Nor is it my intention to discuss the problems posed by language in relation to being. What is of concern is how we think about the provisions of Christianity when it comes to love and faith.

In the nineteenth century few thinkers had considered more deeply the problems that revolve around faith and love than had Kierkegaard. He maintained that all his writings were bound to a specific problem within Christianity (Christendommen) and that he never wrote about anything other than the difficulty of being a Christian in dialogue with the terrible deception: Christendom (*Synspunktet for min Forfatter-Virksomhed* 81).[1] Søren Kierkegaard's interest in the problems of the Christian faith was passionate – so passionate that his writings on the subject raise not only the reader's awareness of the inevitable connection between faith and life but also of the ancient and seemingly persistent difficulties in people's lives in the Christian world. Such is the harvest in Fear and Trembling (*Frygt og Baeven: Dialektisk Lyrik*) which first appeared in 1843 in Copenhagen under the pseudonym Johannes de silentio. In this text, the author approaches the call of faith by putting himself in the shoes of Abraham the day he walked up the mountain in Moriah with his sacrifice, his son Isaac.

Kierkegaard's approach is unique: it is contrary to the whole being of the author of *Fear and Trembling* to follow a beaten path, to talk about magnificent things in a less-than-human way, as though "a few millennia were an immense distance." He chooses to talk about great things as though they happened only yesterday and lets "the greatness itself be the distance that either exalts or condemns" (28).[2] What the author perceives in the story of Abraham is the contradiction between faith and ethics: from the point of view of faith, Abraham is prepared to sacrifice his son to God; but from the point of view of ethics, Abraham is prepared to murder his son. "But in this contradiction lies precisely the anxiety," de Silentio writes, and, without it, Abraham is not the man he is made out to be (24).

The contradiction between faith and ethics in Abraham's story is not easy to deal with. Kierkegaard maintains, in fact, that no field of learning has ever managed to resolve the subject. His interpretation of the story is demanding and not in line with those offered in later decades.[3] But what about love? How is love connected to faith in Kierkegaard's view?

Of various interpretations, Kristján Árnason's comes to mind. In his introduction to the Icelandic translation of *Fear and Trembling* he points out that the book no doubt mirrors Kierkegaard's personal psychological condition during the time of writing as well as addressing more general theological and ethical topics. Kierkegaard's attempt to deal with the problems of faith and love and the connection between them could, in other words, be his own personal struggle, even as it also points to much larger arenas. This is so not only in *Fear and Trembling* but also in *Repetition*, which appeared the same year. At that time, Kierkegaard had broken up his engagement to Regine Olsen, which is not to say that he considered the relationship to be entirely over. It is possible that he toyed with the "idea that everything would turn out right in the end, as was the case for Abraham who got Isaac back ... and Job who got everything back, even twice," Kristján Árnason writes. He also points to Kierkegaard's journal entry for 17 May 1843, which says: "Had I believed, then I would have stayed with Regine" ("Introduction" 30–1).[4]

I will not dwell on ideas regarding Kierkegaard's psychological condition during the time of writing; rather, I will explore his inquiry into the vast domain of faith and love, how contemporary philosophers and writers approach these emotions, and how the story of Abraham (and Kierkegaard's take on it) enters the picture. Derrida

is among those who have written on the subject, and here I consider
his interpretation of the story of Abraham, with an emphasis on how
he explains its relevance to modern times. Bergsson is a fine example
of how a modern writer deals with the story, which, given the discussions in the previous chapters, should not come as a surprise. In
Bergsson's writing, the predicament of faith is an important theme,
and it is discussed in relation to an equally important theme – namely, love. In a discussion of these issues, Bergsson's short story "An
Image of Man from the bible" is unavoidable.[5] I also discuss in
greater detail *The Mind's Tormented Love.*

THE TEMPTATION OF ABRAHAM IS
HIS DESCENDANTS' PROBLEM

People nowadays may find the story of Abraham and Isaac to be too
distant to have any relevance, but there are many besides Kierkegaard
who do not doubt the importance of the story. One man, in fact,
goes so far as to claim that the setting for this story – Moriah – is the
dwelling place of all of us, each and every moment, each and every
day. That man is Jacques Derrida, and, in *The Gift of Death*, a book
that is said to be the most detailed text he wrote on the subject, he
discusses the problems of Christian religion. Here Derrida answers
the call of faith and says: "If faith does not require responsibility, it
requires nothing" (2). When it comes to the relationship between
faith and responsibility, the onus is on each and every person.
According to Derrida, unlike what the moral prophets of our day
preach, those who remonstrate in the press day in and day out, it
would seem that responsibility is of no special concern to contemporary ethicists. We find nothing on the subject in the writings of
philosophers; rather, we find it in people's experience of daily life.
What the story of Abraham shows is that the sacrifice of Isaac is our
daily bread and that the experience of this sacrifice is everyone's responsibility (67).

Kierkegaard would no doubt agree with Derrida that responsibility is not of particular concern to ethicists. However, the question is
whether he would see the sacrifice of Isaac as our daily bread. Before
going any further, it is helpful to review a fragment of what, with
regard to translation and interpretation, is considered to be one of
the most difficult chapters of the Bible:

And it came to pass after these things, that God did tempt
Abraham, and said unto him, Abraham: and he said, Behold,
here I am.

And he said, take now thy son, thine only *son* Isaac, whom
thou lovest, and get thee into the land of Moriah; and offer him
there for a burnt offering upon one of the mountains which I will
tell thee of ...

And Abraham took the wood of the burnt offering, and laid *it*
upon Isaac his son; and he took the fire in his hand, and a knife;
and they went both of them together.

And Isaac spake unto Abraham his father, and said, My father:
and he said, Here *am* I, my son. And he said, Behold the fire and
the wood: but where *is* the lamb for a burnt offering?

And Abraham said, my son, God will provide himself a lamb
for a burnt offering: so they went both of them together.

And they came to the place which God had told him of; and
Abraham built an altar there, and laid the wood in order, and
bound Isaac his son, and laid him on the altar upon the wood.

And Abraham stretched forth his hand, and took the knife to
slay his son.

And the angel of the Lord called unto him out of heaven, and
said, Abraham, Abraham, and he said, Here *am* I.

And he said, Lay not thine hand upon the lad, neither do thou
any thing unto him: for now I know that thou fearest God, seeing thou has not withheld thy son, thine only *son* from me.[6]

In 1981, a new edition of the Bible appeared in Icelandic, and professor of theology Þórir Kr. Þórðarson prepared it for publication. In
one place he discusses the changes that occurred in the above passage in Genesis 22, and how those changes affected the meaning of
the story. In the 1912 edition the wording is: "after these things, that
God *tried* Abraham and said unto him"; but, in the 1981 edition, the
passage has become: "after these things, that God *tempted* Abraham
and said unto him." Professor Þórðarson traces the reasons for this
change and says that the word "tried" is too weak for the important
and terrifying events that are taking place in this chapter. And, with
regard to the moment when Abraham – in his mind – has *already* cut
the boy's neck, Þórðarson says: "It was his intention. He who does
not apprehend the terror and fear of this moment, and consequently

of the story as a whole, is blind. And it is in this moment that we see how the verb 'to try' is incredibly casual for the terror that besets Abraham that day" (133).

The verb "to try" does not, in other words, describe the terror this temptation brings on, not only in the mind of Abraham but also in the minds of his descendants – us. But how? What is the *temptation*?

Þórðarson discusses Kierkegaard's interpretation of the story of Abraham and seems to agree with the viewpoint that there is at work there a terrible and incomprehensible paradox that concerns not only the people in the Old Testament but also the people who live in a Christian culture. Abraham is led into the temptation of turning his back on God's commandment. However, according to Þórðarson, if he performs the task asked of him, he has broken the laws of life: "I think the terror of this story, and its influence over the ages, comes from the fact that here, on a 'higher plane,' and, as with the revelations to be found in a poem or a parable, we find an expression of the ultimate limits – of the furthest recesses a human being can be made to travel to, when it has come to pass that wherever you go, all avenues are closed, and the abyss opens up before you and everything you do is wrong. A deeper paradox cannot be found" (135).

Could the sacrifice of Isaac be our daily bread?

Just like Kierkegaard, Derrida inquires into the paradox of Christianity. He asks about this particular event on the mountain, this moment when a father is prepared to sacrifice his son as a demonstration of the power of his faith. Derrida is asking about the nature of sacrifice, or about what he calls (in the spirit of Johannes de silentio) being in the grip of *terror*. This is what you experience after having accepted the death of the particular, that one thing that cannot be replaced, that thing you hold dearest of all. Derrida also reminds us of other basic elements of the meaning of sacrifice in Christian culture, such as the idea that a person can become a substitute for an animal (for example, Isaac becomes a lamb) as well as the connection between sacrifice and the secretive (*Gift of Death* 58).

I temporarily put aside the question of whether the sacrifice of Isaac is our daily bread. However, Derrida's view that, in Christianity, the experience of sacrifice is everlasting (even though this aspect of Christianity has not been adequately addressed)[7] may be shared by others. There are those who doubt that faith experiences have been entirely eliminated from the minds of modern human beings. As

William James argues in *The Varieties of Religious Experience*, the reality of religious experience is no less powerful in later times than it was in earlier times. The only difference is that, with the rise of a reliance on science, many attempts are made to explain religious experience in a scientific way. The experience being discussed here is not, however, one that psychology and the mental health sciences attempt to explain. The experience of the responsibility of sacrifice has never been classified under the rubric of abnormal behaviour. Ethics and theology have spent quite a lot of time on this experience. However, if we listen to the author of *Fear and Trembling*, the results have been inadequate. Faith, says Johannes de silentio, is beyond discourse. Disciplines like ethics, theology, and aesthetics fall short when trying to explain faith.

But can Moriah be considered the dwelling place of all of us, every minute, every day, in the sense that Derrida maintains? In the sense that, in this life, we are always at a critical point of terror? And, if that is so, would not such an idea fall on deaf ears at this time in our history?

In Christian societies at the beginning of the twenty-first century, it appears as though materialism has drowned people's interest in the relationship between faith and existence. This is not necessarily a new condition. In the nineteenth century, Kierkegaard noticed the insufficiency of how people thought about faith and how it becomes tangible, both for the individual and for society. With the rise of the bourgeoisie and the constant pressure of materialism, the question of faith in life lost its power and people's passion for life waned. There are no magical cures for such a crash. The problem, however, is that Christianity continues to be dominant, but only nominally: people only *consider* themselves Christian. This is the deception that Kierkegaard perceives and cannot leave alone.

Another, and no less important, point is that Kierkegaard's criticism in *Fear and Trembling* is directed at certain spokesmen for nineteenth-century theology, as Jóhanna Þráinsdóttir points out. In 1837 a young theologian, Hans Lassen Martensen (1808–84), gave a series of lectures at the University of Copenhagen. The series was called *Prolegomena ad dogmaticam speculative*: An Introduction to Speculative Theology. According to Þráinsdóttir, Martensen wanted to "come to a holistic view of the world and of life where everything of importance in existence – matter and spirit, nature and history, poetry, arts and philosophy – could all be collected together in the temple of the spirit behind the leading light of Christianity instead of philosophy, as Hegel had intended to do." In order to reach this goal, Martensen felt he needed to go "further than Hegel"; he called his theology "harmonious" and, with the help of the foundational concept of philosophy, *both-and*, as his weapon, he felt it was possible to "mediate between all the oppositions and contradictions that rationalists and naturalists found fault with in Christian learning and cause people to repudiate them" ("Historical Backdrop" 231–2). Kierkegaard's criticism in *Fear and Trembling* is particularly directed at Martensen. As Þráinsdóttir notes, Kierkegaard considered himself "plainly called to show the truest form of Christianity ... and in that Christianity there would be no *both-and* but, rather, only *either-or*. With his text *Fear and Trembling*, he stepped into the fray" (233).

Who, asks Johannes de silentio, speaks in the name of the passion of faith? While love has its priests among the list of poets (and, he adds, some of them rise to the task), there is general silence on the subject of faith. Theology "sits by the window all made up and courts its favor, offering to sell its delights to philosophy," that field that wishes to "surpass" religion (*Fear and Trembling* 27). Hegel is considered more difficult to understand than Abraham; to understand the philosophy of Hegel is a miracle, while Abraham is considered to be an open book. But Hegel, de silentio goes on, is, for the most part, easy to grasp. To think about Abraham, however, is exhausting because the paradox that is the basis of Abraham's life is not made for human thinking. According to de silentio, no matter how passionate one's thinking, it is impossible to penetrate the paradox that is the basis of Abraham's life.

Such is the difficulty of Christian faith – a difficulty that Kierkegaard discovers and about which he cannot remain silent. But is this the same difficulty with which Derrida struggles? Before discussing in greater detail how Kierkegaard interprets this problem, I turn to the arguments of Jacques Derrida.

FOR THE DESCENDANTS OF ABRAHAM, SACRIFICE IS TREASURE'S ISLAND

The sacrifice of Isaac, Derrida says, belongs to a common inheritance. This terrible secret is the joint inheritance of the three religions that are called the religions of the Book – Christianity, Judaism, and

Islam. In short, the sacrifice of Isaac haunts all the descendants of Abraham. The severity and demands of this faith compel its followers to do things that seem – and must be – terrible, things that must repulse those who guard the morals upon which these religions are built. According to Derrida, perhaps the kernel of Christianity has not been thought through to the full (*Gift of Death* 64). But how do we approach this treasure, the essence of Christianity, itself?

In the spirit of Johannes de silentio, Derrida makes an attempt to face Abraham's terror: a father prepared to kill his son, whom he loves and who is more precious to him than anything else, because, without explanation, some intangible, unknowable, incomprehensible God tells him to do so. What secret can be as terrifying as this father's/child murderer's, who keeps silent about his intentions without knowing why, even as he goes against his own love, humanity, family, and ethics? (65).

How can this be our daily fare, our everyday affair?

According to Derrida:

> Paradox, scandal, and aporia are themselves nothing other than sacrifice, the revelation of conceptual thinking at its limits, at its death and finitude. As soon as I enter into a relation with the other, with the gaze, look, request, love, command, or call of the other, I know that I can respond only by sacrificing ethics, that is, by sacrificing whatever obliges me to also respond, in the same way, in the same instant, to all others. I offer the gift of death, I betray, I don't need to raise my knife over my son on Mount Moriah for that. Day and night, at every instant, on all the Mount Moriahs of this world, I am doing that, raising my knife over what I love and must love, over those to whom I owe absolute fidelity, incommensurably. Abraham is faithful to God only in his absolute treachery, in the betrayal of his own and of the uniqueness of each one of them, exemplified here in his only beloved son. He would not be able to opt for fidelity to his own, or to his son, unless he were to betray the absolute other: God, if you wish. (*Gift of Death* 68–9)

It seems that Derrida's thinking on the sacrifice of Isaac and the paradox of faith and ethics in the story of Abraham poses a way of examining the idea of sin. Unless we conclude that his discussion of the sacrifice of Isaac is a call to political consciousness and responsibility.

The geographical location of this sacrifice is holy, but it is simultaneously a place of bloody struggle – this place where three variants of religious monotheism have fought, and still fight, in violent battle. Each religion is fighting for its own perspective, and each one makes demands on the same location through historical and political interpretations of the sacrifice of Isaac and the Saviour. The readings, interpretations, and traditions behind the sacrifice of Isaac are elements that, in themselves, contribute to blood sacrifice. And the sacrifice of Isaac continues – politically and religiously – every day (70–1).

This is how Derrida expresses his attempt on the Moriah–experience:

> I am responsible to any one (that is to say to any other) only by failing in my responsibility to all the others, to the ethical or political generality. And I can never justify this sacrifice, I must always hold my piece about it. Whether I want to or not, I can never justify the fact that I prefer or sacrifice any one (any other) to the other. I will always be secretive, held to secrecy in respect of this, for I have nothing to say about it. What binds me to singularities, to this one or that one, male or female, rather than that one or this one, remains finally unjustifiable (this is Abraham's hyper-ethical sacrifice), as unjustifiable as the infinite sacrifice I make at each moment. These singularities represent others, a wholly other form of alterity: one other or some other persons, but also places, animals, languages. How would you ever justify the fact that you sacrifice all the cats in the world to the cat that you feed at home every morning for years, whereas other cats die of hunger at every instant? (*Gift of Death* 70–1)

But what is the responsibility awakened by faith? Does it evoke the unbridgeable chasm that separates faith and ethics in the story of Abraham? Do we get a glimpse of the abyss on Derrida's Moriah? If people are tempted to sacrifice a thing or two now, they have plenty from which to choose; people may believe they are sacrificing something, but they are not necessarily suffering as they still have plenty to love and believe in after the sacrifice has been made. Perhaps Derrida's claim that the sacrifice of Isaac is daily fare cannot be separated from his assertion that responsibility belongs to everyone. If this is the case, Derrida is perhaps drawing attention to the present moment in history: when the tradition of blood sacrifice is preserved without apparent responsibility, at least in the political sense, it would seem that responsibility is a critical issue.

I now turn to Kierkegaard and his struggle with faith, love, and responsibility.

THE PROBLEMS OF FAITH HAVE NOTHING TO DO WITH WORLDLY GOODS

According to Johannes de silentio, one has no ethical obligations to money (Kierkegaard, *Fear and Trembling*, 23). People believe in money, but it has nothing to do with the common treasure of Abraham's descendants. In this context it is tempting to take a contemporary example. A young bank manager who has worked hard day and night for *a whole year* in order to generate funds cannot say to his children: "If you do not perform well, then I have sacrificed the best for nothing!" "The best" in this context cannot be equated with the sacrifice of Isaac; to give someone money (or what may be bought with money) is not the same as to give someone the gift of death. People who confuse these two things are likely to maintain that the experience of death is not possible without actually dying. In the mind of de silentio, this confusion is based on "crass materialism" (39).

A person has no obligations to money, de silentio says, but the duties of a father to his son are the highest and the most sacred (23). How can the father then be prepared to sacrifice his son?

Let us stop at faith, de silentio suggests, instead of going further (31). He admits that his own experience of the knight of faith is nonexistent. After many years of searching, he has found no "authentic exemplar." According to him, usually people travel around the world to "see rivers and mountains, new stars, flamboyant birds, freakish fish, ludicrous breeds of humanity. They abandon themselves to the brutish stupor that gawks at existence and think they have seen something." As for himself, he has no interest in such worldly travels. He would, however, travel on foot if he knew where the knight of faith lived, for "this miracle" concerns him "absolutely" (31).

The point is this: anyone who wishes to follow in the footsteps of Abraham has to commit himself to the absurdity of existence. In the Bible, Abraham makes the leap from the potential of faith to the experience of faith. He does this by believing, without a doubt, in the unthinkable. Abraham, in other words, makes the leap from the paradox of existence (which is the moment when a human being's passion, faith, and responsibility part company) to the experience of faith itself.[8] Johannes de silentio cannot believe in the way that Abraham believes. In order to have faith, it is necessary first to love. But love, like faith, is not all that meets the eye. In order to believe, it is not only necessary to love, but to be able to deny oneself one's love – that love that is unique, that decides one's fate in life. Such is the prerequisite of faith (34–9). But what does de Silentio mean by this?

By denying oneself everything that one holds most dear in the world, he says, one feels pain. And it is exactly this pain that leads one to embrace existence. What we are talking about here is a movement that is related to the movement of faith but that is actually only its prerequisite. This inner development, which de silentio refers to as "infinite resignation," can be experienced by anyone. That is, anyone can train her or himself to experience this transformation that, "within its pain[,] reconciles one with existence." The infinite resignation, he says, is the shirt "mentioned in an old legend. The thread is spun with tears, bleached by tears; the shirt is sewn in tears, but then it also protects better than iron and steel." The secret of life is that each and every person has to sew his or her own shirt. And men can sew it quite as well as women, take note of that: "In infinite resignation there is peace and rest and consolation in the pain, that is, when the movement is made properly." The fact is, says the silent one, that "people believe very little in the spirit, and yet spirit is precisely what is needed in order to make this movement" (38).

In de silentio's mind, love is only the prerequisite of faith. But what does the knight of faith do in this case? De silentio imagines him, sees him in his mind as he has relinquished the love that sustained him in life and accepted suffering. And what happens next? Here is the miracle: the knight of faith makes "yet another movement more wonderful than anything, for he says: 'I nevertheless believe that I shall get her, namely by virtue of the absurd, by virtue of the fact that for God everything is possible'" (39).

Johannes de silentio realizes that it requires strength and freedom of the spirit to perform the movement of infinite resignation. He also knows that this movement is possible, but as soon as he wants to begin it:

everything turns around and I fly back to the pain of resignation. I can swim in life, but for this mysterious floating I am too heavy.

To exist in such a way that my opposition to existence expresses itself at every moment as the most beautiful and most secure harmony with it –, that I cannot do. And yet it must be glorious to get the princess. I say this every moment, and the knight of resignation who does not say it is a deceiver, he has not had a single wish, and he has not kept the wish young in his pain. Perhaps there was someone who found it sufficiently convenient that the wish was no longer alive, that the arrow of pain was blunted, but such a person was no knight. A freeborn soul who caught himself in that would despise himself and begin afresh and above all would not allow his soul to be self-deceived. And yet it must be glorious to get the princess; and yet the knight of faith is the only happy person and heir to the finite, while the knight of resignation is a stranger and a foreigner. (42–3)

What de silentio suggests is the following: "Let us then either forget about Abraham or else learn to be horrified by the prodigious paradox that is the meaning of his life, so that we may understand that our age, like every age, can be joyful if it has faith" (45).

THE FLICKERING BOUNDARY BETWEEN RELIGION AND AESTHETICS

Even though Derrida's interpretation of the paradox of faith and ethics in the story of Abraham may not lead to a great chasm, as does Kierkegaard's reading, Derrida understands faith (in the spirit of de silentio) as responsibility. He also maintains that the secret of faith resides in the fact that it cannot be mediated from one generation to another (Derrida, *Gift of Death*, 80). In this matter he refers to the final words in *Fear and Trembling*, which is de silentio's epilogue, where it is written:

This genuinely human quality is passion, in which one generation perfectly understands the other and understands itself as well. Thus no generation has learned how to love from another, no generation gets to begin at any other point than at the beginning, no later generation has a shorter task than the previous one, and if someone here is unwilling to abide with love like those previous generations but wants to go further, then that is only foolish and idle talk. (Kiergegaard, *Fear and Trembling*, 107)

But what about the story of the other son, the one God himself sacrificed for us? Derrida discusses the connection between this event
and the story of Abraham. In this context, Derrida also talks about
the "sacrificial *hubris*" that Nietzsche referred to as the "stroke of
genious called Christianity (Derrida, *Gift of Death*, 114–5). Because
what is this religion that slays – in silence – two birds with one stone:
humanity's passion and humanity's morality? There are aspects of
Christianity that have not been thought through, especially not by
those who call themselves its prophets. However, Derrida points to
a discourse on this secret in Western culture, a tradition of thought
"that consists of proposing a nondogmatic doublet of dogma, a
philosophical and metaphysical doublet, in case a *thinking* that 're-
peats' the possibility of religion without religion" (49).[9]

Unlike Derrida, Kierkegaard has little faith in philosophy, pinning
his hopes solely on faith. His interpretation of the story of Abraham
serves a clear purpose, which, in Vilhjálmur Árnason's words, is "to
draw out the essence of Christian religion. This is a merciless interpretation which is ill-suited to those who choose to live a bourgeois
religious life without having to face the demands of Christianity."[10]
As Jóhanna Þráinsdóttir points out, faith was, in Kierkegaard's eyes,
the entire world: "The individual could not be truly free unless he
acquired, himself alone, full consciousness of God and His eternal
freedom. It was, however, his own decision whether he used his rela-
tive individual freedom to choose such a faith and the hardship it
cost to make it that far" ("Historical Backdrop" 244).[11]

But what about the role of aesthetics? In one of the footnotes, de
silentio reviews the truths about the untruths of aesthetics and calls
it "the most faithless of all branches of scholarship." Everyone who
has "truly loved it becomes in a certain sense unhappy, but anyone
who has never loved it is and remains a dumb animal" (85).
Elsewhere, he says that the difficulty of aesthetics revolves around its
magnanimity. As soon as aesthetics gives up the illusion of magnanimity it can work "hand in hand with the religious – for this power
is the only one that can rescue the esthetic from its combat with the
ethical" (82).

Here we may have come upon the creation of the boundary between religion and aesthetics, but Kierkegaard is famous for his adventurous camouflage in this matter. According to him, his whole
oeuvre concerns a certain problem in Christianity, and he does not
write about anything other than the problem of becoming a Christian

in direct or indirect argument with that terrible deception: what we call Christendom. But he also writes with such passion on the subject that the boundary of religion and aesthetics cannot easily be discerned. As Joakim Garff has discussed, the works of Kierkegaard have been read in every which way, but foregrounding the subject of aesthetics has not been one of them. Kierkegaard himself may have contributed to this tradition. In his book *The Point of View for My Work as an Author*, this is how Kierkegaard warns the reader who seeks aesthetic enjoyment in "this religious author's writings": "If it is assumed that such a reader perfectly understands and judges the particular esthetic work, he totally misunderstands me, since he does not understand it in the religious totality of my work as an author" (24). In his interpretation of Kierkegaard's writings, Joakim Garff seems to place aesthetics at the forefront and to draw our attention to one of Kierkegaard's footnotes, which has been mentioned earlier. It is on aesthetics and indicates that it "is the most faithless of all branches of scholarship," that there is "little happiness in placing one's faith in it," yet that anyone who has never loved aesthetics "is and remains a dumb animal" (Garff 414–15).[12]

I will not further consider the role of aesthetics in the writings of Kierkegaard. But in a discussion of the relation between faith and love in an era of watered-down Christianity, it might be necessary to take a look at "faithless" science. As noted earlier, Kierkegaard felt that the difficulty with aesthetics had to do with the high-mindedness of the field. As soon as aesthetics abandons the illusion of magnanimity, it can be in league with religion, the one power that can rescue aesthetics from the "combat" with the ethical. This had not come about in Kierkegaard's time, it seems, but what about later years? Perhaps the later guises of aesthetics, which have not given up on the questions of faith, love, and responsibility, may provide answers. The existentialist challenge for the aesthetics of later eras is understandably different from that of Kierkegaard's era. With the advent of modernism, we find in the works of certain poets and novelists a passionate connection between life and art, which is reminiscent of the passionate bond between religion and life found in the writings of Kierkegaard.

In *The Concept of Modernism*, Ástráður Eysteinsson at one point discusses the ideas of the modernist writer Antonin Artaud concerning the relation between life and art, and his ideas are illuminating in this context (232). In *The Theater and Its Double*, Artaud has the

following to say about art and how it can become an "event" in life:
"We are not referring to life as we know it from its surface of facts,
but to that fragile, fluctuating center which forms never reach. And
if there is still one hellish, truly accursed thing in our time, it is our
dallying with forms, instead of being like victims burnt at the stake,
signaling through the flames" (13). What Artaud calls the "fragile,
fluctuating center," this part of life that no form can reach, not only
exists, in his estimation, but is a subject only for those few who dare.
Perhaps contemporary aesthetics can deal with this subject, as it
maintains a passionate loyalty to the problem of life at the same time
as it expresses doubt about the way systems function. Such distinc-
tions do not thrive in an artful flirtation with form. In order to express doubt about the way systems function, it is necessary to go into
this "centre," all the way to where the emotions of faith, love, and
responsibility reside. Perhaps we can say that the search that we
discussed in the previous chapters amounts to throwing oneself on
the pyre of risk. However this may be, it seems that the aesthetics of
Guðbergur Bergsson's writings are distinguished by this.

Another and related factor that is important in this context is that
humanity still belongs to the era of the Book, even though we have
abandoned our faith in it. The modern era may therefore be characterized by a deep-seated experience of ambiguity, and Bergsson's *The
Mind's Tormented Love* contains references to just this conndition.
Another of Bergsson's fictional works, "An Image of Man from the
bible," is no less striking in this regard. I therefore begin the next
section with a discussion of this short story.

"AN IMAGE OF MAN FROM THE BIBLE"

In the story "An Image of Man from the bible," Bergsson not only
takes aim at the Old Testament but also provides an interpretation
of the story of Abraham:

Listen here, brother Isaac, I sometimes say to myself, I whose name
is not at all Isaac: "They sacrifice you on a pile of wood. They allow you to dangle along so you can pay for the oil on the fire, the
oil that is poured onto the woodpile, the wine they drink. They
think they are Abraham." Then I address myself in my own desire
to burn and say: "All right, Isaac, son of Abraham. Who would not

purchase the moment and the friendship and the destruction for a high price, and therefore burn with lust in the flames?" (8)

Here are Isaac (the sacrifice) and Abraham, albeit in a different guise than they appear in the Old Testament. Here, Isaac throws himself on the flames, in full knowledge of the reason for the sacrifice. It is not the belief in God that is behind this. The paradox that unfolds in the domain of faith and ethics seems absent in this short story, as does the problem of responsibility. The stage for the sacrifice is deprived of God, and this moment seems to have little to do with Abraham's experience. What could be the connection?

Without putting the *leap of faith* that Johannes de silentio attempts, but is unable to perform, on an equal footing with the willingness to sacrifice seen in the characters in Bergsson's short story, within a specific context of "Christian" ideas there is an existential challenge to perceive in both. Because of the presence of those ideas, not only are the boundaries between religion and aesthetics made tangible in Bergsson's short story, but we can also still perceive the power faith is able to have in faithless times. But faith in what? What is this image of humanity in a lower-case kind of book?

The setting for the short story (which appeared first in 1972) is Reykjavík in the 1970s. The story is a recollection of twenty-four hours in the lives of a group of friends, and the narrator is the character whose "name is not Isaac." The friends get together, get drunk, go to the restaurant Naustið, and from there to a party at which some of them pass out. Some then beat up on the unconscious ones and some head out into the ice-cold winter night to answer, in their drunken stupor, the pull of nature to procreate. When the story takes place, the girls are dabbling in "translating Augustine," referring to "Simone de Boulevard and her Lay," saying that "everything is existence without stipulation"; they are without makeup, unkempt, and wearing "hardwood-earrings" and "batik-dresses" (13). The boys are celebrating "Russian afternoon," which means they begin drinking after lunch on Saturday and continue as soon as one of them wakes up on Sunday. As the narrator also explains (in fictional monologues that are utilized throughout), the girls later find themselves "leeching off their husbands' degrees" in a radical Scandinavian version of environmental protection, in which they walk home in wooden shoes with the milk in a "green shopping net" (12), just before they take a step into the future "with their eternal sandwiches and pizzas ... natural to their days' end among husbands they could well do without" (13) The boys also change. Take, for example, the one who celebrated Russian afternoon and thought it was "radical to have sex": he later became a lawyer who "dried up in an overheated office downtown" (10). In short, the group of friends represents a generation that has been educated with "the last Marshall-dollar of the nation," a generation that was always going to stay together and avoid "other groups" but that, in the end, could not stay true.

When "An Image of Man from the bible" takes place, the narrator is rejoining this group of friends after some time away. He does not regard them as his friends, referring to them as acquaintances and claiming to want nothing but a "moment's proximity" (7). For that moment he is prepared to pay, as is shown in the fragment quoted above. And this in a noteworthy setting: here we find him, "not-Isaac," himself. But his way of distinguishing himself, if we can call it that, is not characterized by an artful play with form. This character talks about the long-gone past in as human a manner as does the author of *Fear and Trembling* – this "not-Isaac" who claims to be a boor among boors who spends his time with his "equals in degradation" (8). This is how he throws himself on the fire of existence. And what are his possibilities?

As with other Bergsson stories, the complex narrative of "An Image of Man from the bible" awakens a sensibility towards actual reality, on the one hand, and the concept of reality, on the other. The main character of the story is in the process of separating from actual reality. "My view of things," says this "Isaac whose name is not Isaac,"

does not fall in line with those whose idea is that without wine there is no life. I am no philosopher in the grips of Dionysian hysterics, but instead I stumbled into this group the same way I stumbled into this life: by sheer chance, on my birthday in July, into a life I neither choose nor understand nor am able get a grip on. Life is tumultuous for me. And, it is rightly said, that man's greatest misfortune is to have been born. We roam about, somehow, through life, along the uncharted expanse of this slogged and overtrod existence. (7)

And he continues to philosophize:

From the moment a man is born he becomes more and more a corpse every day. Everything is that way: death inside death, and life is a trial rehearsal for death. But I bless my parents for the trouble they took upon themselves in the flower of their youth and in their poverty, when they decided to have me. That said, they now know that I am grateful to them and am full of silent respect, not towards life, but towards the will to create life. There is always some sort of dream involved in that. (8)

The possibilities for this man are nonetheless to be found in the lines of thinking to which he claims not to adhere, and in the kind of society to which he "does not" belong. Where should he go? It is a mark of his dual-standing in this society that it should be in the company of these same *acquaintances* that this Isaac throws himself, blind drunk, onto the fire of existence. And what do we find?

They have just been to Naustið and have arrived home to Iddi's place, whose role it is to "extend the twenty-four-hour cycle." Before the narrator and his acquaintances step into the basement suite where Iddi lives, we read a strange sentence: "Over the crowd hovered an unwritten law: apprenticeship should be prolonged" (13). The graffiti on one of the walls of the basement, which the narrator describes upon stepping inside, also sharpens the reader's sense that there are many layers of meaning involved in this (otherwise average Icelandic) debauchery:

When Israel went out of Egypt,
Jacob's clan from the people who spoke in a foreign tongue,
Then Judaea became his sanctuary,
Israel his nation.
The ocean saw this and fled,
Jordan looked away.
The mountains jumped like rams,
The hills like lambs.
What is it, ocean, makes you flee,
Jordan, makes you look away,
Mountains, makes you jump like rams
And hills like lambs? (13–14)

Certainly the narrator ponders the social and cultural conditions of this group, and this within a wide context. As the graffiti indicates, the similarities between Iceland and Israel appear to be manifold. He asks, for example:

> What did we flee from? Under military occupation, drunk, rich and nationalistic but confused and with pockets full of credit, and singing loudly in English. I don't want to shock you simple souls playing hide and seek, but we were all blind drunk during the end of the Marshall-loan there on the floor in the room. "Here nothing can happen. O god, I am so fortunate. I own everything everywhere. I am so free and fortunate with my man, so happy with my children." That is not how we were singing, but we heard this song everywhere around us, through the open windows of the town, the town that was not yet a city. (14)

The materialism of his countrypeople is about to drown out the sense of judgment. God is called on in ludicrous contexts, as though symbolizing people's freedom to buy things (or even status) with the credit obtained by this new, independent nation. The group of friends, of which the narrator is part, remains removed from this hysteria in its Russian afternoon. Only later does the group come to an ideological end, and its members' views begin to amalgamate with the song lyric: "Oh god I am so fortunate. I own everything everywhere. I am so free," and so on. But where is the narrator at this point? Where is he headed?

At this point in the story, Svanur is mentioned by name. He is in the basement reading a story he wrote while the others were either lying on the floor in a drunken stupor, like logs, or else leaning against the wall "groping each other in a fruitless way." Svanur is a character from Guðbergur Bergsson's Tangi stories, as is Anna, which is Svanur's mother's name in other stories but which in this story is the name of the girl whom Svanur is pressed against (in order to confuse the others as to their real relationship, he says). The narrator's position is therefore dual in nature, both in the narrative and in those events that are described. And when modernist formalism has, in a manner of speaking, achieved dominance in this complex staging, the narrator says: "Then it happened, suddenly and unexpectedly, like everything in my life" (15). What is it that happens?

They sit next to each other "emotional and grim," he and the girl Anna, when he sees the master of the house, whom he calls the "devious animal," come out of his stupor:

He lifted his head and looked around, glared at us like a lion from Judea might glower at sleeping lambs by the river Jordan, slowly rose to his feet in the half-darkness with the halo that his sallowness had produced, and he gave one of the others, who was sleeping with his wretched face on the floor, a fistful. With my sleepless eyes I saw the blood well out of his sockets. I could feel how righteousness seeped into my muscles and streamed in circles around my head inside, but Anna grabbed me, nestled up to me and tried to clean the inside of my mouth with her tongue. It's possible to pound and thrash and abuse sleeping people and commit crimes and injustices, because a well-kissed man will not rise up for any cause in the name of justice. He will sooner rise himself and before long the woman will be licking him all over. That is how it went for me. She cleaned out the anger from my mouth with her tongue. (15)

In the narrator's mind some kind of reversal concerning the idea of sacrifice has occurred: he knows that he himself is not sacrificed this night: "Isaac had become far too old to be involved in such things, or in some sort of sacrificial celebration. If my name is Isaac at all, then" (16). It is he himself who makes the sacrifice. But of what? If he is to be seen as an image out of the Bible, it is only because of his consciousness of his own responsibility. But this consciousness is not altogether biblical. The narrator's sense of responsibility arises in spite of the generative force of the physical: if you feel the passion of love, it is impossible to avoid its grim side as well, emotionally speaking. Such is the concession to an inescapable paradox, which is not exactly the same as Abraham's paradox but still falls clearly within the Judaeo-Christian framework – as if this were an attempt to rewrite a story on responsibility. Despite the still existing psychological fortresses, courtesy of the crass material-ism Kierkegaard sensed some time ago, responsibility cannot be fled. In this story, the subject is addressed in an "open field" at the boundaries of the author, the world of ideas, the work of fiction, and the reader – a field that is, in fact, the basis for the reader's participation in all of Bergsson's writings. Characters and narrators move about within this field, and they are not a mirror image of their author, even though they further the cause of his perception and ideas. In this particular story, the narrator asserts that humanity is "a house full of pictures, and I often go into my own house to look at the stories the pictures on the wall tell, stories of the past that last for the entire future" (17–18).

What is of equal importance in this context is how the field of
writing merges with the arena of the physical body. The narrator and
the girl are in a taxi on their way to her place. The conversation begins on a moralistic tone, and they discuss a man who passed out in
a potato shed and whether he might not freeze there. Then they immediately begin to talk about the list of poets who kept themselves
alive by eating raw potatoes, and from there they turn to a discussion of how the death of Snorri Sturluson might have taken place.
The narrator continues in an assured tone:

> "I know everything about potatoes," I said. "Snorri came to
> Iceland before the potato."
>   "Are you nationalistic?" she asked.
>   I didn't answer. Such gibberish is too much to take.
>   "Are you against the potato?" she asked, and her ice-cold
> hands were fumbling about inside my clothes and groping my
> balls. That was blessedly delightful, to be fumbled with that way.
> I said to myself: "you don't need to be embarrassed over your
> sack of potatoes." But I said out loud:
>   "Snorri's potato seeds are no concern of mine."
>   "Thanks probably to you," she said.
>   "Is he always so sleek and smooth?"
>   "Whom do you mean?"
>   "Svanur," I said.
>   "You should know him better than me," she said. "He has a
> big head and a long neck."
>   "Then that is exactly how he is made," I said. (19)

After this hidden manifesto of our secret poet (for the sentence
"Snorri's potato seeds are no concern of mine" can be read as an attempt by the modern poet to separate himself from this major medieval patriarch, writer, mythographer, and historian), it seems that the
poet Svanur is merging with the sexual organ of the narrator. The
following fragment again shows the connection with the Bible and
the possibilities for creation that may be found in this "much trod-
den" existence:

> "We should never judge people by how they appear on the sur-
> face," she continued. "We only get a biblical image that way."
>   I said *poo* to that, and that not everyone had a biblical surface,
> but I thought about whether we could be a bacterium in the

microscope of some higher being, higher than ourselves; and whether our movements might be only that being's thoughts; and whether that could be the reason why we sometimes rise above ourselves and become greater than we actually are. (19–20)

In this story we discern an elucidation of the problem of responsibility. The paradoxical relationship between faith/religion and ethics is evident here as well, although the circumstances are different from those in the Book itself. However, it is a mark of the atheism inherent in this story's existential challenge that faith runs parallel with the contradictory creative power within the *body* of the narrator: he "rises" physically, and he multiplies himself in the physical body of the woman, after becoming passive and giving himself over "to the power of the unconscious" (20). He knows this, he says, when he wakes up at midday "with blood on the waist" (20). And where is all this going? Marriage?

> "You will become a stiff husband," she cried over her lips. "You will become fretful and complaining: 'how's about dinner? What? The potatoes are half raw. Get yourself into bed, woman. What's the idea staying up all hours? Are you starting to wash the floors at this hour, at midnight?'" (21)

The girl is weeping as she says all this, after she finds the narrator inside a closet. He is hiding from the world, but he discovers several tightly written notebooks that are all entitled "Svanur." If this man is on a journey, his destination is not the creation marriage can offer. Will he perhaps become a poet this very night?

It seems as if the narrator approaches faith and responsibility by way of the contradictory creativeness of physical circumstance: should passion be born, the cruel side of things is inescapable. He is under no illusions concerning his and his friends' standing in cultural history. He himself is not named Isaac, and they "believe" that they are Abraham. He is nonetheless conscious of the problem of faith and responsibility. With this he throws himself on the conflagration of life and gives himself over to creativity. The narrator's sacrifice can therefore be read not only as a variation on the theme of Bacchus-worship among Icelanders but also as an awakening to life on the stage of modern Western culture in general. And, in a time when "the gods are missing," a capacity for dreaming is involved in such a creation.

Another narrator throws light on the manifold creativeness involved in thinking about the emotional requirements of the Christian
cultural world. That narrator is the diarist in *The Mind's Tormented
Love*, and, as has been mentioned, this narrator thinks a great deal
about the possibilities of the emotions, not only on paper but also in
life. I now address that subject.

POET OF THE TERRIBLE PASSION

It is important to realize that the diarist in Bergsson's *The Mind's
Tormented Love* is not necessarily a man who favours any particular
"theology." The subject bores him, he says, regardless of whether it
is "for or against the god of wine, the belief in socialism, capitalism,
or in woman with a capital 'w'" (60). But what about homosexuality? He says it has been a closed book for him since its advent (when
he was still a young man), but he adds parenthetically that, at that
time, he "could find no trace of it" in himself:

> When we are born we disappear from eternal life, which is the
> absence of physical consciousness, and we awaken to earthly life,
> which is the consciousness of the body, its needs and require-
> ments both. To this is added what I heard my childhood friend
> say:
> "Life is a certain negation of that invisible part of the spirit
> that god keeps. While we are alive we can only forget the con-
> sciousness of the body in the amnesia of love by letting lust have
> its way." (61)

Here the diarist makes a distinction between, on the one hand, a
personal belief (or what he *thought* was the opinion of his childhood
friend), and, on the other, the "theology" of homosexuality, which
concerns him in some way. But when we inquire into the beliefs of
the diarist, it is as though he is approaching a consciousness of the
problem of the paradox of faith and love:

> I don't want to applaud wholeness of any kind; I am content
> with fragmentation. I know that if I died, I would not die into
> you or be reborn in your body, but I would maybe get lost in a
> disagreeable god and probably never awaken after that in the
> embrace of the one I love. As I understand it, I have raised myself

in such a way that I can live life here on earth without knowing for certain who I am or where I live, except that my thoughts are often with you; but that is not enough. (61)

As I discuss in chapter 1, the diarist knows no moderation in matters of love. But what does he find concerning the connection between faith and love? At one point he says: "To my amazement I have had the same experience as an artist, even though I am something else, but to love and to withhold love is an endurance, and what lies behind most things in life" (85). This experience of love is not tied to his friend. It is wider in nature and becomes a kind of attitude towards life, and, as such, it reminds us of Nietzsche's ideas on the subject for, in *Thus Spake Zarathustra*, we find the following words: "And certainly it is no command for today and tomorrow to learn to love oneself. Instead it is the finest, cleverest, most extreme and patient art of all arts" (196). The diarist also says he knows that storytelling is generated from "autohomoeroticism, by the poet's contact with himself in a love relationship, where he is lovingly inclined towards that part of himself which is the other man" (Bergsson, *Mind's Tormented Love*, 81).

In the basement in present-day Reykjavík the diarist's friend continually comes up with something new to do with regard to love and, thereby, attains the nickname "the poet of terrible passion" (102). In all this there flourishes an excessive faith in an unusual form of theology, but the body of the friend is the pathway not only to physical love but also to faith:

For the first time in our acquaintance, he kissed me on leaving.
He took me strangely and clumsily in his arms so that I was surrounded by a calm I had not known before, and I wanted to cry.
I heard inside me the rain and was filled with gratitude that some god had proved his tangible existence to the unbeliever and heard his prayers with an indescribable touch which is the basis of all creativity. (102)

In the diarist's mind, the faith in the body is more prominent than the belief that body and spirit are separated, at the expense of the former. The indescribable touch, the touch that the diarist says is the basis of all creativity, must necessarily hold to a belief in the body over a god who would prevent such a generous form of faith. The

friend in the basement is also, as has been discovered, no ordinary
wellspring of passion's original bloom, that which is excessive and
reminiscent of primitive nature worship. These ideas are foreign to
the friend, as opposed to the diarist, who not only ponders them but
also attempts to alert his friend to something called responsibility:

> I cannot see evidence of anything except that he measures his ac-
> tions and thoughts only by his consciousness, and that this is the
> only ethical morality he has. When I try to point out to him what
> it means to be responsible for your actions and that no one should
> let his obsessions rule him, he seems to be clueless and says:
> "I won't listen to such things. You live with a woman and you
> are responsible in your home, but you are not all there. I have
> had three wives and made them all more than happy. I have five
> children to prove it and they are doing just fine in life."
> "What then?" I ask. "Can you do whatever you dream up?"
> "There are not that many things I dream up," he answers. (74–5).

It seems as though the friend in the basement causes both admiration and contempt in the diarist:

> I do not know the art of quarrelling, or of being persistent, nor
> do I deny facts with stubborn and confused arguments. To do so
> goes against my feelings, which are formed according to their
> own logic, and not by some uncertain natural law that causes
> difficulty and defends itself by constructing arguments. My feel-
> ings are moved to tears on account of my friend's behaviour, and
> I am not blind to the fact that I adore him for the accomplish-
> ment of having protected his authenticity, unrestrained passion
> and primitive self-righteousness, either to seize or to be unmoved
> whether one does or does not get fulfilment, depending on the
> whims of one's nature. My senses are contemptuous of such be-
> haviour and I go to pieces when I see how he takes on all manner
> of manipulative actions until I get confused, become nearly a
> dithering fool and give way in order to get rid of him and not go
> mad. And yet I am in admiration of all this. (153)

It is possible to live originally, in unrestrained passion and primitive
self-righteousness, but only without reflection. The diarist's problem
is therefore significant since his struggle is with faith and a longing
for authentic love.

These circumstances are not a surprise to the diarist. He says he knows this from his own experience and he is facing once again "the same difficult life challenge – the problem is that I have to, in an uncomfortable way, look myself in the eye" (154). And his response this time is as follows:

> If I believed in god or that he existed regardless of faith or faithlessness, then I would no doubt lean on him with my suffering in the hope that he would allay it, or I would inflict myself on him like a son, ask him to take away this cup, which is more like a well than a cup, a deep well where I struggle with the angel of the water as I swim between the battering walls of hatred for my existence. (154)

The diarist is, he himself says, "a son of the world, society, and nation" (154). In this he is no different from his contemporaries. Quite the contrary. He lives, like a few others in the Western world, in secular times. There is no question about that. But even though many people choose to ignore the development that has taken place in the last two centuries or so, when it comes to the peculiar and influential interplay between religion and greed in the still up and running scheme of Western materialism, our diarist is unable to overlook it. Even though he does not believe in god, he says, he nonetheless respects people and understands "their weaknesses and their need for a power that is higher and hopefully more helpful than earthly powers" (154). What he himself is incapable of is "approach[ing] god anew with a faith that is based on [his] own interests and look[ing] for solutions from [god] for things that [he] should be able to solve without help, with [his] own intelligence and the experience [he has] been through" (154).

When trying to believe in love, the question of responsibility is a confused one for the diarist. He has the following to say about the possibilities of the emotions in life (and this is reminiscent of the words of de silentio): "Men have to be, above all else, their own shelter; they have to be the protective garb that hides that which it is unnecessary to shield" (155). And he continues in the same vein: "One should not tramp around the world pointing like an ignorant child, neither at god nor at nakedness, wherever it is found, but instead one should endure both compassionately, for it is uncertain whether either god or nakedness actually exist" (ibid.).

Is he then a poet of the terrible passion? Is it the diarist himself who awakens a belief in and a longing for that which is authentic in love? For that which is unrestrained and reminiscent of primitive natural law in matters of love?

LOVE IN A TIME OF PROLONGED DESTRUCTION

One of the things the diarist confronts is that he will never arrive at an answer to his obsessive questions. He accuses himself of "having gotten things distorted in his so-called education, by never learning from life and being unable to live comfortably with things he cannot understand; among them love and its uncertainties" (Bergsson, *Mind's Tormented Love*, 75). The search for the possibilities of the emotions therefore continues, as does the thinking about the requirements of faith and love.

What he sees in his marriage with his wife concerns the requirements of "a half-true virtue":

> I have become painfully aware with my wife that we are no longer children in our marriage; we have lost the child's grimness, the naughtiness of the prankster boy and the whims of the girl, but have taken up virtue instead – maybe not as a lie, but we live according to a half-true virtue that came to the fore after the Christian faith waned. (76)

But there is something else that requires loyalty and that also concerns certain problems within the marriage. This is not about the requirements of Christianity, as such, but, rather, about something in a person that is there from birth and that Christianity has not managed to fully control. It is a particular quality people have of rejecting love as soon as their wishes have been fulfilled. It is tempting to call this quality "ingratitude," but that would be the wrong word. The issue runs deep but continues to seep to the surface. The diarist wonders about the potential he and his friend have in this regard and whether their relationship might be free of unfaithfulness in the classical, Christian sense:

> If everything were evidently obvious, this relationship could go the way of our marriages: our wishes are fulfilled, but with time gratification ruins the relationship.
> Still it is possible that our lives might turn out so that if we lived together we would start to be unfaithful to each other,

because that is man's nature, and this of course with our former wives, to make the act complete. (76)

How does one live love?

The diarist knows of two kinds of truths in life: the truth of truths and the truth of lies. And he discerns two kinds of animal: the domestic pet and the predatory bird:

> In the truth of lies there is a need for the variegated game, which is as desirable as it is necessary in order to enjoy the poetic in the flight of life; but the truth of truths is fine for daily use and offers security, which is the pleasure of the domesticated pet, and not of the bird that flies along in its predatory nature without full consciousness that he is free and happy in his endless soaring search for something to eat, full of desire to find quick prey and snatch it for the sheer pleasure of it. (77)

As the diarist explains, there is a considerable difference between these two truths. He who chooses the truth of truths opts for order and regulation over the possibility of soaring above the earth. Those who cannot resist the flight of life, however, and choose the truth of lies, eventually risk crashing. The question is how this difference between truths has come about and whether it is possible to live with this disparity.

Such thoughts have beset others as well, for the diarist's concerns are reminiscent of Nietzsche's in "On Truth and Lie in an Extra-Moral Sense." Nietzsche wrote this essay in the summer of 1873, but it did not see print until 1896. In it Nietzsche looks at the thinking that enables human beings to go about their business in this world, and he considers how their definition of reality is dependent on metaphors that become concepts. The difference between the truth of truths and the truth of lies – which can simply be called the difference between the intelligent being and the intuitive being – is much discussed here. On some occasions, Nietzsche says, the intelligent being and the intuitive being are parallel in that one is fearful of the intuitive and the other of abstraction – the latter is just as insensible as the former is uncreative: "They both desire to rule over life; the former by knowing how to meet his principal needs by means of foresight, prudence and regularity; the latter, by disregarding these needs and, as an 'overjoyed hero,' counting as real only that life which has been disguised as illusion and beauty" ("Truth and Lie" 60).

Nietzsche goes on to say that sometimes the intuitive being's methods are more successful than are those of the other, that the intuitive being handles "weapons more authoritatively and victoriously" than does his/her opponent, as perhaps was the case in ancient Greece. There, art reigned over life. Creation itself, whether it is about habitat, physical movements, dress, or household objects, does not imply any need: "It seems as if they were all intended to express an exalted happiness, an Olympian cloudlessness, and, as it were, a playing with seriousness" (61). However, the intuitive being pays for this: "To be sure, he suffers more intensely, when he suffers; he even suffers more frequently, since he does not understand how to learn from experience and keeps falling over and over again into the same ditch. He is then just as irrational in sorrow as in happiness: He cries aloud and will not be consoled. How differently the stoical man who learns from experience and governs himself by concepts is affected by the same misfortunes!" (61).

The difference between these beings cannot be considered alien to us. But Nietzsche's interpretation of what they have in common shows the originality of his thinking: unlike what many think, the masterwork of illusion is just as immediate for the sensible being as it is for the intuitive one. The only difference is that the former acquires its illusions through misfortune, not with a "quivering and changeable human face," as is the case with the intuitive one, but with the aid of a mask (61).

Nietzsche, like Kierkegaard, has an unshakable interest in the actual possibilities of humanity in life, not least in the context of the alleged truth of Christian teachings.[13] In the following chapter I discuss Nietzsche's ideas in greater detail. For now, however, it seems clear that the question of the possibilities of faith and love gives Bergsson's diarist an occasion to confront the age-old problem, the conflict between reason and emotion, in his search for the possibilities in his own life. At the same time, he cannot help planting seeds of doubt in the minds of readers concerning how various dogmas approach the problem.

The diarist in Bergsson's novel has doubts about the value book learning has for life. He also has grave doubts about the usefulness of the itemization of things when human life is part of the figuration: "I do not think it is healthy or useful to understand everything" (*Mind's Tormented Love* 103). But it is not a simple thing to throw off the inheritance of reason, however mistaken it might prove to be. When the diarist looks at his friend and one of his women, sitting together wolf-ing down cake at the restaurant Come Tonight, he is of two minds:

> Both of them seemed to be enjoying themselves royally and I enjoyed seeing that such people still existed in society. But at that moment I had no desire to get to know them better and I approached the table disinterestedly when I heard they were discussing where would be the best spot to go camping on Labour Day Weekend to hear what people in the next tent were doing. (110)

The question that arises is this: what is there to look for? It is of considerable importance in this context that the diarist is not after a moral solution to the conflict between reason and emotion. His search for the possibilities of emotion concerns life itself and litera-ture's possibilities in this matter, not the notions of the "learned" re-garding what is right and what is wrong. What he sees in his friend's life can almost be called the reality of literature rather than the fic-tional web that "beautiful, educated, and famous people" create round their lives. Here we discern not only the aesthetics of the everyday but also a pointed criticism of the lives of those who are able to choose the best but, instead, make of their lives a nightmare:

> The public, or ordinary people, to whom you pay no attention on the street and who you think are everyday-grey in the soul and who live an uneventful existence, often have a more varied and happy life than those others, whose lives may be beautiful, educated, and famous. A large portion of the common popula-tion turns life into a true work of art or a living poetry for daily use with unfaithfulness, lustful shenanigans, and all kinds of wonderful and human merriment. This is of course common every-day literature, something on the level of a kitchen thriller, but at least something happens in the story that is fast and ob-vious, even though it is little more than getting a hold of this or that, gambling with cars, condo buying, and the art of getting away with things, or envy and harmless indignation over this or that person who allows himself more than others. Then there are of course other people, especially educated and moral ones, who are constantly choosing the best but never acquire anything, or who turn their lives into a nightmare by making up loyalties that they spice up with the sins of the mind. (117)

Just as the diarist admits that he will never get to the bottom of what obsesses him – love – he comes face to face with his powerlessness against his partner, who most resembles life. For who is the winner here? It is the partner who is "the oil, the mainspring, and the engine of everything," while the diarist feels he himself is little more than the "engine-blast" of what he is writing (117)? This does not mean that the diarist settles on any kind of conclusion to so major a problem as the conflict between reason and emotion. He fully admits that he is more advanced than his partner in one thing:

> I can be with him in a way he probably can never be with me. In this it is the intelligence that matters, and neither physical vitality nor the strength of flesh and blood comes into play. Whenever I like I can be with him in written text, and in whatever way the mind desires; there I rule over it all and do as I please, as I am now doing. (117)

The aesthetics of this paradoxical existence are not at an end, however. What the diarist in fact realizes is the following: I can be free, and in fact more free than my partner in love, because I can be with him through writing, whenever and however I like. But to be with a living being through writing is in fact "to play alone with oneself. And if someone only exists in written form, then he is for the most part an imaginary creation and a fiction" (117). Fiction, he says, is "to be able to stutter yourself towards the barely known. That is why the connection between the language and the writer is truly a form of masturbation" (ibid.). And reading? "Reading is the reader's longing to masturbate with the writer and his few ideas; nothing more" (ibid.).

The large questions, then, are these: Is it the partner who wins out both in life and in love? Is it more satisfying to be able to lose yourself in another person than to lose yourself in the reading of books and the pursuit of writing? Whoever wishes to live a full life, the diarist says, lives in another and neither reads nor writes books of fiction. The diarist-narrator's partner lives life that way, unlike the diarist and the reader of his writings. Or is this so?

In the wake of these reflections another question comes up, and it is this: is it certain that the diarist's partner lives in an important way through the diarist? It could be that he "does not dare to admit to himself or to others that he loves in more than one way, or he does not dare to admit that he does not dare to dare" (118). If this were the case, it would not be a surprise to the diarist. That is because the consequence of such courage "is terrible":

> Courage is an antiquated, old-fashioned form of daring that leads to tragedy. To my mind we are not living in the era of tragedy but, rather, in the age of a long, protracted destruction. Therefore, when it comes to love, should people not behave in accordance with the times? (118)

What, then, are the possibilities, emotionally speaking?

> We know that, while we are alive, death has continuous intercourse with life, but we have hope in the light behind the darkness that, in this way, we will escape from death in the end and be granted eternal life in the beyond.
>
> I often thought about this issue while I was a child and listened to the talk of the village women. Ordinary people were then continually thinking about the boundaries between life and death, and in fact the dangers in life were greater then, both at sea and on land, and many illnesses were incurable. (95)

As is the case with Kierkegaard's philosophy of religion, the aesthetics of Guðbergur Bergsson's writings contains a passionate allegiance to the individual's attempt to be human at the same time that it doubts the construction of systems of thought. As a result, it can be said that Bergsson's existentialist thinking bears certain similarities to Kierkegaard's. This does not mean that the paradox that Kierkegaard takes as his subject matter is the same as the issues with which Bergsson grapples. It is Kierkegaard, and not Bergsson, who advises his contemporaries to learn to fear the "prodigious paradox that is the meaning of [Abraham's] life." In this way, according to Kierkegaard, people can at least understand "that our age, like every age, can be joyful if it has faith" (*Fear and Trembling* 45). The characters in Bergsson's fiction do not possess that kind of faith: but faith they do have. They are not only conscious of the problems of the emotions but they also admit to the insurmountable contradiction inherent in physical creation. We could add that they admit to their own responsibilities, not exactly in the spirit of the Bible but, rather, in a Christian sense, such that we are able to discern the above-mentioned transformation in the role of responsibility and its refusal. Such are the possibilities of modern aesthetics. And, in light of modern aesthetics, Bergsson's contemporaries can understand that, in this kind of creation, some kind of dream is inevitably involved.

Nor does the diarist's search lessen the impact of such a deduction. He follows the thread of the problem of life, along the path of "knowledgable" ignorance, beyond the rule-binding ideas prevalent in the era of diluted Christianity concerning what is supposed to be true and right in love and faith. At the same time, we may deem the creation of his passion to be a duel with the times in which he lives, in which tragedy is absent and a long drawn-out destruction is in place. In this matter, we can talk not only about the roots of the individual in Guðbergur Bergsson's aesthetics but also about the ethics of this aesthetics. And these are the issues to which I now turn.

The Roots of Individual Aesthetics: On The Creative Boundaries between Life and Art

The first thing in my life that I remember clearly was that one night, shortly after we arrived, when we woke up in a panic because someone had poured a bucket of cold water on us through an open window. A sheet had been covering the window and dad pulled it aside, looked outside, but did not see who had done this. It was bright everywhere and the migratory birds had arrived. There was no oven there and we could not cook food or anything, not even dry our clothes. That did not matter, for we had acquired a generator and we were given water which we kept in a wash tub. It took a rather long time to dry ourselves in the sunshine of the night, and after we tried to go to sleep once the window had been closed and we could no longer hear the sound of the sea or the birds. (Bergsson, *Like a Stone*, 44–5)

This is not the beginning of a biography. Nor is it the beginning of the first volume of Guðbergur Bergsson's fictional autobiography *Father and Mother and the Mysterious Power of Childhood*; rather, we find this fragment in the second volume, *Like a Stone the Sea Polishes*. But where does the first memory of one's life belong if not in a biography? Can the concept of a *fictional autobiography* do away with the age-old tradition that holds that literature relates the narrative of a human being's life? And the metaphorical gale off the sea in the inner life of a family that shivers in the damp night on the southwestern coast of Iceland just before the middle of the twentieth century, is that cold sea wind perhaps life itself, and is the sunlight of the night the poetry written about it? How can we approach the incomprehensible boundaries between life and art?

As has been mentioned, some interpreters of Bergsson's works have expressed doubts about the role played by humaneness, as though his works are somehow "inhumane." His fictional autobiography stirs up those doubts once more. In this work, the humanity of the author cannot be denied, possibly because the aesthetics of his fiction is the aesthetics of the everyday. In Bergsson's writings, not only is art seen from the vantage point of life, but we can also say that he tests out his aesthetics in life, which is altogether unprotected and exposed.

Exile has been of considerable usefulness to Bergsson. The roots of the individual in the aesthetics of this writer therefore rest not only in his thoughts about a village on the southwestern coast of Iceland and the lives of its residents but also, to a large extent, in his dialogue with poets, novelists, and philosophers who are prominent within the history of ideas and world literature. In this chapter I discuss, in particular, the creative connection Bergsson has with Nietzsche. Both are concerned with the boundary between life and art, with how art relates to a possible knowledge of life and the suffering that comes as a result of such knowledge.

But, some might ask, what about the part played by Icelandic culture? Does Bergsson's native culture not influence his aesthetics, he whom we might call a key figure among modern Icelandic writers? At the end of this chapter I address this matter.

ART ACCORDING TO LIFE

A born artist who is careful about his nature never lives in the commotion of the present unless he has his eye on eternity. Everything else is a betrayal of his nature. (Bergsson, *Father and Mother*, 82)

In *Father and Mother and the Mysterious Power of Childhood*, the reader meets a man who has come to his parents' house in the village of Grindavík in the southwestern corner of Iceland. The man is "Guðbergur Bergsson," and he has decided to make his origin the subject of a book about a father and a mother and the mysterious power of childhood. As the following description of his upbringing shows, this book is not a traditional autobiography: "A man's origin is everywhere and nowhere, and is mostly to be found in thoughts and words" (27). The reader is also reminded, over and over again, of the transformation of form and content. Already in the introduction to the text we find the following: "This work is historically wrong. Its main intention is to be somewhat right, emotionally speaking, as far as the author is concerned. This is therefore a fictional autobiography." These words find an echo in later words concerning the author's intention: he claims to want to create "an analogy to what is past" in the memory of his parents through the use of written words (12). Biographies, he writes on the flyleaf, are, strictly speaking, non-existent because "few things vanish as completely as a man's life, so it is only possible to express in words man's desire to capture life's aura."

The man has returned roughly half a century after the occurrence of the events he wants to relive. His mother has died, his father is in an old folks' home: life and the people he knew are mostly gone. But what does he want to find?

The man claims not to want to find anything that is lost. We seldom search, he says, for anything other than what it is not necessary to find: "I look for stories that I know cannot be found in their correct renditions, and in fact, I have not lost them as much as changed them; on the other hand, it is necessary to remove them from their natural settings [within memory] and place them in the unnatural garb of language" (*Father and Mother* 16). This man wants to discover stories to retell, and the stories come in three parts: about the father, about the mother, and about the mysterious power of childhood. But just as the border between fiction and reality cannot be considered clear, neither can the chapter segments. The setting is not clear either, in the the same way that the time is not singular. In the spirit of someone who wishes to acquire spiritual maturity and independence later in life, of one who is fearless in the face of the holy realm of the parental sagas, the man asks: Who is my father? Who is my mother? And he asks these questions in order to find his own way.

But, the reader may ask, what is the aura of a human being's life? What is a fictional autobiography? Is this work perhaps closer to art than to life? How are we to think of these boundaries?

Throughout Bergsson's writings there is a relentless focus on the margin between life and art. *Father and Mother and the Mysterious Power of Childhood* is, therefore, not an unusual work as far as Bergsson's subject matter goes. In it, we find many of the major questions posed in his writing as well as their aesthetic position. The observations about the subject of origin – namely, that it is everywhere

and nowhere and that it may be found in words and thoughts – bear
a likeness to sentiments found in Bergsson's first published works:
the poetry volume *Repeated Words* (1961) and the novel *The Mouse
That Skulks* (1961). We see in the former a poet introducing himself
as a writer on the stage of repeated words – words that rely on the
idea of an authorial god (the author of existence) and that, at the
same time, demand freedom from that idea in order to create an image of humanity. In *The Mouse That Skulks* we see a novelist aiming
for the surroundings and inner life of a boy who seems to become
prey to existence after the iron-clad power of his mother is gone.

Such is the nature of perception in Bergsson's works: it is an experimental perception of existence that takes on creative images necessary for the possibilities of repetition on the outskirts of Europe.
In *Father and Mother and the Mysterious Power of Childhood* not
only do we sense this perception but it also becomes the focus of the
author's search for the origins of life and art. Through the profound
questions that the work raises in this area – What is the relationship
between the imagination and death? What is it about life that injures
the inner being? How does a person maintain faith in life in the relentless company of death? – the reader participates in the author's
search for his own origins, beyond historical dogmas concerning
right and wrong, and beyond rule-bound public notions about what
is true in life. This is the mindset of a modern writer thinking about
art from the perspective of life:

> I know that a thought can travel widely through the air, settle on
> the gravel and grow, many-coloured, wherever it takes root. A
> thought is not a prayer to life, life does not need a prayer; it does
> what it wants and has no sympathy for the living. Life is bereft of
> laws, it is only us who make them up. (*Father and Mother* 232)

In further discussing the boundary between life and art, I explore the
creative force of this thinking, first in relation to Bergsson's fictional
autobiography and then in relation to Nietzsche's *The Birth of
Tragedy*.

FICTIONAL AUTOBIOGRAPHY

According to Bergsson, *Father and Mother and the Mysterious
Power of Childhood* is not an instructional novel from the beginning

of the century intended for those who take pleasure in self-delusion and pretend to be righteous and good. The novelist wants to be able to ask: who am I, especially when I look at myself as the offspring of my parents? In order to do this he must tell stories of their upbringing, the unfairness that was their lot in life, and the shadow of death that made its mark on their experience of life:

> I think people who have had a difficult experience in childhood and who continue to be deprived and oppressed in various ways throughout their lives, the so-called poor, have always felt as if they were in some way dead, that they are living a life in death even though they draw breath and appear to be alive. Most poor people in some way inhabit a shadow, and to be poor is to possess only a shadow. (205)

The author also needs to take a position on the human qualities of his parents. How does a son or daughter who is a novelist deal with the qualities of his or her parents? How does one approach a telling of the human condition? "Is it better to dream than to think about people in the midst of their circumstance?" (14). This is what the man asks his father as they sit together in the old folks' home in Snæfellsness, the setting of the father's youth. The father has returned, finally, to the place that always nourished his longing and desire. And he addresses his son's question:

> "Yes, judging from my experience," he answered.
> "Then I will never think about you after you are dead, but instead make even more things up," I said.
> My father laughed. Because he is intelligent and enjoys half-recited verses. (14)

This is what the author is thinking while in the house his father built in Grindavík. There he first perceived the importance of rising up against one's father and seeing his faults through the eyes of one's mother, and yet not losing respect for one's parents but instead see them as one's centre. His father's lot, as far as emotion goes, was different from his own, and it was in his house that the man searched for stories about the common man, about the subservience of the underdog, and about learned conviction confronting authoritarianism. And what did he find? He relives his emotions concerning his

father's destiny, which is to be the victim of ennui, a plaything in the
hands of the powerful, and feels that he is a witness to the mechan-
ism of the world's injustice, revisiting the stories of a father living in
poverty on the fringes of the world during the Second World War.
We see how the son acquires knowledge of his geographical place-
ment in the world and the possible influence this might have on his
thinking and outlook. We also see how he acquires a feeling for one
of the paradoxes of Western culture:

> What was once an uncertain surmise about the world became a
> certainty: that beyond the ocean, which we wanted to play on in
> childhood, there were other civilized worlds, much better than
> the peaceful one we lived in, even though people there had wars.
> The warships that sailed past along the horizon south of the pen-
> insula were proof of that. (35)

But the narrator is aware of the distinction between fiction and reality as well as the limits of his ability to think about his father's life
and their relationship. He recalls how events in people's lives sometimes wrestle with incursions of fiction, and how literature awakens
people to a consciousness of the possibilities of what he calls "an
incomprehensible power." Literature raises a consciousness of the
"creative urge" itself, which springs from a "seething life-anxiety"
and "melancholy" – this incomprehensible will to raise oneself up
from "stupor and anxiety, up to the light that is sometimes called
inspiration" (12). He remembers his longing for his father's company and his guidance at the same time as the stories about his father's emotional distance are pressing on him. As a child, he could not
show his father more than a fragment of that part of his emotional
life that is "absurdly" not made for oneself alone "but is intended for
giving" (46). He also comes to see how work filled his father's need
for company, and how he came to believe that the highest form of
companionship was knowing the art of being alone with oneself, of
working without being lonely and without the need for destruction.

Along with this, the man also recollects the stories about his mother and his relationship with her. She was a woman who had, in a
certain way, never been a child – a woman who was embarrassed at
having an opinion of her own parents, who made her a working girl
before she was a teenager. He recalls the bitter-tinged words of his
mother, but who is she? She never actually knew what she was, only

that she was not a child; and, just as with his father, her upbringing did not, for the most part, offer her a chance to express her emotional life.

In the old house, the man remembers stories of this woman, who was tired of children long before she had any herself but who became, unavoidably, a mother, at least physically speaking. And what does he find? He finds a life lived in order to be useful, but it is a form of usefulness that does not derive from generosity and consideration, either in the life of individuals or of nations, but from obedience to parental powers. Like his father, his mother never got a chance to seize her rights. Her destiny was to live her own mother's fate, a woman who waged her life struggle against the senselessness of humanity and nature. What the man remembers about his mother's life are her contradictory statements: "My mother preferred me to everyone else. Everything was loaded onto me" (38). While he is thinking this, he feels remorse about his mother's fate and thinks about what it means to be the son of a mother who was made to suffer the crime of nature against women – to bear children because of their nature and not because of their desire. And he thinks: "Birth became some sort of sin, a general crime against women, and perhaps procreation and birth into the world are nothing other than an evil deed, a complete wrong against the freedom of women" (38). What the man also finds in the stories of his mother is how pathos rules human experience, how parents sow in their children loneliness and emptiness (what he calls the parents' eternal bestowal on the souls of their children). God and his son are of little consequence when compared with the influence exerted by those who are ceaselessly near. As the man explains, the mother's playful whisper in his ear in the evenings, just before sleeping, was much more powerful than the distant Christian gospel. Mother, the boy senses, fills god's vacuum. That is why he needs to protect himself from her.

But the damage of parental influence has been done, and the man retells the story he heard his mother tell, again and again, when he was a child, the story of when his grandfather threw his wife out:

"You no longer live here."
My mother cringed. Her childhood was suddenly at an end on hearing those words. She could tell, somehow. They stopped and stood still and waited, almost overburdened by the weight of the sewing machine.

"You no longer live here," he repeated in a lower voice this
time and looked calmly at grandmother.

She did not answer, but he walked out and did not look at
either of them.

"What on earth is this?" grandmother asked out into the blue.

"I don't know," my mother answered, as if the question had
been directed at her.

From this, grandmother could feel she no longer existed to her
husband, but my mother could feel that she existed neither for
her father nor her mother. The siblings did not dare move. No
doubt she no longer existed to them or to the world, so she sank
into her own depths the same way children do in order to save
themselves when swimming through the seas of emotion. They
expect nothing from anyone.

It did not matter how many times my mother told this story,
the colour seemed to disappear from her eyes and one was
drawn into her loneliness and vacant vulnerability. The way only
parents can bestow emotions onto the emotional lives of their
children, they seem to do it automatically, of their own nature
rather than by design, and it seems as if the natural flow of life
were unthinkable any other way. (146–7)

The man in the house – who has not only created different conditions for himself and lived for long periods of time far away from the
lava fields and the village of his youth but has also made life his
subject matter in fiction and poetry – has this to say about humanity's hope in life: "The only thing man can hope to control is his
work; almost everything else is uncontrollable" (93).

In his narrative of his father and mother, the man in the house
would like to approach something that is true, emotionally speaking, in regard to himself. To arrive at this kind of truth, he remembers the mysterious power of childhood. Childhood is a particular
condition of the inner life that is characterized in his mind by the
equal jostling of fulfilment and emptiness. When he was a child
he felt:

[It was] much more secretive and fun to sit up against the wall
and feel how the dry sand in the clenched fist would trickle along
the palm of the hand and fingers tickling, more and more so as

the sand emptied out and streamed faster out of the hand, which seemed at the same time to fill with emptiness. I found in this simple game an insight into the equal measure of fulfilment and emptiness in life; that emptiness is also a form of fullness, but of course only in its own way. There is a balance in this, and a similarity between the material and the immaterial; the tangible and that which is impossible to touch except through thought and sense – that is how form and content come together. I could lie there for hours, sometimes all day, with this activity; discover the pleasure of feeling the material and the immaterial both in my hand and in life and perhaps in the arts as well; how form and content run together in existence. (31–2)

The man says the only role that both writing and children play in life is "to have no purpose other than enriching life with what is otherwise non-existent for adults" (292). When he has grown up he feels the emptiness, the same that he felt in childhood when the house was unfinished and the expanse was so wide and open. He feels his melancholy search for something that can never be found and that does not exist in order to be discovered but only in order to create a suspicion of its presence. As a child in the unfinished house he discovers what will later form his aesthetic perspective on life and art: how what is unfinished and half done awakens special enchantments; how existence is characterized not by what is fulfilled and emptied out but, rather, by its imaginable possibilities (91).

IS LIFE LITERATURE?

In his search for "the imagined possibilities of existence" in the house of his youth, the man thinks about the sorrow that life engenders and how human grief has no other purpose than to water the emotions so that they do not dry up. He also reviews his mother's deathbed experience and how he felt a sense of deep shame at her bedside. His mother's battle with death recalled to him a story by Borges concerning a woman who was about to die and whose face suddenly lit up with the blossom of youth. He remembered that he felt he was in the power of literature, as though his own reality were the reality of literature. "Was life then nothing but literature?" he asked himself. "Is that which awakens stories always some kind of battle with death?" In this context he remembers the mysterious power of youth, and how ideas about literature and his own nature were born and how a writer dies in his works so that they can live independently.

I am not maintaining that the mysterious power of childhood can provide a conclusive answer to the question of whether life is nothing but literature. What the man in the house calls "something" and what his mother says no one can comprehend can perhaps show the reader the way: "We are lying in a cluster in a bed that is a huge bird. I know we are using it to fly together out into something, out into what is 'something,' and mother says no one gets to know what that something is. Never ever" (229).

The only thing the man claims to have learned from the world and from those of whom he has been most fond is to "not want to be like them, but instead, unafraid of punishment and exclusion, to stand alone and not even desire that which can be had with obedience to their ideas" (271). Here we can see the kind of creativity this perspective on life and art entails. We see how *Father and Mother and the Mysterious Power of Childhood* narrates the author's witnessing of a father and a mother: these are not just stories of poor people waging a life struggle in a world of injustice; rather, they are stories that are repeated to us from the vantage point of life sprung from the soil of human living, unprotected and naked.

But can we further clarify the boundaries between life and art? What is the creation of such a perspective if the subject matter is not only human life but also those human-made laws concerning life that people either struggle against or obey?

Thinking about art seen from the vantage point of life can be richly rewarding. And, like the fund of stories the narrator's mother has to tell, "a bottomless well of mysterious pleasures, a certain kind of sorrow, and mysteries" (205), the latter volume of Bergsson's fictional autobiography, *Like a Stone the Sea Polishes*, answers the call should the reader wish to continue to follow the author's journey along the boundary of life and art. The setting is still Grindavík in the fourth and fifth decades of the twentieth century, and the same man in the same house searches for more stories from his childhood and youth. At the same time, we see the formation of the perspective that forms the author's aesthetics – a perspective that comes from his dialogue with a few of the major laws of Western civilization. Here we inquire into these laws insofar as they touch on the soul, faith, and beauty.

LAWS OF LIFE

The narrative persona Guðbergur is almost seven years old, the Second World War is at its close, and no one is at home in the village of Grindavík except for the women. Later in life, the man cannot understand how he could listen endlessly to those women: "But whom was there to listen to – the wind?" (Bergsson, *Like a Stone*, 197). Their sense of literature was unique, he tells us, and built on a state of mind that was based on stirring the flesh and the soul until out came a "greyish yogurt-like life substance with insidious bacteria, colourful organs, and death that had the flavour of crime and murder potboilers" (206–7). And what did life feel like to these people? "People saw life as some kind of ogre that god created," for it was an open wound "but it was possible to lessen the sting of it with an endless run of stories from morning to evening in a place where no one knew how to compose poems or to sing songs" (207). He felt, the man says much later, that this was the right way to live. And he recalls how he listened endlessly to the "ode to the body and the grief over it too" – that the body "is life and the soul is something on the margins of life and death. In the body there were the adventures, and outside of it there was almost nothing" (ibid.).

That perspective that the narrator calls "the right way to live" – with the body being thought of as "life" and the soul as "on the boundary of life and death," with the inside of the body being thought of as where the "adventures" reside and the outside of the body being thought of as "almost nothing" – can be interpreted as one of the main features of the aesthetics of Guðbergur Bergsson's writings. The stories that have been discussed so far evoke such a notion, wherein the ode to the body and the grief over it are continuously see-sawing in an almost dream-like state of balance. But here we are not really talking about an art of balance. Is it perhaps the flesh that enacts the spirit?

Perhaps we have here the central feature of the aesthetics that characterize Bergsson's work, and which is discussed in greater detail below. But what about the scientific disciplines concerning the soul and human psychology? Do they not explain the human condition? Has Freud nothing to say about this?

At the time in which the fictional autobiography is set, people in Grindavík knew nothing about Freud and his writings and the dialogue going on around them in the cultural milieux of Europe. But,

the reader might ask, what about the conversations of people outside the village? Were there no learned people in Iceland? What
about people in the capital city, Reykjavík? Regarding the discourse
that the boy heard in Reykjavík, when he and his father went to the
old folks' home in which his grandmother was living, he says as an
adult: "Usually people were doubling up with laughter when the
'delicacies' were offered and the discussion came around to Freud,
but I noticed a despondency in myself over how intelligent people
could sometimes make good use of poor but hopefully knowledge-
able stories" (287–8). The fictionalizing going on in Grindavík is
what is real, and we can see here a trace of the roots of the author's
thinking about the soul. At that time, he says:

> No one knew about Freud or his fictions built on the women of
> Vienna – fictions that were to spread around the world and dis-
> tort more than explain and change human nature. Instead he in-
> serted a new kind of terror among the learned and even among
> the ignorant, whom the industrial societies of our day have de-
> prived of their life blood, giving them instead childish thinking –
> ludicrous ideas about how a natural anxiety and various feelings
> that arise in the life of the soul from the interactions people have
> with themselves and others, their thoughts and one's own – that
> these are all neurotic complexes. (189)

People in Grindavík just before the middle of the twentieth century
knew nothing, it seems then, of the speculations of Freud. If we consider the perspective towards humanity and human nature and the
laws that have been generated to benefit humanity, we see the auth-
or's dialogue not only with these but also with the creativity that is
involved in the dialogue between literature and scholarly learning.
According to the narrator:

> [It was Freud who destroyed,] in his own way, the unrestrained
> enjoyment of life, so people instead live and enjoy themselves ac-
> cording to specific rules. He argued for behaviours that in earlier
> times one was most likely to find among nuns, monks, priests,
> and evangelicals who have always maintained that everything
> that is deepest in our nature, especially the joy of play, is animal-
> istic; that is how we have become prey to mental illnesses. Our
> animalistic qualities need to be eradicated as if they were evil

spirits, not with flagellations and torments in cloisters, but with scientific superstitions and medications in hospitals. Because it is neither natural to enjoy ourselves nor to suffer according to our real natures. That is how this messiah of the psyche, who intended to eradicate mental illnesses, instead managed to increase them as well as the agitation of the emotions, and also increase instability and sicken society with a terror of human nature in order to create a kind of new church service for people, a form of work in the area of the soul that has always made human beings human and was never meant to be cured. Do not cure man of himself, for then he will stop being human and will change into a utilitarian object with the correct genes according to the theology of these mentally ill sciences. (189)

Words like these give the reader a clearer picture of the kind of creativity involved here – a creativity that emerges from the interactive dialogue between the author and two of the most influential tenets in Western culture. We see not only the author's doubts about the science of psychology but also his opposition to specific ideas of god, especially when it comes to the creative potential inherent in the human being. From the vantage point of literature, it is as though certain kinds of ideas reduce not only the expression of those emotions inherent to the flesh but also the depth of the human being. In this context, it is as though humanity has fallen prey to a theological diagnosis.

Are human-made laws antagonistic to that which they regulate? And what about the dizzying prospect of living itself? Why should people not be able to find relief in theories of the psyche? Why should the god of the sciences not attend to the bleeding wound caused by life's sorrow?

Perhaps what Bergsson is opposing is the approach to the subject of the human being. If Bergsson's perspective is tied to the search for the origins of life and art, then it seems that something as complex as the human soul can awaken and thrive only on a boundary that no one can comprehend – the boundary between life and death. Is it the same with the idea of god?

In the fall of 1937, the author, as a boy, observes his mother, who is heavily pregnant, scouring the floors and, at the same time, coping with intrusive guests. They are the brothers from the Westfjords who, after suffering various hardships, have been saved by faith.

They sometimes find their way to the house and fill it up with a view
of life that has "characterized Icelandic thought as if it is nothing but
getting ahead or obeying and knowing how to be ashamed so
thoroughly that the disobedient one in the end has to yield to those
in power" (23–4). After they have overwhelmed the mother with
their god, she lies

> flat on her back with her face pressed against the wall and she
> answers nothing and seems to have gone to sleep. While she lay
> that way without moving, with her eyelids closed and shaking, I
> felt disappointed that she had given in. She should rather have let
> herself be killed, as she so often said, but she probably didn't
> mean it any more than others who pretended they would do one
> thing or another and in the end did something completely differ-
> ent. I also felt disgust for a faith that made it possible for people
> to use it to shame and destroy our self-respect, make us wretched
> with the insidious ways and machinations of domineering
> people. I saw the brothers-in-faith use the opportunity whenever
> someone was sick, like mother who was almost helpless. Instead
> of a faith that raises a person up and shines its noble light on
> you, if the intention is to make you really human, this faith hu-
> miliates you in your weakness. Somehow I could tell then that it
> seems as though faith in god clamps down like a bird of prey on
> those whom life has diminished with all its laws, when they are
> least able to help themselves, and then it pretends to offer them
> relief when they are cowering in the corner. (32–3)

Here the complex subject of faith enters the stage, a subject upon
which Guðbergur Bergsson again and again throws light in his writings. In the preceding chapter I discussed the paradox of faith, especially as it concerns the issue of love. Here we see the paradox again,
but in a different way. Here, we see how a religious dogma undermines a human being's capacity for self-preservation. And the reader
asks, if faith in god is to raise a human being up, to shine its light on
her/him and make her/him a "real human being," if faith is to strength-
en a human being's faith in life, then why does it confine itself to
interventions that evoke only humiliation and crushing weakness?

But it is not only the limitations of a law of god that occupies the
mind of the narrator. Early on in his life he is thinking about the
complicated nature of the need for faith. This throws further light on

the limits of human-made laws concerning the inner life, and the
dialogue the author wages with the reader sheds light on the aesthetics under discussion:

> "You are completely obscure," is what I thought might be the
> only truth about myself.
>
> Thinking this way, or in that frame of mind, I learned early on
> that the tendency towards faith is an individual thing; it is not re-
> lated to religions, and inside ourselves there is a more sorrowful,
> clouded, happier, and deeper way than theirs, with more light
> and longing than there is in nature and the sunshine, and the in-
> ner man is more complicated and expansive than the fields of
> home or the world. It is worth getting to know that inner person;
> to dwell in the mind with him more than with nature or even the
> flowers and other people, let alone to practise a religion or to
> trust in the gods. Least of all should you trust in those people
> who are said to be your closest. (218)

Unlike the need for faith, which is individual in nature, it seems as
though, in the narrator's description, the laws and religious estab-
lishments of humanity are not of much consequence to the inner
being. We discern here the creation of an individualized aesthetics,
which is at once radical and graced with what we might call cautious
humanity. If we talk about the communication of an individualized
aesthetics, this is what we see in Bergsson's writings, where art is
thought of from the vantage point of life – a perspective that does
not shy away from the frailty of human life. This is also a novelist
who thinks:

> You demand nothing of god and your faith originates from an
> inherent non-belief.
>
> You know that no one but you is the glimmer of light with the
> rose; you are also the brightness.
>
> You are the sea and you are also the daylight within yourself.
> (77)

But how does one live with such thoughts concerning art, if life has no
sympathy for the living? What is beauty in this kind of creativity?

On the subjects of the barren beauty of his childhood (which he
thought about at night, with his head on his pillow, after his father

had left to go to sea, not in Rapollo but in the district of
Þorkötlustaður) and of the sadness he experienced following a still-
born desire, the man in the house has this to say:

> I felt a sadness that I had lost something that I never received
> and had never seen and thus imagined all the more clearly. I tried
> to focus my mind on how good it is to see the light of the sun,
> the natural daylight over the earth in the mornings, white snow
> and a deep blue sea after a winter night. Then it became confused
> with Rapollo in my grandmother's picture. The region was en-
> dowed with a barren and stony kind of beauty, which is easy to
> visualize by thinking of imagined places. Everything is different
> from what you can see with the naked eye. (75)

Not until much later, when he had visited the countries he had
seen in his dreams, did the man realize that it was there, in those "so-
called beautiful places," that he found "nothing more beautiful than
what appeared time and again in the sleeping hours; the stone-clad
wasteland by the sea. Those things are sometimes most beautiful
that no one can see except ourselves, and it is best to see them with
closed eyes or at night in the darkness or when the inner vision
dwarfs everything outside. That is how selfish and concealed beauty
can be" (75).

Here we see how the search for the origin of life and art takes the
man to the kind of beauty that cannot be comprehended except with
"closed eyes or at night in the darkness when the inner vision dwarfs
everything outside." But if beauty is so selfish and hidden from
others, how can it be revealed?

> It was in this small, stony heath I am thinking of now, that I
> made the first draft of my sense of beauty. Few people would
> probably think of looking at things that way or believe that this
> desert south of the house, that this nothing, as most people
> would say, was in my eyes and to my senses the wellspring of
> beauty. No one except maybe someone who has been raised on
> another heath and who thinks his is the only true one, or the man
> who spent his childhood on the green or in a big city could say
> such an improbable thing about my heath. Whoever talks that
> way has no idea that only in childhood, and after that in litera-
> ture, can we appreciate most what comes close to being nothing,

quickly glimpsed, and then everything when considered more
closely. The child lives in the beauty of that which seems to be
made of nothing, or of the most simple or the smallest. (102–3)

This writer is conscious of the illusion of the senses and asks himself such questions as: "Can it be that I looked at life and its beauty
wrongly yesterday?" "Am I squint-eyed or cross-eyed when it comes
to my speciality, to have a sense of the two?" "Do I in fact have no
sense of what is beautiful, like the mother who finds her own offspring most beautiful, the child she has given birth to, because she is
selfish and blind to the beauty of other infants?" (103). In the wake
of these questions, the man in the house reviews the production of
traditional aesthetics, or those learned theories of beauty that regularly see the light of day, and talks about the attempts to find "reasonable and certain laws concerning beauty, in order to avoid beauty, or
rather taste, from being too free in relation to lasciviousness" (104).

If we believe these words, then this novelist does not want to con-
vey the kind of beauty that is the result of traditional, systematized
aesthetics. In other words, he is as doubtful about the human-made
and institutionalized laws concerning beauty as he is of those theories that are supposed to encompass faith and the soul. From this
perspective, systematic aesthetics diminishes not only the potential of
beauty but also taste, and its involvement with the "history of lust" is
at risk. Later I take a closer look at this issue and at how Bergsson's
thinking about taste is tied to the view that the body is life and that
the soul can be sought on the boundary between life and death. For
now, we are left with two questions, and they are: What if the feeling
for beauty and ugliness cannot be measured? Is it possible that beauty
resides not in the material but, rather, in the immaterial?

Now I understand that the beauty of the heath was not based on
the landscape itself but, instead, was outside of that. Such is
beauty and its nature. Beauty did not reside in the heath but,
rather, in an idea I had of the heath, and maybe it will also reside
in the words I make about it, if I am careful. From this it is possible to see that I have often said that the beauty of a thing is not
in the thing itself; not in the idea of the thing or the notion one
thinks up of the thing, but, rather, it is in the desire to see the
thing in the right light. For that matter, beauty is not independent
but remains at a comfortable distance from that which one is

thinking. In other words, it is in the consciousness and the talent
to enjoy that as a form of truth. Only in that way can everyone
enjoy it, high and low, ignorant as well as learned. Even animals
and birds sense it, and become happy or sad at it. (104–5)

In his thoughts about the frosty mornings of his childhood and how
they were "the most beautiful in the world, here in this place, if
memory does not deceive, and is trustworthy and pure in the same
way as the breath of dawn," the writer allows the reader to participate in his wish. He wanted to be able to look at his childhood place
objectively, "like a work of art that has no relation to anything other
than that which induces a fusion between he who looks and that
which is looked upon" (393). But how does a wish like this get realized? Do the boundaries between life and art perhaps reside in the
entirely unnameable? A writer who uses the right names, the man
says, will soon be singing his last. The writer who makes them up
can, on the other hand, expect to "get to live his narrative like a
dangerous accident in word and style." This art, the man says, is not
based on fear but, rather, is "a search for the fusion of something but
the writer does not know of what" (392).

Is it perhaps the ability to enjoy beauty as a certain kind of truth
that enables the writer to live, in words and style, his thoughts on art
as seen from the perspective of life? Or is distance the key to beauty?[1]

Perhaps the following fragment can give a clearer picture of the
way this writer approaches the boundary between life and art. He
recollects a moment from his childhood concerning his father and
mother, their poems, and the suffering that parts reality from fiction:

I shuddered to think [father] could not reach outside the material
world and did not have a taste for beauty or an ability to sense
the suffering that parts reality from fiction and turns even an
ugly mindset into a pure spirit with the right mood. Perhaps he
tried to make his mother hurt him like my mother was when he
destroyed her book. Her suffering had no prototype; it originated
from her nature the same way as the precious poem.

Was he jealous of the poem in her book?

Did he tear it up in order to practise on mother; to see her
suffering?

In the trips to Reykjavík he has not found it appropriate to
take up the square wooden pencil and a sheet of paper in the old

folks' home or in the parking lot and write a note to himself that
he could use later. He believed in memory and found no use in
anything other than what could be gathered in memory and in
his limited power over alliteration and rhyme. He did not know
that the nature of suffering is not built on anything; it just lives
inside us and is created in our nature. Sorrow is always in its
place even though life may smile. (312–3)

Truth may perhaps reveal itself in thoughts about the division between reality and literature, about this grief that, in the writer's sensibility, can make an ugly state of mind turn into pure spirit, a grief
that has no paradigm but is instead generated by human nature and
lives inside of us.

But can the world and existence then only be justified as an aesthetic phenomenon? This question can also be found in the form of
an assertion in Friedrich Nietzsche's *The Birth of Tragedy*, a work
that first appeared in 1872.

THE REBIRTH OF TRAGEDY

We have seen how the roots of Bergsson's individual aesthetics are
embedded in a village on the southwestern coast of Iceland and the
lives people live there. But they are also to be found in his dialogue
with a few poets, novelists, and philosophers. The idea we see unfold
in the fictional autobiography – the idea of art seen from the perspective of life – is also prominent in Nietzsche's *The Birth of Tragedy*.
Bergsson himself discusses the generosity of writers and how we find
in art only what already exists in the artist. In this context, he mentions
Nietzsche's understanding of this subject. Ever since he was about
twenty years old, Bergsson claimed a resemblance between his works
and Nietzsche's.[2] This much is certain: the boundary between life and
art is equally riveting to both of these authors. As is the case with
Bergsson's fictional autobiography, Nietzsche's *The Birth of Tragedy*
raises profound questions about the incomprehensibility, as well as the
formation, of this boundary. Both Bergsson's fictional autobiography
and *The Birth of Tragedy* awaken in the reader a consciousness of a
certain kind of knowledge of life, the grief that is its consequence, and
question of whether and how art has anything to do with this.

Are we then talking about the *re*birth of tragedy? What is the
connection?

Many who take *The Birth of Tragedy* as their subject eventually long to understand what Nietzsche means by when he says "art is the highest task and the true metaphysical activity of this life" (11). Nietzsche does not explain this assertion. But there is more here that confuses people, something upon which many Nietzsche scholars have dwelt, and that is the question of Nietzsche's position on reason, on the one hand, and art, on the other. Do we find him changing positions in his earlier and his later works?

In brief, several interpreters disagree on whether there is any discrepancy between the ideas of the younger Nietzsche and the ideas of the older. Did the ideas in Nietzsche's first book, *The Birth of Tragedy*, become the groundwork for his subsequent writings? Peter Berkowitz is one of those who casts doubt on the traditional interpretation of *The Birth of Tragedy*.[3] He sheds light on a problem that other interpretations more or less ignore – a problem that he says Nietzsche alredy took seriously in *The Birth of Tragedy*. Unlike many critics, Berkowitz suggests that the main subject of the book is not artistic creation. On the contrary, he claims its main subject is the question of knowledge, or wisdom – how knowledge is achieved and what it uncovers. He also discusses the overwhelming influence knowledge has on the individual who is "exposed to it" (44). The question lodged in *The Birth of Tragedy* is, he maintains, whether art is more helpful than philosophy in understanding the truth about the destiny of humanity and the world. And he says Nietzsche's answer is clear: art wins out. Nonetheless, the question Nietzsche seeks to answer is Socratic in nature: what is a good life? The answer is also in the spirit of Socrates, or at least in the spirt of his conviction that life without thought is not worth living. And, if we ask about the spirit of Nietzsche with respect to the dignity of humanity, we see that it is based on wisdom (Berkowitz 45).

But is this not a contradiction? How can art be better suited than philosophy as a way of understanding the truth about the condition of humanity and the world if life without thought is said to be worthless? Berkowitz answers this by saying that Nietzsche "portrays art (the tragic myths of the Greeks) and philosophy (Socratic rationalism) as fundamental orientations towards the truth about the fundamental character of existence" (Berkowitz 47). Nietzsche, Berkowitz says, nonetheless considers the superiority of the Greek myths to be due to the fact that, through this medium, the Greeks came face to face with the terrifying truth about existence (and thereby showed courage), whereas Socrates' theories are only good for covering up the terror of the human condition (and thereby represent cowardice). The contradictory reasoning found in Nietzsche can therefore be described something like this: by removing the veil from the true character of existence, art does what reason and science promise but do not deliver (ibid.).

What matters here, not only for those interested in *The Birth of Tragedy* but also for a discussion of the rebirth of tragedy, which we see in Guðbergur Bergsson's fictional autobiography, is how Nietzsche sees the conflict between science and art: he sees science from the perspective of the artist, and he sees art from the perspective of life.[4] This, Berkowitz maintains, is what Nietzsche indicates in the foreword to *The Birth of Tragedy*, and he begins the discussion of what will become the central argument: the relationship between ethics and art. The ethics of art is front and centre when it comes to an inquiry into the hidden width and breadth of existence. This is because the ethics of art is grounded in a deep understanding of the "true or real needs of human beings" and a "precise knowledge of the fundamental character of the cosmos in which they dwell" (Berkowitz 48–9).

If we consider Bergsson's fictional autobiography in this context, it is indeed possible to discern a rebirth of tragedy. The understanding of the man in the house engenders a tragic sense of humanity's needs and the nature of the world in which it dwells. It is also proposed that the reader of the story is given an opportunity to come face to face with the poverty of those people in the man's childhood. And this comes about not by creating sympathies that are tied to time and place (which would make the reader think "What injustice the common people of Iceland had to endure in the first half of the twentieth century!") but, rather, by awakening a consciousness of human nature, whose senselessness manifests itself in a sweeping echo of life. As a consequence of such a thought, not only is the need for human-made laws made tangible, but so is the problem and extent of human existence. If we believe this story, it seems that the laws of our time concerning the soul, faith, and beauty do not take us very far.

Is it only art that can answer the call of human nature and existence? Are the ethics of art the only permanent ethics?

WHAT THE GREEKS LEFT BEHIND

In *The Birth of Tragedy*, Nietzsche explores the ideas of the ancient Greeks on faith and how these ideas are presented in their tragedies.

He approaches the question of the actual needs of a human being, of the fundamental characteristic of the world of human beings, and of the part faith has to play in this. In other words, he asks about the powers that lie behind the Greek tragedies. Those powers, Nietzsche feels, not only relate to the fundamental principles of the nature of life and the soul but also reveal human nature itself.

If we accept Nietzsche's ideas, then tragedy comes to be when two opposite powers merge: these are personified in Greek mythology by the gods Apollo and Dionysius. Greek tragedy, the height of artistic achievement in Nietzsche's mind, is the fusion of Apollonian art (which has to do with form) and Dionysian musical art (which has to do with passion). The actual fusion of these powers does not occur, however, until they have wrestled for a long time. Their merger is no small matter when you think of the chasm that separates them – a chasm that Nietzsche describes as that between passive dreaming and unrestrained, violent intoxication.

Nietzsche's ideas about the different creations of Appollo and Dionysus are no less interesting. The Appollonian artist requires distance from the ever-interfering drives and instincts, from the surging maelstrom of the world. He or she requires some kind of philosophical separation that is accompanied by an awareness of the difference between reality and appearance. The Dionysian artist, on the other hand, needs to be far removed from this kind of dream-like creation, this artful illusion. The expressiveness of the Dionysian artist rests on the rudiments of stimuli and passions – here and now – and reaches its highest point in those famous orgies. Instead of formulating stimuli and passions in form or in repetition, the Dionysian artist gives them free rein, engaging in a seemingly unrestrained freedom of expression. The artist is therefore not only an artist but a living work of art. While the Apollonian artist needs to remove him/herself from the eruption of his impulses, the Dionysian artist needs those impulses to be gratified on the boundaries that separate them from him/herself. In other words, the Apollonian artist is taken in by beautiful illusions, while the Dionysian artist pawns his or her intellect in order to become a rank plaything of the wild forces of nature.

In and of themselves, the gods are subject to limitations, but what Nietzsche does in *The Birth of Tragedy* is to show the relationship between those limits and the requirements of faith. What Nietzsche sees in the Greeks is that their faith is a beautiful work of the imagination. And he asks: what colossal human needs created this handsome assembly of Olympian gods? Those needs seem to have sprung from their knowledge of the human condition, but that condition has to be considered problematic and hardly desirable in itself. It is for this reason that Nietzsche asks: how did the Greeks manage to say "yes" to life? And, roughly, his answer is: the Greeks knew and felt the terror and dread of existence, and, in order to endure them, they placed between themselves and life a dream-like panoply of Olympian gods. Thus, what lies behind the creation of the Greek gods is the Greeks' need to live (Berkowitz 51). This being the case, their religion is enviable in itself, and it leaves something behind for we modern people to desire.

But there is more that the Greeks left behind, things that the limits of the gods uncover and that touch on one of the main subjects of this book – the connection between aesthetics and faith. If the role of Greek mythology is to say yes to life rather than to cower from the miserable contradictions that constitute humanity's fate – a fate that circumnavigates the discrepancy between human desire and the possibility of its fulfilment – then something has been won. But, as Berkowitz points out, Nietzsche also illustrates the insufficiency of Greek mythology and its gods: they are nothing more than a symbol for the reconciliation of beauty and necessity. With their gods, the Greeks created an image of redemption, which is, at its best, simultaneously aesthetic and literary. And that is not enough (Berkowitz 52). A redemption that takes place through delusion is an incomplete solution to the problem of human desire and the possibility of its fulfilment. In Greek mythology, a solution outside of the terrifying meaninglessness of life is possible, but only in dreams. As a result, we see how Apollo, without the aid of Dionysius, imagines a form of relief but is unable to provide it. The solution has to take place in the midst of life itself, not in a soaring illusion of life. Dionysius is, on the other hand, a god of gods, if we consider life here and now. That is why the dreamer must side with Dionysius if he is to fulfill the powerful Greek need to love life. A Dionysian artist lacks the ability to "profit" from the knowledge he has acquired in life. While Apollo is, so to speak, only presented as imaginary, Dionysius is presented as change incarnate. Alone they are unable to fulfill their basic requirements, but together they can do what is necessary, and this occurs most completely in the form of tragedy. And here tragedy comes to the full, with all its wisdom (55).

But what is the wisdom of tragedy and what effect does it have on she or he who acquires it? Nietzsche says it leads to knowledge of the true nature of the natural world, rather than to the deceptions of culture, which is a well-known theme in many of his works.[5] But is this kind of wisdom good for us?

The main argument that Berkowizts offers against Nietzsche's ideas is this: if human suffering is the yardstick of insight, might such a perspective on the human condition not lead to insanity? For if we accept Nietzsche's ideas about the superiority of Greek tragedy when it comes to possessing an exalted knowledge of the human condition and of existence, then we must accept that this same knowledge seems to end in complete devastation. The fulfilment of human nature for which Nietzsche is looking seems to reside in the total humiliation of humanity. The question is, therefore, how the fulfilment of human nature could possibly be built on what one might call a "lethal comprehension" (Berkowitz 59).

These kinds of disagreements with Nietzsche are nothing new. It has, for example, been claimed that Nietzsche's ideas are more indicative of a sickness than they are of a cure.[6] But does Nietzsche present himself as a doctor offering cures?

Other interpreters of *The Birth of Tragedy* take a different position. One of these is Alexander Nehamas, who, in his *Nietzsche: Life as Literature* interprets Nietzsche's ideas on what tragedy tells us about the nature of knowledge. What tragedy teaches is nothing other than the opposition between the truth of nature and the lies of culture, and it is the latter that considers itself most significant. Tragedy shows, in other words, how the world we live in and respond to is our own construction, and how this created world cannot turn without the aid of the perspectives, values, and desires of those who live in it. But what makes tragedy even more significant in the eyes of Nietzsche, Nehamas says, is how it offers comfort for the terror and dread that grips us in the wake of this insight. Tragedy shows that humanity is not separated from nature, that it is part of nature and belongs fully to nature. It shows that life is, in the end, the basis of everything. In spite of continuously changing images, of continuous transformations, life contains an unmistakable power and provides pleasure: the blind and meaningless flow of life's high and low tides is worthy of joy and astonishment (Nehamas 43).

What matters is that these interpretations of Nietzsche's ideas about the nature of knowledge that tragedy elucidates can just as easily emerge from the investigation of the aesthetics involved in the fictional autobiography of Guðbergur Bergsson. The aesthetics of this fictional autobiography, as of *The Birth of Tragedy*, seems, in other words, to allow room for the points of view of both Nehamas and Berkowitz at once. But how can that be?

The safeguard we find in Berkowitz concerning the "lethal knowledge" of tragedy reminds the reader of the difficulty of the kind of thinking that has been discussed here: that is, how is it possible to live with the knowledge that, in all likelihood, it is not only human life but also life itself that is senseless? The fragment of the chapter that has been alluded to from the first volume of Bergsson's fictional autobiography may better explain the subject. The grandfather welcomes "Guðbergur's" mother and grandmother home after the two of them have carried a heavy sewing machine across a field of lava and says to his wife, "you no longer live here" (*Father and Mother* 146). The child (the narrator's mother) not only carries inside herself the seeds of loneliness and vulnerability but also generates it in adulthood in the emotional lives of her children, as if this were the "natural flow of life." On the other hand, we see how this kind of knowledge has in it a seeding of sorts, which reminds us of Nehamas's interpretation of Nietzsche's ideas about tragedy and the knowledge it contains: nature is not separate from human beings but, rather, is integral to them; therefore life is, in the end, the basis for everything. Another fragment from Bergsson's fictional autobiography reflects this idea, a fragment that has already been discussed and that can be found in the book's second volume. It deals with the moment when the man in the house talks about the stories with which he grew up and how he eventually found the right way to live (*Like a Stone* 207).

The fictional autobiography is not, any more than is *The Birth of Tragedy*, a blind ode to art. It is more true, in a sense, to say that the aesthetics of this book is characterized by an inexhaustible search for the possibilities of art, seen from the perspective of life. In the autobiography we also discern a striving for the individual's existential–artistic domain in direct opposition to some of the most dominant human–made laws known to the modern individual. In this way Bergsson's fictional autobiography is reminiscent of Nietzsche's *Birth of Tragedy*. In his introduction, "An Attempt at Self-Criticism," Nietzsche states that there is "no greater antithesis of the purely aesthetic exegesis and justification of the world, as taught in [his] book, than the Christian doctrine which is, and wants to be, *only* moral, and which, with its absolute criteria ... banishes art, *all* art, to the realm of lies, and thus negates, damns and condemns it" (9). According to Nietzsche, views on art are clearly not to be underestimated. For him, the Christian doctrine's kind of "thinking and evaluating" reveals "hostility to life." But why? Describing himself as an "advocate for life," it seems that our opportunity to approach, and embrace, life itself could be at stake: all life rests on "semblance, art, deception, prismatic effects, the necessity of perspectivism and error," Nietzsche writes. The problem with Christianity, however, is the endorsement of and the belief in a supposedly better place. What Nietzsche perceives behind this wishful thinking is "hatred of the 'world,'" a condition that he also defines as a "curse on the passions, fear of beauty and sensuality, a Beyond, invented in order better to defame the Here-and-Now, fundamentally a desire for nothingness, for the end, for rest" (ibid). It seems that Guðbergur Bergsson is not unfamiliar with such a heart-felt experiment. Consider the fragment on the possibility of thought in life: "I know that a thought can travel widely through the air, settle on the gravel and grow, many-coloured, wherever it takes root. A thought is not a prayer to life, life does not need a prayer; it does what it wants and has no sympathy for the living. Life is bereft of laws, it is only us who make them up" (*Father and Mother* 232).

A SELF-PORTRAIT THAT REFLECTS
AN IMAGE OF THE WORLD

In one of his essays on literature and aesthetics, Bergsson discusses his view of literature in Iceland. He says that this literature has always been special and that, in Iceland, there has "never existed any classical literature," that "the utilitarian point of view" has been dominant in poetry and other genres, and that "Icelandic literary theories" and "inane aesthetics" have gone astray and "never reached an intelligent foothold" ("Sæmundur the Wise" 93–4). He also talks about the aesthetics of "progressive" literature:

By only concentrating on the words and sometimes their sound, rather than becoming acquainted with their meaning or the thoughts they might entail, readers and critics do not see the aura of the works that are individual in nature and are perhaps not engaged in any other battle than the one waged with human nature, and are not written in order to await their day in the sun, with a following of fans and goings on among those who reign over the market purse. They may not even be created for the memory, the common sense, or the understanding; and least of all for the one correct understanding. Instead, they spring from a longing to search for the reflections that investigate the nature of the endless road to the incomprehensibility of life, which seems to recede as soon as the steely memory thinks it has found that unwavering certainty. Just as humanity resorts to its forgetfulness, life seems to renew itself by automatically awakening the incomprehension of those who are living according to specific rules. Progressive literary works are similar; they create incomprehension of the right form of understanding, and the disinterestedness of the public is the foundation for all viable books. This kind of literature leans simultaneously towards its nature and away from it. They paint a self-portrait and at the same time an image of the world. (95)

This feature of progressive literature, according to Bergsson, is based on an individual aesthetics, and he mentions a work by Rembrandt to illustrate this.[7] But it is not only in Iceland that readers and critics become confused about the aesthetics of the individual. If we believe Bergsson, then this is the case throughout the world. The general crisis in this matter is not necessarily tied to an Icelandic version of utilitarianism. Quite the contrary, if and when the subject matter is life itself, and humanity's relationship with it, the crisis concerns the nature of modern thought:

When a crisis occurs in the spiritual world, the human spirit risks seeing life in its various specific parts; the human spirit then specializes. This is evident in the practice of modern philosophy. Philosophers think they can see all the natural features of the human being, perhaps in language and its use; others see the entire panorama of human life in behaviour; others in politics or in the party politics that reign in the world instead of democracy. Philosophy no longer sees life as a whole; it does not view man from all sides. The great systems have come to an end. There is an effort to convince us that man has become so complex that no human being can acquire a full knowledge of him. Therefore man must be scrutinized one feature at a time with a scientific

bent. But man is and will always be a living form that you can
walk around and look at from every vantage point you like.
("Critique of Criticism" 559)

As has emerged, we can say that the aesthetics of the individual
that we find in Bergsson is rooted in the village on the southwestern
coast of Iceland and the life people live there; however, the profound
dialogue this author has with certain key issues in Western culture
also mark his thinking.

But what about the part played in Bergsson's aesthetics by Icelandic
culture and society? Bergsson is clearly a European author and the
aesthetics of his writing offers a self-portrait that is simultaneously a
portrait of the world. But, in his works, Icelandic culture and society
must be something more than a stony heath on a southern coast? Is
he not located on the Saga Isle? Are Icelanders not a nation guarding
a literary treasure? Does their literary heritage not matter at all to this
novelist's aesthetics? And what about the part played by cultural politics? Is there perhaps a specific political position in Iceland with respect to culture involved in Bergsson's calling the village of Grindavík
his Florence? Although he addresses himself to the whole world, does
he not also, and no less so, address himself to the representatives of
Icelandic culture in Reykjavík, the capital?

Dialogue with Icelandic Culture and Society

In the foregoing chapters I discuss creative repetition as it is found in Western cultures, how Bergsson's writing unveils an existential sensibility that is hidden but not forgotten in his part of the world, and how this subject concerns both art and life. The creative force of repetition does not place limitations on the aspects of modernity in Bergsson's writing. Quite the contrary. Bergsson's works powerfully observe the streams and trends in the sciences and arts of modern times. In Bergsson's writing, Icelandic culture and society are not left out of this dense arena of "repetition." The question is: how do Icelandic readers respond to this aesthetic?

As we have seen, Bergsson's perspective takes a specific aesthetic position. It concerns not only his ideas about the laws and limitations that are placed on people but also the body and how taste, which is constantly changing, stirs up and confuses laws and limitations. In one place, Bergsson discusses this issue and how "the wondrous power of taste" not only confuses the way people look at things from one day to the next but also "truth" itself and "the teachings of Christianity concerning eternity":

> Nowadays everything is so that nothing is either right or wrong unless it is seen from a preconceived point of view, and that is how we look at most things. But since neither truth nor the Christian right and wrong last for eternity, what was right today could be wrong tomorrow on the strength of the wondrous power of taste. The changeability and waywardness of human taste are not always the result of new inventions, which are inevitably right compared to the solutions reached previously; but

taste also comes from the nature of desire and/or fulfilment.
(Bergsson, "Afterword" to *Love Life*, 227)

In Bergsson's aesthetics we see a persistent and fearless exploration
of taste and its influence on life as well as on art. Whether it is in
content or form, the capriciousness of taste thrives in an excitable
but often chaotic environment that finds its renewal and recreation
more in the instincts than in reason. In this light we are able to talk
about the struggle between the flesh and the spirit, even though that
struggle does not occur in the spirit of classical ideas on the subject,
the classical/theological notions of body and soul. In Bergsson's
writings, the flesh enacts the spirit. This is even more noteworthy
when we consider the reception Bergsson's writing has had in
Iceland, whose aesthetics has, at times, been viewed as anti-human.
One of the reasons for this could be that, in his writings, Bergsson
cares little for "approved" ideas of social responsibility and, instead,
propounds a form of responsibility that is only found in the freedom
of literature and can appear there – in complete opposition to the
judgments of learned people – as an ethics of aesthetics. Whatever
the reason may be for the, at times, curious reception of his work in
Iceland, it is necessary to take a closer look at some of the extra-
ordinary quarrels that have ensued here as a result of its aesthetics
(mostly in the 1970s and the 1980s). I only look at a few specific
features of these quarrels as the width and breadth of Bergsson's
works is extensive.

Here it is worth keeping in mind the above-mentioned fragments
that deal with the history of aesthetics in Iceland. It is also important
to remember that, in Bergsson's writings, the reality of Icelandic culture and society is interwoven with elements of the literature and the
history of ideas of the West. I have emphasized the pervasive thinking concerning the boundary between life and art, reality and imagination, flesh and spirit, creativity and death. And the dialogue
Bergsson has with the laws of Western culture on subjects such as
love, faith, and beauty reveals that nothing is assumed, that everything is the material for creative search and creative thought.

Already in Bergsson's first books we see the characteristics of that
aesthetics, and they also occur with great clarity in *Tómas Jónsson
Bestseller*. The latter shows a crackling perception of the individual
in Icelandic society and in the culture of the postwar era. The time of
the story – socially, culturally, and aesthetically – is, however, more

far-reaching than the milieu of the 1970s. It is clear that this story marks the beginning of a certain fictional world in Bergsson's oeuvre, the so-called "Tangi stories," which was to include five more novels: *The Love Life of a Compatible Couple* (1967); *Anna* (1968); *It Sleeps in the Deep* (1973); *Hermann and Dídí* (1974); *It Rises from the Deep* (1976); and the short story collection *What Is God's Kindling?* (1970).[1] As in his first novel, *The Mouse That Skulks*, Bergsson creates a setting reminiscent of a village on the southwestern coast of Iceland. Besides being a focused, modernistic experiment in form, we discern in this fictional world a continuing examination of Icelandic society and culture in the middle of the twentieth century. Here Bergsson also strengthens the ethics that will characterize his whole aesthetics: nothing is either wrong or right except insofar as the vantage point is preconceived.[2] The characters in this fictional world unmistakably bear witness to the author's aesthetics – as does the society to which they belong – on the boundaries of reality and imagination, fiction and actuality, the present day and eternity.

With the appearance of the Tangi stories, interest in Bergsson's writing began to grow among readers, critics, and publishers in Iceland. Antipathy also grew, however, and some described these works as "formless" and "pornographic." The antipathy we see for his work in the 1970s and 1980s had become significant by the time he had completed this particular fictional world.[3] This "death peal," however, has been unusually lucrative, as is evidenced by Bergsson's opus. The dialogue between Bergsson and Icelandic culture and society, the public discussion of his aesthetics in Iceland, and his fictional world are all explored here. I discuss the novel *Tómas Jónsson Bestseller* and the complicated era from which the aesthetics of this book derives. Then I consider the same subject in *The Love Life of a Compatible Couple*, along with the ethics of its aesthetics. I also discuss *Anna* and how Bergsson's ideas about the need for renewal in literature are tied to his attitude towards repetition in life as well as in art. Finally, I consider Bergsson's aesthetics in his writing in general and show how, by touching on a much larger world, it concerns Icelandic culture and society.

THE TIME OF TÓMAS

When *Tómas Jónsson Bestseller* (1966) was republished in 1987, Bergsson wrote a foreword in which he said, among other things:

I suppose, even though I do not know it for sure, that I harbour somewhere deep in my monstrosity a hidden hatred for literature, even though it is the main feature of my life. Perhaps the disgust I feel comes from the fact that I have on occasion had to yield to my imagination and do whatever I had to in order to get rid of it; for example, to waste it by relentlessly spewing it into works of literature. For what are works of literature other than a bottomless pit of the imagination and, in fact, the wasting of it? In me there is a very busy man who is "one against all." And he is also up against me, myself. Tómas Jónsson is born with these qualities too, and he is one who both wastes and is wasted, not only like my life, but like life itself. It wastes and is wasted and it yields to other things. (3)

In the same foreword Bergsson says:

I have been reluctant to give permission for the republication of this book; in fact, I maintained the belief, and still do, that the book has value only to the generation it was written for.
   Then one fine day, when I was asked to, I decided to say:
   "Go to hell, Tómas Jónsson, and try to make it, you old devil, among those who have never met such a bastard as you, who hopefully will never appear again, neither in literary form nor in society. Live as a symbol of your time."
   That's how it was. (6)

Not everyone agrees that *Tómas Jónsson Bestseller* has value only to the generation for which it was written. Ástráður Eysteinsson has discussed the subject and maintains the opposite, maintaining that *Tómas Jónsson Bestseller* is not at all a testament of a former time but, rather, is even more provocative and relevant now than are most of the new novels of recent years ("First Modern Novel" 56). Before turning to this matter, it would be helpful to look more closely at Bergsson's ideas about the book and the soil out of which it sprang. In that way we may approach not only certain ideas about the literary scene in Iceland in the 1970s but also an interesting and possibly relevant connection between Icelandic literature, culture, and society.
   In the foreword, Bergsson discusses different ideas about form and how an author has to be graced with a sensitive and expansive sense of it if he is to get anywhere in his work. This is also the case for the

writer who wishes to break with traditions in form and to change it "so that it sings in the wider formalities of time" (*Tómas Jónsson* 3). With the appearance of *Tómas Jónsson Bestseller* people already heard this song, loud and clear.[4] But what was the Icelandic sense of form like in the 1970s, and what did this say about the sense of form among Icelanders in general? If we accept Bergsson's words, then Icelanders' sense of form had gone astray. Politicians had locked themselves in argumentative circles and had little hope of escaping their rhetoric. The case was similar for literature and society as a whole. The reason, Bergsson says, was a stagnation, which, in his view, came from "too rigid a sense of form" and that appeared equally in the areas of religion, politics, and literature.

Bergsson says he has avoided this kind of stagnation in his own writing by uprooting himself. He says he has quelled the traditional sense of structure in himself and suffocated the storyline, the potential perfection of his works, at its inception. He wanted, in short, to avoid preying on an old-fashioned product, even though such wooden works of art were often showered with "praise and admiration." This is also an author who claims to have avoided applause. Not even literary scholars have been able to get him on their side. Indeed, for Bergsson, acquaintance with them is pure poison: this is "not only because they are just like goats, hankering after wooden nettles, but that they have no interest in the newly sprung greens, unless it is in fashion. The goats just go for the nettles or the greens or whatever literary stew is trendy" (4).

Bergsson states that, in the Icelandic literary scene, before *Tómas Jónsson Bestseller* appeared, there were quite a lot of "old nettles," and these old nettles got a lot of praise. Politics – which was "locked in rhetorical circles" – had generated wooden poets and novelists. Of these the right had two, as did the left. By writing *Tómas Jónsson Bestseller*, Bergsson did not intend to chase down those "old nettles," who, for him in his youth "and in his best years," had been quite necessary. The character Tómas is by nature a writer, but in spite of that Bergsson goes about creating "a symbol of all the sterile powers in the nation's garden ... a man of the much-discussed 'centennial generation'" (4). The centennial generation, the generation that was dominant at the turn of the nineteenth and twentieth centuries, was a fertile creative force, especially with regard to Icelandic independence. But at this time, in what Bergsson calls "the social reality of Iceland," this generation becomes an obstruction to progress. It had even become "a threat to independence, which [it] had fought for in its time" (5). Bergsson says that this generation had been letting the country slip out of its hands. The character of Tómas springs from this kind of background, but his apartment is, according to the author, made up to appear symbolic of its time. The complexity of everything is, however, foregrounded: the symbolic image is simple but not readily evident.

With a complexity that people intuit rather than understand, the publication of *Tómas Jónsson Bestseller* created animosity among Icelandic readers and critics. Deep down, among those who were most angry, this animosity presented itself as a need for renewal. For this reason, the novel of Tómas became a milestone work about a turn-of-the-century man, and, after its publication, all moulds were broken. This does not mean that *Tómas Jónsson Bestseller* started any "special new trend in Icelandic literature" (5). Nor was this the author's intention. But what does Bergsson mean by the idea of renewal in Icelandic literature? Let us look at a fragment from his foreword:

A wise man who releases the chains does it in such a way that it will never again be possible to confine what has been let out. I know of few things as despicable as when someone who has been oppressed but then rises to power himself begins to oppress others (in this regard we might mention upcoming writers). He is despicable because he knows in his own body and mind what suffering there is in oppression, and that is why he is actually more wretched than those among the powerful who have inherited their position, because they do not know oppression from personal experience. The slave, however, does.

As an illustration of this, I can put forward the reminder that there was a whole generation of Icelandic writers that got lost between the turn-of-the-century generation and my generation because the petrified book industry was all-powerful much longer than they had life in them to be. (6)

Aside from indirect references to the history of aesthetics in Iceland – and in this context one is immediately reminded of the stilted sense of form that, ever since the era of romanticism, a few poets and aestheticians in Iceland have taken as their subject and set themselves in opposition to – the setting for *Tómas Jónsson Bestseller* is Icelandic culture and society from the middle of the twentieth century to its seventh decade. What remains is a persistent question, which is whether the era of "petrified Icelandic literary styles" is altogether over. Another equally persistent question is whether the view of literature, culture, and society held by the generation from the turn of the century has, in fact, lost all its powers of influence.

Bergsson has written on this subject in other contexts, and in "Is Literature a Path to Salvation?" (1991) he discusses at great length the influence of what he calls the "golden authors" on Icelandic literature, culture, and society – dominant writers from the first half of the twentieth century who were sometimes influenced by Marxist ideology. It seems as though, at the inception of the twentieth century, people again glorified the era of history from which *Tómas Jónsson Bestseller* springs, which Bergsson calls the "golden past," the time when writers "knew how to write and had something to say about poor people in stories written for the wealthier of society" ("Is Literature a Path" 443). In the works of the golden authors, Bergsson goes on to say,

> we see the battle over earthly treasures and lovely sounding
> words that make it possible for people to get into the holiest of
> holy grandstanding. There you could find some of the elect –
> those who were baptized in the arts, politics, and educated in the
> correct understanding of society and the future of the world. This
> was the time of the last old boys' clubs – those monasteries of
> culture where men sat modestly and discussed the correct beliefs
> while women were allowed to serve them, like nuns, newly baked
> doughnuts and "refreshments." (ibid. 443)

Whether or not the era of the old boys' clubs is behind us, the consequence of the fraternities about which Bergsson writes is still visible in contemporary society. If we accept his ideas, then it is possible, to some degree, to trace the apathy of our times towards art, especially towards the written arts, to the golden authors. But how? They were the ones who "failed miserably in mankind's continuous search for his own limits by raising the concerns of mankind in a well-known format, in a specific social and artistic manner. The result has been that regular people do not trust 'real writers' and they run to other sources, which can offer them an escape which they know beforehand is a mirage, a lie, and an illusion" (444). As a consequence of this, Bergsson sees the continuing marginalization of

literature in Iceland. If this is correct, then the following might interest people of our day:

> The betrayal of the "great" writers will not be felt by them, for
> most of them are dead, but instead by the authors of today, who
> have to sip on the bitter dregs of the golden fame of their pre-
> decessors, without being able to learn from their style or the con-
> tent of their works; the only thing they can learn from them is
> how to avoid being like them. The writer of our day is not ostra-
> cized because of his love of truth or his total need to express his
> opinion whatever the cost, but because others used public ex-
> pression to create two kinds of insolent trends: one was the in-
> solence of men who came from above looking for an outdated
> power structure, and the other was the insolence of those from
> below who were trying to make of themselves a new power class.
> Together they managed to choke all the ideas they pretended to
> be fighting for in the name of the whole of society, which in real-
> ity was only a clique of a few.
>   The decline of education and art has hardly ever been greater.
> (445)

In *Tómas Jónsson Bestseller* we find specific chapters (which are itali-
cized insertions) wherein the formal mannerisms of the golden authors are actually the target. The inserted chapters are a parody of
Halldór Laxness, but we also see how Bergsson investigates the art of
classical narrative itself – a tradition of realism with strong romantic
underpinnings. We could say that this connection between realism
and romanticism is pervasive in the work of Laxness, and it is dominant among the writers in the generation after him, as in the stories of
Indriði G. Þorsteinsson. The seriousness behind the parody is significant, whether it concerns Icelandic culture or society, for behind the
following text (which reminds us of Laxness's *The Great Weaver of
Kashmir*), Tómas discusses the "strange ignorance" he grew up with
"in the midst of dried fish and sheep," and how the country, "as far as
its size goes," is well suited to experiments in the area of "social sciences and politics." Is there then no hope for the literary arena? Let us
look at the following interpolation, one of Bergsson's parodies of the
classical form practised by those gilded authors and their followers:

> "No, stop it," she said and looked gently at her friend.
>   He drew back from her. She edged her body towards him,

filled with the healthy creative needs of a young woman.

"Remember," she said. "We should have children," she added, "life for tomorrow. I love children who will create new times."

"Yes," he answered, "but not until our house has been built."

"Then we will hurry up and get started on it," she said full of happiness, enthusiasm and desire to get to work. "Then what?"

"And the night – the first night after the housewarming, in our new house, which we own we two together, you and I – I will remove the contraception."

"Every night from then on will be complete ecstasy."

"My dear, you are a lovely child. Wonderfully child-like and naturally endowed".

"And I will become Þorbjörg Sóldal, the wife of Guðmundur Sóldal the famous doctor, whom all other doctors envy on account of his full waiting room. What do you think people at home in Þarafjörður will say then?"

She rose up from the bed, the bed of poverty-stricken youth, with the torn covering and creaking springs, which prevented the inertia of the night hours. She walked dignified as a deer in the woods across the floor, covered her breasts with her hands, and lifted the curtains. The cold street lights shone in the eyes of the proud, conquering woman. He followed the doe with his eyes, a young buck in the forest of life. The lights of the city seemed to be a distant glow in the mist of the rain.

"We are the Iceland of today, free and strong," he began to think while he kissed his young wife for the first time before the open curtains of the world.

"Come," she whispered, and gently pulled him back to the bed.

Firm breasts. Loins. Eyes in the dimmed room. Eager, groping hands. Messenger. Ocean breakers rose inside them. A lonely fish dived into the depths.

The wave rose and fell in the red darkness.

Athens–Mikanos–Milan–Madrid–Vík in Mýrdalur, summer 1949 (Bergsson, *Tómas Jónsson*, 91)

It would be a simplification to say that Bergsson is trying to debase the golden authors, but he definitely shows his power over this rhetoric by focusing on the form, by going into it and thereby getting a handle on the tradition from which he springs as an Icelandic novelist.[5]

In another interpolation in *Tómas Jónsson Bestseller*, Bergsson may be imitating Indriði G. Þorsteinsson:[6]

When night fell the veil of twilight settled over the withering
earth, and the autumn leaves of the trees curled up like shrivelled
pages of a book, they ambled lovingly along Sóleyjargata. He,
Haraldur Sóldal, newly minted doctor, led his fiancé Todda, bursting, as the boys in the village yelled after her when she came near.
("Here we have the conflict between critique and beauty," he
says). The lights blinked sleepily in the pond like the sadness that
flickered in her eyes when he parted with her many moons ago
and went away across the seas. (The next spring she followed him
to the big city of Reykjavík, where the terrible urban contamina-
tion appeared before her in the guise of a merchant's son full of
pleasure on the one hand, and on the other in the drug addict, the
drinker, the wretch, the homosexual, the poet Tjafsi Í. Vaffs.)

"Þorbjörg, I want you to know that in my life there have been
many women. I do not want to deceive you."

"I know, Halli, you always loved Vala Storð."

"Tell me, did you ever go with Ólafur Magan?"

"No," she answered in a low voice.

"But what about the poet et cetera, Tjafsi Í. Vaffs?" She shook
her head.

"I felt sorry for him. He was just miserable. He was a poet, but
life and human ignorance gave him a hard time."

They had now arrived home. He sighed tiredly after a difficult
surgery in the hospital, where the force of life waged a hopeless
battle with the almighty power of death. They still did not know
if the operation was successful; whether life would conquer and
give the patient a bit more time.

In the silence, which came after her answer, there was a veil
that lay over her innocent love as on a street puddle when the
film of the first night frost grips.

Then he went to her on the sofa, and the night embraced them
and remained silent over the interplay of their naked bodies,
which searched for each other's love like a creek searches for a
river, continually growing bigger in the stream of water that
flowed out into the immeasurable sea.

Silence.

The grass bowed its head as night fell. (87–8)

Attention should be drawn to the passage just before this interpolation, in which we read about the view high school students (who

are "future lawyers and ministers") have of literature. Christmas is coming in Reykjavík, and the students have just finished writing a class essay about the "great financial holiday for the merchant." The subject of the story is the conflict between poverty and wealth, and the students feel they have done their bit "by offering their sympathies with the poor wretches in an artful way." In fact, it is the boys who think along these lines, and when they approach the "ladies" in the hallway they make themselves "important" and tell them that "Nietzsche and Rilke are out of date" and that Nietzsche was nothing more than an "erudite phraseologist" (87). It seems as though, if anything, the tradition of the Icelandic narrative arts found in the golden authors supports this kind of attitude and the status quo.

The time of *Tómas Jónsson Bestseller* is certainly tied to a specific era in the history of Icelandic culture and society. At the same time, the story contains an indirect reference to the history of aesthetics in Iceland, which can be seen in the attitude of the turn-of-the-century generation. But the novel is set within a much wider time frame than this.

TÓMAS, THE OFFSPRING OF "HEALTHY, BLUE-EYED VIKINGS"

I have noted Ástráður Eysteinsson's view that *Tómas Jónsson Bestseller* is far from being a memorial to a time gone by; that it is, rather, more significant and more contemporary than most new novels of later years. But how is this so?

Tómas Jónsson Bestseller is the autobiography of a writer, and it begins as follows:

Autobiography

I am the offspring of healthy, blue-eyed Vikings. I trace my lineage to court poets and victorious kings. I am an Icelander. My name is Tómas Jónsson. I am old
no no. (7)

Clearly, this is no traditional biography. And the autobiographer is no ordinary writer, never mind an ordinary person. Consider these words of Ástráður Eysteinsson:

A host of people are speaking through the narrator, who uses the discourse of his own time and of the past, of the nation and of his own territory; chatter of various kinds; memories of events that seem to be of no importance; various tellings in the form of diversions, gossip, and ancient saga tradition. All this is flowing through Tómas but is always on the border of meaning. The monologues become a text without him being able to focus the subject for the reader. Most of these monologues have no sharp outlines but seem to be constructed in such a way that each of them could, theoretically, continue to go on endlessly; they stop some place rather than end. And Tómas is always on the border of evaporating as a character in this textual overflow. We can perhaps understand the title of the novel to be saying that Tómas is, actually, a Book. ("First Modern Novel" 84)

I would agree with this. But how is it possible to read this book as *more modern* than most new novels of later years?

One way of approaching the ever-shifting present of the story is to look at its form. As critics have discussed, the novel is fragmentary. The question is: what is the nature of these fragments? Upon its publication, Sigfús Daðason said that *Tómas Jónsson Bestseller* was a "'story in compartments' with a great many interpolations: 'Folk tales,' satires, horror stories (*histoires macabres*) that have few comparables in Icelandic literature, and the only thing that brings these various discourses together in Tómas Jónsson is that he appears to the reader to have collected them in his memory" ("Expression of Negativity" 424). Eysteinsson agrees that these are fragments, but he does not agree with Daðason that this is a "story in compartments": Tómas certainly desires organization and orderliness, and he thinks he has a pretty good grip on his life. But he fails, in Eysteinsson's estimation, to concentrate his thoughts and his world outlook: "the interpolations are not interpolations because they are not elements of another discourse at work in the book" ("First Modern Novel" 84). Tómas is the symbol that holds the whole work together, Eysteinsson continues, but he also negates the work by being full of texts that refuse to line up on the ladder of meaning, which would make it easier for people to make continuous, holistic sense of it.

The form of the story therefore tells a great deal about the protagonist and his fate as a sentient being. In Eysteinsson's opinion, *Tómas Jónsson Bestseller* is one of the works that is characterized by deeply radical doubts about the ability to maintain a holistic, never mind an independent, meaning. Even the worldview of the work is fragmentary.[7] This does not, however, mean that the narrator is untouched by a worldly longing. Quite the contrary: we can talk about the "expansion of the self" and how the text shows a person's need to "balance his own central position and his complex world view" (Eysteinsson, "First Modern Novel," 85). Tómas could therefore be a satire on the critical, informed, and independent bourgeois citizen, as Eysteinsson has suggested. The satire would, however, be without any bite if it were not possible to see the prototype in this character: "Tómas is a man of reason; he is good at many things; cares about the world. His memory – the wellspring of the text – is a collected memory, in its own way encyclopedic in the spirit of enlightenment. But this independent cultural work of his is also the root of his 'ideological crisis'" (86). This is a man who longs for a "well-ordered, differentiated picture of reality, but he has at the same time thrown it overboard by piecing it together himself, in his own eccentricity, which is incapable of orderliness" (ibid.).

The structure of *Tómas Jónsson Bestseller* can therefore be built on a type of thought that Eysteinsson refers to as "integrative" and "cosmic." However, according to Eysteinsson, aside from the novel's having certain characteristics tied to realism, it is marked by a romantic kind of chaos. The views of Sigfús Daðason are pertinent here: "Various things about the form of the book are more reminiscent of a romantic outburst than of the detail-fetishes of '*nouveau roman*'" ("Expression of Negativity" 423). Do all rivers then flow to Jena? The underlying force of the thinking that lies behind the fragmentary form of *Tómas Jónsson Bestseller* can be related to the thinking that lies behind the fragmentations that came out of Jena romanticism, which had no greater desire than to write a holistic poetic work that could overcome the growing emptiness of the time. As has been noted, this was a failure, and romanticism has been called an art form without works.

But is this actually a viable connection? Is it not far-fetched to read into the thinking behind *Tómas Jónsson Bestseller* the adventurous failures of the Jena group? What about the dialogue between the author of the novel and Icelandic culture and society?

The fragmentary structure of *Tómas Jónsson Bestseller* not only breaks with the form taken by Icelandic literature in the 1970s, so that it "sings in the wider formalities of time" (*Tómas Jónsson* 3),

but it also reveals a far-reaching outlook that was created by romanticism and then left behind. This "unworked" romanticism influences those poets, novelists, and philosophers who take as their subject
matter the acknowledgment of finitude and the limited nature of human understanding. As discussed earlier, fragmentary writings (or
non-writings) can be viewed as introducing "into the Subject a certain impotence and passivity that escapes the movement of comprehension" (Critchley 38). In other words, as introducing an element
that lies outside human understanding in a reality that is, in some
way, deprived of meaning. In *Tómas Jónsson Bestseller* we see clearly
what we might call the finitude and limits of human life. This concerns not only the constant and overwhelming proximity of the body
but also, and no less so, the admission of the limits of the spirit.

This thinking regarding the proximity of the body and the limits
of the spirit, which simmers within the novel, is not particularly related to the ideas of twentieth-century Icelandic scholars and writers
regarding the greatness of Icelandic culture and literature. The following fragment might explain how deep the thinking in this novel
goes and how powerful its criticisms. Not even the most steadfast
scholar of Icelandic studies can shake off the helplessness of the re-
searcher before the enigma of medieval Icelandic literature in this
Bergssonian satire of Icelandic scholarship pertaining to Old Norse
texts, upon which the foundation of national literary pride rests:

On Kimblagarr

Kimbli is by many scholars considered to be the son of Broki, but
Finnur Jónsson presents very interesting arguments in opposition
to this, even though most of them are speculation (as is so much
of what Finnur says). But if Finnur is right, then Kimbli ought to
have existed in the seventh century (was the poem composed
then?) according to genealogical research, since the names
Blágarr and Garr often occur, but these names originate from
Úlfsteinn hretur, and from this, and especially the Blágarr-name,
we can in many ways consider Kimblagarr to have been composed no earlier than the thirteenth century, and perhaps even
later. The name Bölvi (and probably Mildís as well) occurs first
in the genealogy of Yngli. And Glámur lived out east in
Mikligarður. It is probable that Saint Olaf sailed with him to
Garðaríki, but it is hardly possible to guess with any real

evidence (see Heusler), what Yngli was thinking at that time. i)
... The use of the word "vilmögun" is very peculiar in this context, but it does not prove anything about the age of the poem
or its origins (no proof has been found about Kimblagarr since
Finnur died; no author has been found, the scribe is unknown,
and nothing is known of its history ... If all these studies are
carefully examined, it seems the poem was composed in the elev-
enth century, or perhaps earlier. ii) But if we consider the poem
to have been composed before or after this – then when? Here,
as might be expected, no ideas will be supported with any specific arguments, but a few simple things will be pointed out for
contemplation by those who wish to read the poetic shreds. The
poem as a whole is lost to us; nothing about it is mentioned in
the Codex Regius, and there is little evidence for it except the
oral history of the eighteenth century, although Finnur seems to
have heard something about the poem in paper manuscript form.

   As might be expected there are a legion of articles and doctoral
dissertations concerning the age and origin of Kimblagarr, which
is considered one of the most remarkable farts of our medieval
Icelandic literature. (141–3)

In this fragment we see a well-known methodology go astray, and
not just slighlty. Or does the stagnation of form rise any higher in
Iceland than it does in Medieval studies? As is the case in the texts
cited above, in which Bergsson satirizes the golden authors and
thereby stirs up long-standing notions about certain classical literary
values, we see in this fragment how he goes into, and undermines,
the kind of rhetoric that has been thought to secure cultural values
in Iceland.

   As has already emerged, Bergsson says that *Tómas Jónsson
Bestseller* is both an example and a satire of modernism and that
so-called modernism typifies the freedom of the twentieth century
as, in the modern era, the individual (i.e., the novelist) is allowed to
do anything regarding subject, style, and language. He is also of the
opinion that never in the history of the arts has the romantic feeling
of the individual for him/herself been as unrestrained as it is in modernism. But at the same time he feels that this freedom invites ridicule: for a free human being is, more than anything else, comic. He
or she often acts stupidly and we laugh when things go awry, as is
the case when we imagine ourselves being free. An unfree person is,

on the other hand, confined, and Bergsson thought he knew a thing
or two about confinement.

In a textual fragment, a "folk tale" entitled "Katrín Jónsdóttir
Soprano," the narrative form gets just as lost as it does in the scholarly text quoted above. The story is a sort of meta-fiction about the
reputation of the Katrín–character in Iceland. She was said to be the
greatest Icelandic singer in the years between the wars and was highly regarded in German opera houses. She was at the height of her
fame when the government of Germany fell and Hitler came to
power. Hitler heard of this singer's glory and, after having listened to
her singing, he was gripped by an unquenchable longing for this
Valkyrie and chased her to her yacht. There they are sitting one evening over a meal and talking about art, the difficulties attached to it,
and the difference between German and Icelandic food. After a little
while, Hitler asks about news from Iceland as he had always wanted
to visit the country:

"I so much want to get command of the language," he said.

His desire for that was not due to the influence the Nonni-
books had had on him in youth, even though he thought very
highly of Nonni.

"But it is the Sagas of Icelanders, their kernel and human
value, that tempt me. This heathen clarity, uncontaminated by
Christian morality. That is what ... I immediately thought of,
when I saw you in the floodlights and you looked at me," he said
and laughed:
Why are they soulful
the eyes of Freyja
I think from the eyes
Fire burns.
They laughed heartily at this little comedy.

"Strange," Katrín said, "you have almost the right pronuncia-
tion; for Icelandic is such a difficult language – the oldest living
language in the world."

She said this not only to flatter him. Hitler was rather good at
the Icelandic language. He could manage well. Katrín lifted a
spoon and Hitler said "spoon"; Katrín lifted a fork and Hitler
said "fork." That way, one after another. (Bergsson, *Tómas
Jónsson*, 217)

No wonder readers see in the book's style something new in relation to what is well known about Icelandic literature and culture. Whether *Tómas Jónsson Bestseller* is the first modern novel in Iceland or not, it is difficult to deny the view that it is an even more pertinent modern work than are most novels of later years. In this connection it is possible to go further and talk about a break from tradition in literature, culture, and society – not because of Bergsson's refusal of tradition but because of his dialogue with it. If this is true, the rupture takes place not only in historical time but also on the boundaries of reality and fiction, the individual and society, Iceland and Europe.[8]

But is this possible? Can the fragmentary structure of the narrative of one modern novel carry such a heavy load?

As Sigfús Daðason points out in his review, courageous authors have, in spite of everything, some roots in the past. With their courage they reap the harvest much more thoroughly than do those who go along well-trodden paths, *wanting*, as Daðason says, "to write classical works." The heritage revolves not only around the unrestrained emotional existence of the individual towards him/herself but also around Icelandic culture itself. As noted before, the author's dialogue in this matter is not built only on ridicule. If we accept the words of the author of the book about Tómas Jónsson (see chapter 6), then Icelandic readers do not need to look far afield for the method: "This is one of the many characteristics of the Sagas of Icelanders," he says, for in them the same names crop up again and again; events and materials are woven together with the same places and the same names of people. And, furthermore: "The method is Icelandic, even though it is similar to the habits of classical tragedy, weaving together events, places, and times in the web of fate" (Ásgeirsdóttir, *Guðbergur Bergsson*, 117). Not all Icelandic critics have, however, explored such a connection in Bergsson's stories.

THE MONSTROSITIES OF THE POET LAUREATE
IN PLACE OF WELL–MADE POPULAR SONG LYRICS

The year after the publication of *Tómas Jónsson Bestseller,* the novel *The Love Life of a Compatible Couple* (1967) appeared. Shortly after the latter's appearance the journal *Tímarit Máls og menningar* (*Journal of Language and Culture*) published an article by the Reverend Gunnar Benediktsson. Bergsson's *The Love Life of a*

Compatible Couple is one of three works he chooses to discuss; the other two are *A Feast Under a Stone Wall* by Svava Jakobsdóttir and *Mixed with the Black Death* by Steinar Sigurjónsson. Benediktsson claims to have heard on the radio that these three young novelists were the representatives of a new narrative method in the Icelandic language and delved most deeply into "the concerns and the depths of the soul of our amazing times." Setting the reviewer's overall distaste aside, the books by Jakobsdóttir and Sigurjónsson receive an almost respectful response while that of Bergsson is treated differently, as is the author, whom Benediktsson calls "the poet laureate himself."[9] The following fragment shows the tone of the review:

> The book is called *The Love Life of a Compatible Couple*. That title is completely ludicrous, for there are no love scenes and hardly any human interaction. These are said to be twelve connected narratives. That is also ludicrous; the narratives are thirteen in number and their connection is nothing more than disconnected discussions about nothing. The narratives are altogether independent of each other. (Benediktsson, "Three Young Novelists," 89)

There are more passages in Benediktsson's review that are worth looking at. The following, for example, unquestionably reminds us of the problem Sigfús Daðason tries to think through in his essay "In Defence of Poetry":

> Certainly this book is very original in every way. New times demand new forms, but new forms do not guarantee good writing. Good writing only occurs when the subject matter finds the form that suits it best. I think that our young novelists spend too much energy on their ponderings about form and are not as careful as they should be that every new poetic idea will bring forth of itself a new form, in as natural a way as the earth when it takes on the changing colours of a new day. But some kind of new, abnormal form seems to be the main requirement of these three, who also take it upon themselves to criticize and correct things in the name of art. (Benediktsson, "Three Young Novelists," 91)

Here we see the attitude that Sigfús Daðason was struggling against in the middle of the twentieth century, when he came to the defence of modernist writing. Here we also see an example of the attitude of the turn-of-the-century generation that Bergsson says set itself up against *Tómas Jónsson Bestseller*. It seems as though the argument about modern literature was in full swing in Iceland in the 1970s and that it revolved, as ever, around form. But is this revolving door going backwards in time?

In his critique of the structure of *The Love Life of a Compatible Couple*, Benediktsson says Bergsson is one of the young artists who feels it is enough "for an artistic achievement to exercise some sort of trickery that no one else has thought of doing"; he also says that the form of the chapters in the book, along with its style and language, is "so unusually done that it is clear the author thinks that is the most important thing" ("Three Young Novelists" 91). In an indirect way, Benediktsson hits the nail right on the head: Bergsson not only places great emphasis on form but also gives those "trickeries" of taste free rein. And he does so with an instinctual rather than with an intellectual emphasis on renewal. Benediktsson is critical of all this, and his interpretation of the form of the book is enlightening with regard to at least two related matters: (1) the ignorance that Sigfús Daðason notices among critics of modern writing in Iceland and (2) the "law of resistance" as it applies to the reception of modern writing. In Benediktsson's estimation, the form of *The Love Life of a Compatible Couple* is "the main feature of [Bergsson's] writing. The storyline becomes confusing and not believable; the narrative is unclear and foggy and does not throw light on the subject. He is usually far too busy with signs and symbols, so it all becomes a bottomless endlessness" (Benediktsson, "Three Young Novelists," 91). Instead of reflecting upon things like "a confusing storyline" and a "foggy narrative" that can become a "bottomless endlessness" – and in *The Love Life of a Compatible Couple* we do see these features (and in a very realistic context considering the social reality described in the story) – Benediktsson critiques the novel's form as though he were discussing a different type of writing.

The subject of the story is alien to Benediktsson. He says that Bergsson answers the requirement of the times for bluntness and that he tries more than most young writers to outdo the writer Þórbergur Þórðarson in this. But Bergsson, Benediktsson continues, does not seem to have realized that "lack of affectation is one thing, but vulgarity is another matter altogether" (91). He talks about the "choice of language" in the book and says it is vulgar in the extreme.

Nothing less than the truth will do in such an unattractive matter, and to prove that what he is saying is not nonsense, he is forced to present some examples, apologizing "beforehand for allowing such rude language to be found in an article that is connected to [his] name" (ibid.). And here is the example that Benediktsson offers to prove his case concerning the vulgarity of Bergsson's language:

> [Bergsson has] special admiration for the noun 'penis' and the verb 'to piss.' It does not seem like he has paid attention to the talks of Icelandic scholars on the radio, which warn people against the overuse of certain words. In one story he says four times about one and the same character that he lifted his testicles while sitting on a chair. Since this man finds that activity so poetic, why in heaven's name can he not change the wording a bit and talk about adjusting the genitalia or fiddling with the dick? (91–2)

What so upsets Benediktsson? According to him, it is revolting work "to collect all this together, but now we will have to bite the lip and keep in mind that we are talking about an award-winning book here" (92). Where others see an award-winning book, Benediktsson sees "vulgarity" and feels "disgust." He also says that the book is "lacking" and that it contains so many grammatical errors that he has never before seen "anything like it in the writing of recognized authors" (92). This, he continues, "should be proof enough that this poet laureate has no special sensitivity to the Icelandic language" (ibid.). And again we see Icelandic logic rear its head: "My harsh criticism of *The Love Life of a Compatible Couple* might first of all be pardoned for the fact that my observations are true. To this we might add that it is impossible to let that truth remain unspoken, when such an average and squalid book has been judged the best book in the Icelandic book market in the Lord's year of 1967" (93).

Clearly, this rampage is very defensive. But what does Benediktsson wish to defend? He asks the critics of "art writings" to take "their job sufficiently seriously, since such a heavy responsibility rests on them concerning the future of literature in Iceland" (93). And he continues:

> On the cover it says, among other things: "He (the author) takes the reader through ceremonious glossaries and key words of modern times into the emptiness behind it all." What do they

mean by the "key words of modern times"? I make a thorough search of words that have not been common in our literature so far, and I first and foremost run into words like "balls," "cunt," "asshole," "penis," "horny," "crotch." I do not know where those keys fit, except in the emptiness and the vulgarity that lie behind the words themselves. (93–4)

Again the article by Sigfús Daðason rears its head for, like Benediktsson's critique, it too is clearly an act of defence. However, Daðason defends modern poetry against the inertia within the Icelandic literary heritage, aesthetically speaking, while Benediktsson, for his part, keeps hammering the cooled iron. Could it be that the subject has to do not only with the reviewer's aesthetic taste but also with his political conviction?

At the close of his review, Benediktsson mentions the awarding of the art prizes for 1967 and goes straight to the polemic of the time: "The jury for the arts prizes accidentally overlooked Guðbergur [Bergsson] when they donated their merciful gifts. Then we heard much heaving and crying, and one of the loudest outcries could be found in the socialist paper; that is the vehicle for those ideas that many have sacrificed their lives for" ("Three Young Novelists" 94). Benediktsson's words do not, in short, concern Bergsson's writing or his aesthetic subject but, rather, the writings of other authors and the apparently eternal political argument in Icelandic literary discourse.[10] The words that go right to the mark are actually enlightening for the ingrown literary concerns in Bergsson's country: Benediktsson notes: "it so happened that, seated with us, was a certain Kristján from Djúpilækur [an Icelandic poet], who has done more than most men to treat the youth of the land to national and well-made song lyrics at social gatherings" (94).

Yes. It is the "national" and "well-made" that is "suitable for the youth of the land" at social gatherings! Here we have taken an aesthetic leap back not only to before the middle of the twentieth century but all the way to the nineteenth century and, possibly, even back to the time of Benedikt Gröndal Sveinbjarnarson. How is this attitude to be explained?

We cannot accuse Gunnar Benediktsson of a sloppy reading of the novel. He himself doubts anyone has read it as carefully as he, and he claims never to have read any book as "closely as this – not excepting the Bible and Sturlunga Saga" ("Three Young Novelists,"

89). Þorgeir Þorgeirsson says that Benediktsson wishes to make his critique "even more weighty" by putting these three books together; however, in an open letter to Benediktsson, which is entitled "About the Cunt on the Cliff and Clerical Aggression," Þorgeirsson discusses the review and its author's preconceptions and workmanship. If we believe the letter, then Benediktsson's attitude comes not only from a moralistic–linguistic ethics but also from a deep-seated conservative national politics.

In Þorgeirsson's estimation, the intention of the publishing houses is to publish nothing in modern Icelandic writing except works that are written according to a "strictly determined sentimental style, in which the stagnated political theories of the day are presented in 'lovely imagery' or with a 'gentle adventurous air'" ("Cunt on the Cliff" 4).[11] Þorgeirsson says that the preference is that literature should have no special meaning for people under forty and that a publishing house should make a rule of rejecting all the most lively writing in the country.

But Þorgeirsson is not only talking about Gunnar Benediktsson's attitude towards literature here. He also looks at Benediktsson's "sloppy" workmanship: "You go through the book like a neurotic grazing animal and chew on vulgar words here and there, tear them up and then heave them out again in the face of the reader when you have had your fill of this disgrace. Such methods might be found in Velvakandi [conservative paper column] and other such columns of persecution, which are written for naïve people and ignoramuses in order to make them self-satisfied – but hardly in a respectable literary journal" (4).

Here Þorgeirsson makes clear the requirements for those who write about literature. The question is not whether Benedikstsson is up to the job but how such a widely read man can be so blind to the creative repetition found in Bergsson's writing: "Do you not want to dive head first into the prophet Ezekiel for a moment with the same mind set and prove to yourself that the Bible is not talking rubbish when it says: 'Search and you shall find?' I will let one sentence suffice: 'And she burned with lust for their lovers, who were as licentious as donkeys and the jet shot from them as from stallions'" (4). According to Þorgeirsson, not everything in a newly published book is new, even though the book may be in many ways original: "When a modern writer compares his country to a cunt spread out over a cliff, we know there is a precedent for that in the Bible where nations or cities have been given such likenesses before, and it is unnecessary for an old and respected cleric to let hypocrisy and narrow mindedness confuse his judgment towards such an old literary method" (ibid.).

Let us look a little more closely at the "monstrosities" in the form-breaking writings of the "poet laureate" and how they not only mirror the attitudes towards literature in Iceland but also reflect aspects of Icelandic culture and society.

LITERATURE AS A MIRROR OF ITS TIME

When *The Love Life of a Compatible Couple* was republished in 1989, Bergsson wrote an afterword for it. We have already seen the writings in which Bergsson discusses the wondrous power of taste and how its changeable and fluctuating nature can stir up preconceived attitudes. It is not necessarily the "new inventions" that affect tastes but, rather, and invariably, those things that Bergsson says come from the "nature of the instincts' hunger," or "this feeling of saturation." In a discussion of novels such as *Tómas Jónsson Bestseller* and *The Love Life of a Compatible Couple*, this perspective on what affects taste is important. What we might call the aesthetics of the eternally hungry and constantly capricious taste is also an important aspect of the social side of those works. What some people call "disgusting" and "vulgar" seems to be, in the mind of this author, derived from a deep connection between the aesthetics of words and the responsibility of the individual. And this connection concerns both culture and society.

What is it that literature mirrors?

When *The Love Life of a Compatible Couple* was being written, Bergsson says he had the feeling that "most of our ideas, those of us living on this island, and the nature and purpose of society, had become deformed and false," that we had not taken upon ourselves "the responsibility that comes with acquiring the real independence and financial responsibility of a nation that cannot put its own obligations, accountability, and mistakes on anyone's shoulders other than its citizens, and on the nation as a whole" ("Afterword" to *Love Life* 271). A nation that is not spiritually independent will tend to blame those nations with which it has associated most closely for its "ignorance," "spiritual dependence," and "comfortable illusions." Such responses, Bergsson continues, carry with them a fear of the mirror and of what the mirror reveals: "Afterwards, if it has been a colony or in some way subject to another nation, like a patriarchal power, it will not want to see the love life of the former relationship again in the longest-lasting mirror of time: Literature. That is why the nation wants to be like a child who blames its parents for all its own mistakes in life – some continuing to do so into old age, right to the edge of the grave – or like a couple after the end of the marriage" (272).

This is a hazardous situation, both for the individual and for the nation. For if we believe what Bergsson says, literature (while it is "alive and sharp" and before it becomes "a testament of the past" or "research material" or "even classical") is, in many ways, "like a mirror that encourages and inspires readers to look in their own eyes, and at the same time to acknowledge what they see in literature, if they want to search for explanations for their inner and outer problems, which exist inside every man and appear in our works and deeds" (272). With this in mind, Bergsson says he began to write a book about love between a compatible married couple. For what, he asks, "is the outer and inner reality of a nation and an individual, other than a form of marriage and revolt against certain relationships?" (ibid.). This was at a time when the large ideas that had triumphed in the Second World War "were finally getting worn out with their huge intellectually and scientifically proven symbols for the freedom of man and his wealth" (ibid.). Bergsson says he also knew that the novel is not only a symbol for the outer events of the world, but that

> it [also] enjoys its own independence and behaves for the most part according to its own whimsical nature and laws, which only exist for the novel, and it offers possibilities for various kinds of machinations and structures. Most of all, the novel is just something the novelist has thought up. It comes both out of his inner voice, his whispers and secrets, and the outer world of society and the noise of the working world. Still it is, first and foremost, the narrow reality of the novelist while he is writing; a monologue and confession to the blank page or the emptiness, wherever it is found. (273)

It is the shallowness of the eyes, the visual language, that leads us away from the deeper world of existence. A work that has nothing but visual imagery to offer is "doomed to death as soon as the earth and fashion turn the next revolution around its axis. This kind of work lacks the enduring idea, that is, the 'perspective' towards the image we see with the naked eye" (274).

Here we find not only a criticism of the deep-rooted literary tradition of Iceland, or the heavy-handed tendency to emphasize and to judge the value of literature on the basis of its "visual imagery" alone, but also an indirect reappearance of Bergsson's aesthetic perspective: "A born artist" lives in the events of the present moment while keeping an eye on eternity. At the same time we see how his feeling for Icelandic society in the 1970s is woven in with the outer world of literary creations. About the origins of the latter, the author says in the same afterword:

> I remember the afternoon in the attic at home, when the drops fell at first like light smacks on the corrugated roof. Then the water came down in torrents. Then the endless drone of the rain, and with it the drowsiness that comes with the feeling of security of being sheltered and protected by the roof of the father's house, even though inside there might reign even worse weather than what is heard on the roofs.
>
> And all of a sudden I had a vision, as if I walked into a museum whose existence was in literature, even though I have never actually understood anything about either literature or existence but, instead, only the need to be able to live with the incomprehensibility and the unnameability of life. (275)

If literature is judged by its visual imagery alone, we see how readers cringe not only from the reflection of themselves and their society in living literature but also from how they might miss out on the possibility of taking part in the world of creation.

But why focus only on visual imagery? Where does this obsession originate?

LANGUAGE, TASTE, AND THE ETHICS OF AESTHETICS

As we see in the response of Benediktsson, it is first and foremost the "language" in *The Love Life of a Compatible Couple* that does not stand the test of ethics. In the afterword to the novel, Bergsson discusses responses of this type and says that it is common for people to talk about the language in a book in order to avoid thinking about the subject matter. But an author, he continues, does not think about right and wrong in relation to grammar and sentence structure. In the writer's narrative, it is his "ethical judgment – that is, the ethics of aesthetics, which is very complex and consequential when it comes to how the writer composes his work" (Bergsson, "Afterword" to *Love Life*, 277). What is at stake here is, therefore, the complex area of the aesthetics of the individual and how it is woven into the ethics of the artist Guðbergur Bergsson. As is by now clear, taste is not unchangeable in Begsson's mind; rather, it is a constant force. Poets do not even think of writing endless romantic poems because their "aesthetic sense and sense of beauty, together with a satiation of romantic poetry, prevents them from doing so. After a certain time, the writing and the ethics of the beautiful have had more than enough of that kind of trend" (277–8). And, offering a more detailed explanation of this position towards aesthetics, Bergsson says that this is true not only for literature but also for politics.

If we accept the writer's words, it was the "aesthetic conscience" that chose the language of *The Love Life of a Compatible Couple* and not the will alone: "My will seemed to know, that if anyone tried to undermine tradition, the best and most effective way of doing so would be to use new methods, so people would not be able to continue applying the same kind of taste, which had become completely tasteless and ridiculous over time and which defended itself with eternally right arguments and perhaps a petrified way of thinking" (278).

But the conscience of Bergsson's aesthetics does not just concern what we might call an acceptance of the capriciousness of taste in life and art. We also find here what Bergsson calls "a sense of the class structure within the language." This echo of Marx should not be confused with the watering down of ideas to comfort people. But what does he mean by this? All stages of language are derived from the "working class vernacular" – speech. The same goes for society and its class structure: according to Bergsson, both spring from the ground of the common people. Nations and their survival are built on the "health of the common people," on their ability to work and to think. And, unlike what the "lazy Marxists" maintain, nations crumble when the "populace sickens," not when the upper class stops being healthy and becomes degenerate. This does not mean, however, that the author can write in a "clean and uncontaminated vernacular." What is possible, Bergsson claims, is to search for "some aspect of speech, or to create a speech of one's own that could appear to be a way of talking or some variant of talking, but at the same time different." He often solves this by attempting to alter the written language, to stylize it, to "flay it so that it shines in its skinlessness. In this way the written language can be made 'strange' or 'artful'" (279).

But what is the intention of this many-layered aesthetic position? According to Bergsson:

If the writer wants to arrive at a new truth and test it out, even though the truth might be old and perhaps even eternal (but never classical and dead), he will have to realize that truths get old and are in need of review. He also has to know that the new truth is only new while it has not been dethroned by time or been beset (or buried) by various laws of a certain time and fash-ion, which I am not saying is negative in nature. My view of the ethics of aesthetics is like this; and so are the aesthetics of my conscience when I write my books. (279–80)

As has emerged, not all critics of Bergsson's fictional world have read against this aesthetic aim. And this has not completely fallen on deaf ears in Iceland.[12] In this context we might mention Jóhanna Sveinsdóttir's interpretation of *The Love Life of a Compatible Couple*. Even though the aesthetics of the story is not her primary subject, in an article titled "A Bergssonian Regeneration" Sveinsdóttir suggests a possible key theme. She discusses the connection between literature and ideology and finds Bergsson to be an "unveiling" au-thor, unveiling the myths of the power elite in a capitalist society. In order to break the spell of capitalist ideology, the modern human being must understand the nature of class society and thereby see through the illusions of its web of myths (283).

In other words, Sveinsdóttir examines the social affinities of the scenes of the story, and she sees, on the one hand, the family, and, on the other, Icelandic society during and after the Second World War. She sees how the proximity of the American base is tangible in all the stories and how most of the stories concern themselves with family life. This way she reads something different into the connection between the scenes than does Benediktsson. The same goes for Sveinsdóttir's interpretation of the title "*The Love Life of a Compatible Couple*." In 1941, the first American soldiers set foot on Iceland and thereby "came the beginning of a fateful relationship between the Icelandic nation and the American occupation forces, and soon the influence of American money became felt in Iceland. The stories of

the book show how those financial and cultural influences, which
began with the arrival of the forces, have coloured the family lives of
the inhabitants; how 'the smell of money' has soaked into the home
and formed a new lifestyle of individualism and greed" (Sveinsdóttir
286–7). What Bergsson does, in Sveinsdóttir's estimation, is to uncover the myths about the independence of private life in relation to
public, national life. The connection between these two is frequently
mystified, but the myths that are uncovered in *The Love Life of a
Compatible Couple* are various, and she mentions some examples:
(1) the myth of a peaceful life in the embrace of the family; (2) the
myth of the special status of Icelandic culture; (3) the myth of the
loving, warm mother tongue; and (4) the myth of "the individual's
right to live and work in a democratic society" (287–97).

We have not come to the end of all there is to say about the culture
of individualism and greed in Iceland, or, for that matter, in the entire "Republic of the Kiosk" – the consumer empire we call the West.
But what about the myths that Sveinsdóttir says Bergsson is trying
to unveil and the values of the society of consumption and competi-
tion that drives the characters in the novel? These features are not
stuck in time and place. As is the case with the subject of "time" in
Tómas Jónsson Bestseller, they allude to a far-reaching "unveiling."
In Bergsson's novels, no matter how bleak and forsaken the present
appears, the past is always part of it. It may not be uplifting to acknowledge the greatly flawed experiment we refer to as modern society; however, Bergsson's equally revealing analysis of the past
provides the reader with a sense of both continuity and wonder. This
does not mean that Bergsson offers any solution to humanity's problems. If that were the case, the aesthetics of his works would not
bear the view that nothing is either wrong or right unless the perspective is preconceived. As Sveinsdóttir notes, he leaves the reader
to "reflect upon the qualities that would be most likely to benefit
human society" (299). The question is, therefore: how does the reader discover these qualities? It could hardly be done in the spirit of the
golden authors, those who "failed in man's search for his limit" by
raising the issue in "a well-known format" and in a specific, traditional "social and artistic way."

In this context it is worth pointing out another element in
Sveinsdóttir's article: its "slogans." Sveinsdóttir talks about the after-
word to Bergsson's Icelandic translation of *Lazarus from Tormes*
There, Bergsson says:

The need for regeneration is not a destructive force; instead its harshness and subversiveness at all times and in all situations come from the resistance it meets before it conquers. And its victory must always be inevitable, because man's adaptability seems to be stronger than his resistance. Generally writers do not write out of a desire to kill, but instead they carry forward other social and spiritual forces, merged with primitive ones, and a never fully definable need of the individual to renew and create. (Bergsson, "Afterword" to *Lazarus*, 109)

Let us look a little more closely at Bergsson's ideas about the need for regeneration and how this need is tied to the ethics of his aesthetics and the possibility of the reader's participation. Here another novel emerges out of the fictional world we are discussing.

ANNA AND THE REPETITION

In 2001, Bergsson published the novel *Anna*. This is not an ordinary publication but, rather, a novel of the same title that he had published in 1968 and rewritten. But why publish the book again? The new version is almost twice as long as the old, and its title is not *Anna* but, rather, *Anna: The Icelandic Book of Fairy Tales*. What lies behind this renewal?

In the interview entitled "The Deep Surface," which Sigurður Ólafsson and Sölvi Björn Sigurðarson conducted with Guðbergur Bergsson and fellow writer Thor Vilhjálmsson, Bergsson says he is a great believer in renewal. He also discusses one of his novels:

My favourite work is a book called Anna. I have reviewed it and changed it into what is called an epic work. I think all books should be in A-version, B-version, and C-version. There should be many versions of the same work because the writer's mindset cannot fit into one work, even when the writer tries hard to get it all in. I think people are so multiple, actually. And this novel of mine, which I have turned into an epic work, is the book of which I am most fond. (43)

In the same interview Bergsson also discusses his thoughts on writing and how they are tied to the subject. He talks about three layers in all writing, which, he says are geological layering: (1) the

"deep surface," which the reader gets hold of immediately; (2) a
layer below – the middle layer – which is more difficult; and (3) the
incomprehensible layer, which is a little bit like life and humanity
itself. And Bergsson says he hopes that people will "always be so
complicated that this [latter] layer will be incomprehensible" (43).

Let us look again at the novel *Anna* and how Bergsson can be considered a reviewer not only of Icelandic literary tradition but also of
his own works. Aside from the return of the works that have been
discussed already, there are more works from Bergsson's fictional
world that reappear. The stories in *It Sleeps in the Deep*; *Hermann and
Dídí*; and *It Resurfaces from the Depths* have all been republished in
the book *True Stories* (1999). Is it possible to publish the same book
again and again? Let us take a look at what Bergsson writes in his
afterword to *The Love Life of a Compatible Couple*. In fact,

> one version of a book is only one of its versions, but never the
> final version, always the incomplete one. Because few things are
> more incomplete than art. Art is the festival of incompleteness.
> That is why there is nothing more fitting for renewal than art,
> even though works of art may be able to withstand the passage
> of time and become classical – that only means that the author
> has stopped changing them of his own free will and others have
> taken it up and recognized it as it is. (280)

Another textual fragment from Bergsson can shed even more light
on this practice for, on the flyleaf of *Anna: An Icelandic Fairy Tale*,
it is written:

> Most novels acquire a [ghostly] following the same way certain
> people do. With people, the following becomes obvious first with
> other people before it does to the one being followed. It is sel-
> dom a question of which one is closer to reality, the man or his
> following. In narrative, it is often difficult to figure out what the
> writer is doing for the reality out of which the novel comes is sel-
> dom simple and usually complex. The novel and its characters
> are created in many guises. In fact, there should be published at
> least two versions of the same novel, so we could compare the
> first one with the following one as a kind of final version.

Anna and *Anna: An Icelandic Fairy Tale* are about one twenty-
four-hour period in the life of an Icelandic family, guests who have

just arrived from the United States, Americans on the base, and the inhabitants of a village on the south coast of Iceland in the latter half of the twentieth century. I make no effort to compare the two versions of the story but only to look at the human and poetic realities and the fluctuating boundary between them. As the text above notes, the reality from which the fiction springs is not as clearly defined as is the reality in which humanity tries to get a foothold. But what is the significance of this difference for fiction itself, for humanity's reality, and for the connection between them?

In *Anna: An Icelandic Fairy Tale*, the married couple Sveinn and Katrín/Anna are talking after a hard day's and night's work. Katrín says that story is repetition and that the times in which we live matter not at all:

> Humanity is going to hang on eternally to the Book of Moses as far as behaviour goes, with the same instincts and guilt as in Eden – not of former days, because then there were no days but only eternity – when married people went at it childless in the garden. It is the same now, even though there are now so many people that man is no longer his own amusement, but his biggest pest, and it is almost unbearable on the earth because of him and the consequence of his goings on. (360–1)

Katrín sees, however, some sort of faint gleam in the repetition, and she says she is "free from all concern, a holy woman wandering from book to book because of the wonder that there are things life cannot create out of reality but the spirit can transform them into reality in literature" (361).

Getting a handle on these fluctuating boundaries between fiction and reality is not a simple matter. But if we consider the tradition of Icelandic culture, we see how the deeply rooted idea of the completeness of a work by which we measure things is at odds with the above ideas. In Iceland there seems to be only a very limited tradition of looking at art as a "festival of incompleteness." As discussed earlier, one reason for this can be traced to the lasting influence of the turn-of-the-century generation on matters of culture and society.

But what if Icelanders cannot resist the repetition and, like other people in the Western world, need to have the "festival of incompleteness" at work? Is Bergsson perhaps right when he says: "Of course art is always, like mankind, repeating the same things in a different way.

The content is the same, only the atmosphere, the style, or the form are changed" (Ásgeirsdóttir, *Guðbergur Bergsson Bestseller*, 117)?

GLEAMING REFLECTIONS ON AN ICELANDIC STAGE

If we again turn to Bergsson's *The Mind's Tormented Love*, we see a forceful dialogue with Icelandic culture and society. The stage for this dialogue is not the inflexible Iceland and all things Icelandic. The theme of repetition has a much wider sweep and concerns life as well as art in the whole Western world. The question is not whether Iceland is outside of this stage but, rather, how it comports itself upon it.

Towards the end of the novel, the diarist/narrator has gone on a trip to Spain with his wife, daughter, friend, and his friend's fiancée. There the lovers test their relationship, with varied results. The women – who have no idea why they have come to Spain – make trouble. But there is more that goes wrong. After having got rid of their partners (accidentally) during a two-day trip across the mountains, the two men stay together overnight. The day after, they "threaten their conditions" by taking a taxi and following their partners. They book a room in a hotel in which their partners are staying in and, after having fulfilled themselves "in each other like strangers who meet by accident in an alien town and know they will never meet again after they part" (*Mind's Tormented Love* 246), they go out. The diarist wanders about in the garden around the hotel and "breathes in existence." The place is "wondrously beautiful"; he has never seen "such beauty, or rather, any such symbol of beauty and life in the same instance":

> The threatening precipice increased the beauty and the admira-
> tion for its life, for something followed after the end of the bridge
> and continued beyond. There I saw a forested hillside that rose
> steep from a broad chasm and then the mountains, covered with
> scattered tree growth. While I stood amazed and looked at the
> landscape, I sensed that my friend was walking along the same
> path I had, but he became aware of me and bent down back into
> the garden. I would have wanted him to come look at the view
> with me, and after that we would have thrown ourselves over
> into the chasm itself, although I knew there was no way to com-
> bine the nature of the earth and one's feelings for one's own
> nature and that of another, and the nature of beauty. (247)

This awareness of the chasm within that separates the human be-ing's love from the loved one is, in a way, more difficult to handle than are the apparent shackles of marriage and cohabitation. It proves also to be a greater challenge for the characters than the rules and regulations society has created. Not even gay studies can find a solution to the problem the chasm evokes, and the solution is not in sight. This awareness that the diarist expresses has deep roots in both the history of ideas and aesthetics and is of no consequence to the specific nationality of the protagonist.

The double-edged nature of Bergsson's dialogue in *The Mind's Tormented Love* sharpens not only the "un-national" features of the inner life but also those that lie on the surface and that create, on occasion, a feeling for, or ideas about, nations. Another textual frag-ment may give an idea of the letter. Shortly after the diarist turns over in his mind the nature of the chasm that seems to reign over the heart of his existence, the women see their men and shout "almost simultaneously: No, look who's here!" And the partner of the friend adds: "No, the farts have arrived, we sure don't get to be in peace very long; that's how it is to be popular" (247). Whatever the partner of the friend is thinking (she is almost a closed book to the diarist), for his wife, the happiness is not a long-lasting one. Happiness is re-placed by grief and disappointment as the family sits together eating dinner at the hotel. At the end of the meal, the diarist roams about in the hotel garden with his friend in tow. Nothing happens other than the silence between them, and then we read the following:

When I turned around again towards the hotel and sat down on a chair outside in the square gleam from the window in the res-taurant, the tourists had begun to get drunk on red wine. The men had become meek and cared for nothing except embraces and enjoyment over being in their own non-existence and talking nothing but nonsense that makes no difference. The women were quite noisy by now and their clothes were in disarray. The for-eign waiters watched us in amazement, but there was no way to determine what they were thinking from the looks on their faces, whether they were surprised at or envious of our freedom. If they thought we were free, they were wrong. Free people never create such a ruckus. Only to know and to admit to yourself that every-thing born is chained, that is being free. But only rarely does this occur. (250)

Here the point of view of the diarist makes visible a certain predicament in Icelandic culture and society: even though the behaviour of
these people is judged on the varied stage of repetition, they acquire
a strange and foreign air, an imagined freedom. This is a key feature,
not least in light of Bergsson's ideas concerning the direction of
modernism in art and the freedom of the individual within modernism. It is one thing to test yourself in a form-breaking artistic movement (and acquire a view of the petrified forms of the past, whether
in the arts, politics, or religion), and another to find a foothold in the
age-old existential arena of the inner being by taking the route of
non-existence and the chaos of inebriation. At one point, the childhood friend of the diarist says: "In this country in which we live, no
one can find himself; the art of losing yourself is practised in a very
artless way but with lots of energy, especially under the influence of
alcohol" (166).

Before the friends go to Spain with all their baggage, the diarist
travels in his mind to Höfn in Hornafjörður, where he has an imagined date with his friend. He chooses the road overland for he
longs to "sit in a coach like a man in a holy story about the origins
of the emotions" (202). And what does he find?

> The coach was comfortable and I followed the landscape that I
> was seeing for the first time, but it ran together with the unreal
> material of stories I was made to read in school: stories about
> daring doctors who crossed over ice floes to save a woman about
> to give birth. Now the heroic sentimental stories suited my emo-
> tional life well: in this way everything acquires value sometime in
> life, both what is small in stature and what is large. It was as if I
> could transfer the stylistic tricks of that author to the trickery of
> my own love life. (203)

Here we see how the parody of the golden authors from *Tómas
Jónsson Bestseller* reappears in a dialogue with Iceland's deep-rooted
literary tradition. In the coach, the diarist remembers his school days
(which is unquestionably reminiscent of the spiritual fodder of the
high school students in *Tómas Jónsson Bestseller*) as well as a fragment from Icelandic literary history, recalling its high-sounding style.
But in the coach he also gets acquainted with his fellow travellers.
He quenches their curiosity and tells them the following story about
the reason for his journey:

"I am a West Icelander and am travelling out of homesickness from Winnipeg in order to see the Hornafjörður moon, but preferably the back side of it" ...

Even though the fellow travellers found this hard to believe, they gave me credit for the explanation because of the love of the homeland and the joy over the fact that the moon in Hornafjörður had become world famous.

But someone had it in him to say:

"Yes, but my good fellow, this is the end of April, and there is no moon to see, just the fog from it, because the light is growing and our country is northernmost on the planet, as everyone knows."

"Well," I said, and made as if nothing was wrong, "I have been in the West so long that I had forgotten when the moon shines most strongly in my own district."

Then I added apologetically:

"I offer as an excuse that it does not matter where we Icelanders go, we have always been a nation confused about time, and we do not know what is and what is passing, like other people do."

"How?" someone asked, offended over the fact that a man who spoke Icelandic insisted, without blinking, over coffee in the restaurant under the Eyjafjöll mountains, that his countrymen might be confused.

I had to withdraw my comment and find a saving thought, so I added:

"Excuse me, I only meant that in the short days of the year, night here lasts almost twenty-four hours, but in the summer we have endless daylight all day; the light is our special privilege because of our position on the planet."

Now my fellow travellers were light-hearted and glad to see my love of country, and they smiled at me and bowed their heads childishly. (203-4)

Here we see how the diarist's fellow travellers cling for dear life to their self-image and culture, which is built on the close connection between language and the land. But there is another matter in this imagined journey of the diarist that shows even more clearly the borders that lie around the outer limits of Icelandic culture but that really concern what lies within. This relationship between language and land is deep and has considerable influence on the inner life and its nature. Again we see the point of view of the diarist as it opens up a multifaceted area. He has certain things in common with his fellow travellers, such as the need for self-deception. While his fellow travellers are prepared to deceive themselves on account of their "love for their homeland," the diarist does so on account of his "love for the landscape of another's body" (204). There is a significant difference here. Love of the landscape of another's body demands more artfulness than does love of the homeland, perhaps because the body is life, it contains "adventures, and outside of it there is almost nothing," as the character "Guðbergur Bergsson" asserts in Bergsson's fictional autobiography.

It is tempting to speculate that a great and lasting love for the homeland might exclude participation in life and in its adventures, but here we must tread carefully. Even though, from book to book, Bergsson's characters wander shamelessly, this is not to say that the interpreter of Bergsson's dialogue with Icelandic culture and society must do likewise in order to offer a hypothesis about Icelanders' fateful love for their country, both in life and in art. It is, however, the man "Guðbergur Bergsson" in Bergsson's fictional autobiography who says that the body is life and that in the body there are adventures and outside it there is almost nothing. But is there not a difference here? Are these not different forms of discourse? One fiction and the other fictional autobiography?

In *The Mind's Tormented Love* the diarist has the following to say about the body and its adventures:

When all is said and done, you sail alone with your heart on the ship of your body in search of a fog of fulfilment. You row in the fog with the hook in the air in order to catch another heart you do not recognize even though it is your own beating in another body. He lets himself be ruled by an unreal dream that it is possible to have that heart and make it the same as the one in his own body as well as in the body of another being and in that way have two hearts at once, in himself and in another. (77)

And he continues:

In that way I sailed in the fog of love and I do not care whether I end in shipwreck and I survive on what is maybe nothing and am destroyed, because the heat from your body has warmed me

about the roots of the heart and I feel all is complete in that un-
fulfilment: I know that man is nothing more than a wretch and
each one of us is alive only in name. (77–8)

And finally:

My desire for you is a longing for the fulfilment of form, shade,
and mist, a phenomenon sometimes seen in the sunshine; it is
possible to see at the same time sun and rain when one is envel-
oped by the golden rain, the holy water from the body of existence that uses up its glow and brings life at the same time.
    Everything that burns cools down and must eventually die, my
friend. (78)

While love in the path of the body lasts, it not only offers participation in life and its adventures but also moves freely from the human
body into the body of existence. The problem with the love of the
homeland, on the other hand, is that its path leads into the seductive
land and fortress of language, away from the fragile human being,
her vulnerable quest in life and her attempts to deal with existence.
That is the arena that is opened by the diarist, and that is what lies
on the boundary between Icelandic and Western cultures. The aesthetics of Bergsson's writings not only agitate the boundaries of life
and art, fiction and reality, flesh and spirit, Iceland and Europe, but
they are by nature opposed to conclusions that are built on the ana-
lytical systems of science. This is so because of the subject matter,
which is an artistic and existential reassessment of life and those
who live it.

If we acknowledge Bergsson's dialogue, then it appears that
Icelanders may have limited interest in these matters and in the possibilities of literature. Aside from Bergsson's social critique and how
it relates to the ethics of his aesthetics, his dialogue is illuminating
because of its inquiry into Icelandic literature and into some of its
characteristics. The search, the thinking about life and humanity, the
creative repetition, the need for regeneration in life as well as in art,
and the participation in the life of writing – all these are things that
sometimes rouse haughtiness rather than interest among the "well
read" in Iceland.

As has been shown, there are many reasons for this. Perhaps what
Bergsson says about the influence of the golden authors, and how

they failed miserably in "man's continuous search for his limits by raising their cause in a well-known format, with the use of a specific social and artistic method," is true (Is Literature a Path to Salvation 444). Is the consequence of this not visible in the Icelandic culture of our day? Is it not still the case "that ordinary people or readers do not trust 'serious writers' and escape to those who can offer them entertainments that they know beforehand are illusions, lies, and pretend" (ibid.)? On top of this, and not entirely unrelated, we can look at the "fluctuating time" in Icelandic culture and history. The idea of a "classical and correct argument" has had its own influence, as has the "petrified way of thinking." History shows these features of Icelandic culture. As is the case for the idea of the importance of literary heritage, the love of country and loyalty to the mother tongue has its roots in the nation's fight for independence.

Did Iceland, then, never become independent?

I will not answer that question. It is worth noticing, however, that there are other nations that shun the mirror of literature, not the least at a time in history that is dedicated to as impersonal and greedy a force as the marketplace. I note this matter throughout, and in chapter 5 I highlight one of Bergsson's articles that discusses the subject within a wide context. To revisit:

> By only concentrating on the words and sometimes their sound, rather than becoming acquainted with their meaning or the thoughts they might entail, readers and critics do not see the aura of the works that are individual in nature and are perhaps not engaged in any other battle than the one waged with human nature, and are not written in order to await their day in the sun, with a following of fans and goings on among those who reign over the market purse. They may not even be created for the memory, the common sense, or the understanding; and least of all for the one correct understanding. Instead, they spring from a longing to search for the thoughts that investigate the nature of the endless road to the incomprehensibility of life, which seems to recede as soon as the steely memory thinks it has found that unwavering certainty. Just as humanity resorts to its forgetfulness, life seems to renew itself by automatically awakening the incomprehension of those who are living according to specific rules. Progressive literary works are similar; they create incomprehension of the right form of understanding, and the disinterestedness of the public is

the foundation for all viable books. This kind of literature leans simultaneously towards and away from its nature. They paint a self-portrait and at the same time an image of the world. (Bergsson, "Sæmundur the Wise," 95)

Among the nuances of this aesthetics we can name Bergsson's investigation of the capriciousness of taste and its permeation of life and art. Not only does this investigation create havoc on the frontier of Christian dualism but it also may be seen as a revolutionary idea in the history of the relationship between body and soul. This kind of revolution is not waged for the hysteria of the marketplace. Nor is it waged for the common sense, the steely memory, or a correct understanding. That is perhaps why these kinds of nuances create a self-portrait as well as a world portrait: Grindavík becomes the Florence of the North, where Bergsson's characters and readers alike are participants in a much larger theatre than that which is named Tangi.

Epilogue: Consecration to Reality

When the diarist in *The Mind's Tormented Love* arrives in Spain, on vacation with his family, his daughter sees him with his friend/lover:

> [She looks at me not] with blame, not surprised, and not even like she knew and understood, but like she suspected something lay underneath because she had often seen this man whom I was talking to while she fed the ducks in the town pond and she clearly recognized him but she said nothing. That is how children react when they understand for the first time from associating with their parents that something is not right in their behaviour and interactions and therefore they have an inkling of life and know naturally that man is created in such a way that something is not right with him right from birth. That way the child waits in suspense without knowing why until it discovers the same ambiguity in itself, and when it turns out exactly the same, no question about it, then it remains quiet but says to itself: "Now I have been consecrated to reality and at this confirmation I have entered the world of adults." (236)

By understanding for the first time that something is not right in the behaviour of her parents and in their interactions, the daughter gets a foretaste of life. Later in life, she will most likely discover the same ambiguity in herself, and that will be the moment of her consecration to reality. With this confirmation she will enter the congregation of adults, who – as the diarist acknowledges – are slippery as eels.

This fragment is not just important for the significance of the daughter's place in the course of the narrative and the way in which the diarist's relentless search for a way to live touches upon some of the most fragile aspects of human lives – the wound of existence itself. It is also important for its illumination of one of the key elements of Bergsson's aesthetics: the consecreation to reality and how that consecration ferries one into the enigmatic "congregation" of adults. This consecration awaits not only children. As soon as someone starts to ask about the possibilities of love, faith, and beauty, it seems that the moment of consecration reveals itself in all its glory, casting a razor-sharp light on the paradoxes from which she/he cannot excape. Such is the testimony of Bergsson's aesthetics, and of the writings of those poets, writers, and philosphers who are discussed in these pages. With Plotinus, Augustine, Kierkegaard, Nietzsche, Blanchot, and Bergsson, we can say that the consecration to reality is an ever-repeated theme, as is the attempt to approach the various paradoxes of life.

The relationship between Blanchot and Bergsson is evident here. At a time in history that is characterized by a deep–seeted ambiguity, by how the modern human being remains a person of the Book but has lost her/his faith in it, both Bergsson and Blanchot are loyal to the (im)possibility of literature. What is unfathomable in humanity is met by what is unfathomable in literature. And what is unfathomable in literary writing is nurtured by the fundamental feature of the life of literature itself: the question. For, in literature, not only are things killed in order to be able to reappear in language and to become comprehensible – functional language separates itself from the world while pointing at it – but there is also a thinking about things before they undergo the negation of language, the clear statement, the answer that shuts language down and kills it. Perhaps this is where we find unrestrained humanity. Whatever the case may be, we look at literary writing as an attempt to awaken the reality of things. And this attempt concerns the search for the possibility of emotions and, thereby, of existence itself, not beyond the unfathomable in the human being and her/his interaction with others, but within the boundaries of her/his reality.

But what about the relationship between Bergsson and Augustine? Let us look at the diarist's words, through which he wrestles with his own life:

For once I face the same problem as when life is most challenging; the problem is that I had to take an uncomfortable look at

myself. If I believed in god or if he existed, whatever faith or
faithlessness said, I would no doubt lean on him with my despair
and hope he would dispel it, or I would wail at him like a son,
ask him to take the cup from me, which is really more a well
than a cup, a deep spring in which I battle with the angel of the
water in my long swim between stone walls in my hatred for my
own existence.

   I am the son of the world, society, and nation, and even though
I do not believe in god, I respect people and understand their
weaknesses and their need for a power that is higher than they
and hopefully more helpful than earthly ones. I could not think
of approaching god again in a faith that is built on my interests
and look for a solution in him for what I should be able to resolve without help with my intelligence and the experience I have
acquired in life. (*Tormented Love* 154)

Here the question of faith is foregrounded in the diarist's struggle
with his own life and existence. If we think about the legacy of
Augustine's existential thinking in Bergsson's writing, it is clear this
legacy is not a timeless one. But as is the case for original sin (and
radical authors turn to this subject again and again), we might say
that Augustine's existential quest shows up in Bergsson's writings.
This is so by virtue of the region of the inner life, this reality that is
both marked by and is the site of creation, where humanity acquires
its potential in life by rejecting existence and becoming "visible" as a
narrative image of humanity. As with Augustine, Bergsson tries out
the narrative image of humanity within a Christian framework. The
circumstances of his thinking are, however, different from Augustine's.
During the time of the advent of Christianity, Augustine naturally
looks to god, while during our day, god's dizzying absence marks the
existential quest. However, in the waning days of Christianity, thinking about faith, humanity, and human possibility has not lost all its
power. The difference is only that, while Augustine looks to God, the
characters in Bergsson's fiction look to earth, to material phenomena, the body, and to life without resolution.

   But all has not yet been said. The requirements we see for the consecration to reality in Augustine's *Confessions* are Christian in nature,
but the influence of neoplatonism is also tangible, and it shows up in
Augustine's existential search, especially when it comes to his interpretation, and confession, of an inner reality and the contradictions to

be found there. Augustine responds to the difficulty with a forceful rejection of everything that is connected to the unfathomable, and he ends in complete isolation and freedom from everything that lies outside himself, including his own body. The radical nature of his negation thereby opens up a space within the kingdom of Christianity and accidentally points directly to the unfathomable itself: not even God can shed complete light on humanity, let alone protect it from itself. Instead of leading to the fulfilment of the confessor here and now, the narrative of his incompleteness is eternal. And even though Augustine rejects his body and its needs in a memorable way, there are few books that awaken such a deep feeling for its presence. In this way, not only is the boundary between life and writing introduced, but perception takes on a life of its own. Such is the power Augustine lets loose on the boundaries of life and writing, creation and death.

Is it perception that ferries Plotinus, the mentor of Augustine, this far? In the consecration to reality about which we read in *The Enneads,* and in how beauty becomes possible with the participation of humanity, we see perception's wondrous influence. In other words, Plotinus's desire for beauty and his search for an authentic existence, we see a great force. The ideas of Plotinus are not obvious in contemporary discourse on beauty, and they may not have influenced Bergsson in a direct way. Nonetheless we can see how the modern writer's search for some kind of authentic existence is not unlike that of Plotinus. So long as he or she makes the consecration to reality his or her subject matter – awakening with it questions about the possibilities of a life full of paradoxes – then the idea of beauty is not only inescapable but also points to the unavoidable connection between the human being and beauty, and how beauty comes to be with the participation of humans.

Like Plotinus, Augustine, Bergsson, and Blanchot, Kierkegaard is also a passionate explorer of that most demanding task: to exist. The aesthetics that is discussed here is not suited to covering up paradoxes, whether in life or in art, and here Kierkegaard is called upon. Further, in the discussion about love, faith, and responsibility, we find the writings of Kierkegaard not only tempting but hauntingly relevant to Bergsson's writings on the same subjects. Both of them think about the consecration to reality in Christian culture with equal devotion, about the requirements for this, and about how love, faith, and responsibility play a fundamental role in an eternally repeated

drama. Thus, their passionate loyalty to the challenge of life is related. The same goes for the reservations both of them have about
the ability of systems to resolve what cannot be resolved in the lives
of human beings. If anything, we can say that Bergsson's aesthetics
answers the call of Kierkegaard's religious philosophy. While the
philosopher looks to faith when it comes to the irresolvable problem
of faith, love, and responsibility, the modern poet looks to the possibilities of aesthetics. As a result, we can see the transformative role
played by responsibility. In Bergsson's writing, the subject of responsibility reveals itself not as a reflection of a Christian worldview but,
rather, as a searching human being in a small-b book.

Nietzsche goes so far as to say that existence is only justified as an
aesthetic phenomenon. There is no final explanation for these words
of his. However, as is the case for the consecration to reality in
Bergsson's writings, and the way it embraces some of life's most
crushing paradoxes, we see that art is foregrounded in certain writings of Nietzsche. The position of art is not one-sided though. For, as
art cannot exist as a subject outside of its connection to life and the
paradoxes therein, art concerns humanity's knowledge of life and
the suffering that comes as a consequence of that knowledge. Both
Nietzsche and Bergsson write seriously about these beautifully demanding boundaries, and about how various world-famous dogmatic systems fail in their attempt to address the human condition.
For example, Christian ethics seems to run contrary to the nature of
life and the living, disregarding the foundation of Christianity itself:
the recognition of the ever-present human need for love and faith.

But where to search for love, faith, and beauty in secular times?
Does the ethics of aesthetics in modern writing reveal a recognition
of and respect for the challenge of life in a time of dizzying atheism?
If the aesthetics in Bergsson's writings contains thoughts on an unavoidable atheism, it does so in direct relation to the always present
need for faith. At the same time, we discern a powerful criticism of
those systems that, whether in the name of faith, beauty, or science,
make little of the difference between atheism and the need for faith.
In light of this we can say that Bergsson's aesthetics combine the
experiments of Plotinus, Augustine, Kierkegaard, and Nietzsche by
recognizing and respecting the need for faith while, at the same time,
rejecting a "holy" hypnotism, thus upholding the intellectual furor
concerning existence and aesthetics.

Does Bergsson then "write with blood" like the others? Is that why he writes untiringly about the limits of those who take humanity as their subject, supported by the dogmatic systems of science, religion, and/or ideology?

Only one thing is certain: Icelandic culture and society are not excluded from consecration to reality in Bergsson's aesthetics. Nor are they excluded from the existential perception that is hidden but not forgotten in his part of the world and that concerns both art and life. The themes of Bergsson's novels, short stories, and poems are set in a reality and society that Icelandic readers recognize. At the same time, we find in his writing an obstacle and a demand for another kind of participation in life and art. However Icelandic readers choose to respond to Bergsson's aesthetics, he adds to the Icelandic cultural inheritance by making his readers participants in a much greater theatre than that which concerns the preconceived ideas regarding the greatness of Iceland's literature, the homeland, and native tongue. The interactions we see in his writings are interactions with existence itself, not entirely free of the love of language and homeland but occuring within a region that does not belong to a fatherland – the region of literature. In this Bergsson not only shatters, for a while, the isolation of the country with regard to culture, society, and literary tradition but also diminishes the influence of the golden authors. Bergsson keeps afloat the fragile, but visible, thread of Icelandic aesthetics. As with Grímur Thomsen, Benedikt Gröndal Sveinbjarnarson, and Sigfús Daðason (to name a few), Bergsson gives his readers a chance to mirror themselves in the times in which they live – in literature.

But there is another matter that separates Bergsson from those poets, writers, and philosophers who have been discussed here. Unlike them (but unquestionably in the spirit of Nietzsche), Bergsson's attempt to deal with the classical dualisms of flesh and spirit, body and soul, is a deadly serious and, in a way, revolutionary affair: in his writings the flesh enacts the spirit. The reverse of the classical argument that the soul governs the body has not come about for no reason. Aside from the dialogue with the age-old themes of faith, love, and beauty, we find in Bergsson's writings a pointed examination of taste and its influence on life and art. Whether it is content or form, the thinking about the capriciousness of taste takes place in an enlivening but irrational environment, which takes its cues from instinct rather than reason when it comes to its regeneration and/or its renewal. In Iceland, this aesthetics has more than once been called hostile to humanity. The reason for this might be that Bergsson does not contribute to piling up preconceived ideas of social responsibility but, rather, concerns himself with a responsibility that is found only in the freedom of literature and that occurs there – in spite of the judgments of learned people – as an ethics of aesthetics. Perhaps Kierkegaard's wish has been granted, in the sense that, if faith in life is possible, then it falls on a certain kind of aesthetics to rescue it from the clutches of systems.

The aesthetics I discuss here is first and foremost an aesthetics of the individual. I find it in the nuances of Bergsson's writings, where love for the way of the body cannot be avoided, and where we are led directly to some of the most significant experiments in the history of Western aesthetics. Here we find both the search for how to acknowledge the unfathomable within oneself and others and how to experience all the adventures of life and art. Perhaps, if we listen to the words of the character Hugborg in Bergsson's *The Search for the Beautiful Land*, this is because "no beautiful country exists except in the body of the one you love" (226).

"Ideas on Beauty"

I do not know for certain, any more than others, what it means when people say "this is beautiful." If you go far back in time to discover the meaning of this it is worth noting that, for example in Homer's time, the concept of beauty was not yet discussed in an intellectual way. Instead the poets seemed to connect beauty with ideas on strength, competence, and perfection. We Icelanders have not thought through the idea of beauty either, neither in art nor in behaviour. We are usually content with seeing beauty as connected to the emotions we carry, or think we should have, towards landscape – in particular the Icelandic landscape. The Icelandic sense of beauty is no more colourful than what we appear to have inherited over the ages from the *Njálssaga*, in which Gunnar is described as saying he thinks the mountainside is beautiful. Then he defines the main reasons for why this is so, particularly regarding colour and texture: because the fields are pink and the meadows cropped. The shapes of things are nonetheless left to the imagination, and it is up to the reader to decide whether they are hills or squares or circles. In continuation of this, it is fairly obvious what the impression beauty makes on the inner life of the person amounts to: a love that shackles. Gunnar's sense of beauty makes him unable to tear himself away and go. That is how the outer world will enchain the inner life; beauty shackles the man to his home fields. We have seldom managed to get over this fact in our art and in our way of life, regardless of how much our society and culture have changed: our understanding of beauty is tied to the landscape and to our sense of loyalty.

When someone says "this is beautiful," what the speaker probably means is that the shape or nature of the beautiful thing has affected his mind in such a way that he is not content with the mere existence of the thing but that it has become something he loves. Perhaps the appearance and construction of the beautiful object agreed with the content and shapes that were already in the viewer's mind. But usually the speaker has compared the object of beauty to something else, similar but worse, which he thinks is ugly. There is no sense of beauty without the involvement of some sort of comparison and contrast.

Assume, in this regard, that we are talking about a coffee pot. We say: "The pot is beautiful!" It is inevitable that we have unconsciously compared this one with another, or at least our idea of what a coffee pot should look like, either more beautiful or uglier than the one we are looking at. If no other pot existed, we would probably have no taste for it because we would have nothing to compare it with, and we would be either impressed or bored with the invention. Our disposition would mostly be conditioned by whether we were for or against the drinking of coffee. In this case our ideas would be governed by functionality, but the usefulness of something is seldom tied to a higher beauty. Beauty only has value in and of itself. If we were coffee drinkers, we would *need* this coffee pot; it would either be useful or useless.

In most aspects of life, we do not take an aesthetic position towards anything, even though we are all philosophers of aesthetics and enjoyers of pleasure and beauty from morning till noon – also at night, for dreams are not simply the confusions of the soul thrusting forward but, rather, the aesthetic life of the senses displaying itself. When we walk past buildings, we are not always contemplating their beauty, even though we are enjoyers of beauty. Most houses are ordinary; only when we happen to see an especially beautiful house do we think: "This is beautiful" and the opposite if it is ugly. The aesthetics of the ugly is much more complicated than the aesthetics of the beautiful, but beautiful ugliness, or, rather, 'what is beautifully ugly,' in man's demeanour and in his acts is much more common than the other. The beautiful ugly is the most common aesthetic in the creation of art, and it is there on purpose. No work of art is completely beautiful.

It is not by accident that artists hold this type of doubtful beauty in high regard. Doubtful beauty is a special style borne of the need to change things; it is a remonstration and comes from the necessity of dividing the one into many. The artist knows that inside the ugly lies an amplitude of forms – more so than with beauty, which is always at risk of being one-sided and repressive. That is why people say something is "disgustingly lovely" if the monotonousness of the thing is excessive; the addition of "disgusting" evokes mystery, different responses and different forms.

Even though some form of the elevation of the ugly has existed from the beginnings in art – for example, when every new object from the artist's hand appears to others to be at least *unusual* and is therefore to a certain degree ugly in their eyes but then, with the passing of time and greater familiarity, acquires the ability to be considered *beautiful* – this elevation of the ugly still did not have a big impact on our culture and society until the Industrial Revolution. Things made by man began then to compete in earnest with nature, which was there originally and which belonged there. Nature was considered to have been created by god and was therefore worshipped next to god. The work praises the Maker in this as in other matters, and receives as much praise as Him, even though it deserves more praise and is actually more useful. The elevation of the ugly in aesthetic thought has been more noticeable after the end of the nineteenth century, and especially in the twentieth.

The veneration of the ugly has usually been associated with progressive trends in the arts. But now, when the avant-garde has, since the beginning of the twentieth century, been acknowledged and made somewhat classical, acceptable, and has created its own traditions so it can pay homage to itself, worship itself, and die – or, rather, refuse to accept its own death – artists have understood the problems they face if they are to sail the ship of new ideas and new styles into the next century in an artful way – a way that has a future in a world where everything concerning the earth and man has become known. In the future it will be almost impossible to forge into the unknown, which was previously thought to be life's greatest adventure. The "unknown" will no longer exist.

Up to the Renaissance in Italy, which reached its peak and began to dwindle in the fifteenth century before it changed into *an art of artifice*, a special perspective and style regarding the ugly had been prevalent in the arts. The ability to see the ugly was tantamount to having a Christian aesthetics. In the Middle Ages people were of the opinion that everything was ugly except god and his kingdom. Man was considered to be contaminated by sin and to be born into original sin. Only the unrelenting worship of god could make a man's soul beautiful in this earthly life. Except the soul always had an ugly frame: a body that could in no way be made more lovely before it died and turned into fog and acquired the asexuality of the angel.

It was not because the painters in the Middle Ages were not skilled enough that people in their paintings were rendered in a style that made them look deformed. This was done because of their religious view of beauty, which derived from a spiritual comparison with that which awaited the body: man would be rid of it in heaven. Physical deformity is the opposite of the beauty of the soul, which is invisible, as god's kingdom is also invisible. That which is invisible was considered beautiful, and therefore there was great emphasis placed on symbols of beauty and delight found in heaven, which was achieved by applying a lot of gilding to the painting. Heaven was the mine of light and the riches awaiting the soul if its owner practised obedient devotion to god during life.

This aesthetic – or this warning to man's spiritual beauty of what awaited if it went astray in pursuit of earthly greed – also pertained to the body of Christ. He was rendered in oval-shaped form, the symbol of the kingdom of god and of spring in the Mediterranean, with hardly any distinction made between him and the bodies of the sinners who tumbled to hell or the chosen who rose to heaven in the hues of clouds and mystery – that is how the bodiless were clothed. This was not done because the artists lacked the ability to distinguish between the body of Christ on the earth or in heaven and the bodies of other men in their works but because the style they followed and had learned had become so rooted that their work habits were defined by it, the same way that the work habits of avant-gardism today became entrenched in the first years of the twentieth century. These are practices that go into blind alleys if they are not renewed and reinvigorated.

When the theories of the Medieval Church receded from dominance in the Renaissance era, artists began to see the body of Christ, as well as human beings in general, from a perspective on beauty that is not altogether different from what is found in the methods used in advertising today: bodies of human beings and of Christ were now depicted with beauty, so that Christ seemed to lure the viewer into thinking "Enjoy me in my earthly state!" or "Buy me in the church and it will save your soul!" Everything concerning the Christian faith was turned into a commodity.

The physical body was not allowed to remain in an earthly Paradise for long, however, because by the end of the Renaissance artists had begun to stretch the extremities in a certain way, and it was made to look more *spiritual*. This was especially so when it came to the baby Jesus and women. Sometimes they even stretched the bodies of men. The beings in the works of El Greco are therefore more spiritual than corporeal in that they resemble the bearing of mortal human beings. These are complete mental fabrications, which reflect the aesthetic view of the painter.

A painter sees his subject perhaps less with the eyes than with the perspective he has on beauty. He probably sees the tangible world only to a slight degree with the subject matter in mind or with the tools with which he is able to work. The vision of a painter that comes through in his work is the perspective he has on things, and not the opposite – that he acknowledges the natural and normal form things take when he sees them. The same is true for artists in other areas. Novelists are usually not in the habit of *luring* their prototypes off the street and into their novels, where they are rendered in lovely sentences on the page; instead, writers verbalize their inner vision. To write is to "distort" both daily speech and poetic material.

The idea that an artist would try to reproduce or "capture" a prototype in real life comes to some degree from the belief that the caveman tried to "catch" his prey in a picture before he could ensnare it in a trap or slay it with his tools. This idea is of course absurd because, if this were the case, the caveman would not have caught much food for himself; there are in fact relatively few petroglyphs around compared to the food requirements of a normal person, not to mention the needs of a whole clan. Or did he perhaps also hunt the hands for food – the hands that he painted more often than he painted the animals?

If we wish to find an example of a painter who portrayed his perspective on beauty, then it is easy to find one in El Greco. We see this clearly in the painting of Saint Stephen, who was killed by an arrow. The painter's arrows are made to slide through the holy, beloved, and spiritual body without harming the flesh with wounds. The flesh is full of shots but there is no wound. Such is the holy nature of the saint and the view the painter has of him and of art. El Greco did not do this because he was stupid or because he thought there was no blood in Saint Stephen's body. Blood would have tainted the beauty of the forms, especially the colour red; and you cannot paint flowing blood without it.

It is often asserted that art and the need for art come of the idea that an artist finds in himself a power that is greater than himself. Art is great; the artist is small by comparison with that which awakens within him or that which he creates with discipline and practice. But is that power he finds inside himself the spirit of god?

No one knows the answer to that. Most likely there is in the artist, as in others, a human inheritance – a memory that resides in the physical cells, especially in those of the brain. But why does this power burst out in the form of art in the case of only a few, and not of everyone, if it is rooted in the inheritance of humankind? This I do not know. But I do know that this hidden memory glides into the mind on account of what we might call a restless murmur. Some might call it the need for faith. I do not know. Whatever this murmur might be, it is not directed at some specific god by the means of prayer, or to a certain political power, even though it is possible to manipulate this power and use if for purposes of propaganda. Perhaps the talent for creating art is really a hunting instinct, where the artist captures unclear ideas and slays them in his works. Every artist must recognize how he chases after ideas. Either overtly or covertly, he tries to entrap them and redress them in recognizable garb, which is usually dependent on the spirit of the times and changes accordingly. Upheaval in the arts and the forms they take are dependent on the times and the prevailing aesthetic perspective, even though the ideas themselves and their content remain more or less constant while the style changes. Both of these are to some degree in a hide-and-seek game with the sense of beauty, so that in each case the appropriate style allows the perception of the idea and its content to come through.

The same subjects come up again and again out of the depths of time and human sentiment. These are rendered in artistic form and live for a while and are thought beautiful or ugly, and then they sink again into the depths in some mysterious and undiscovered way. It is therefore not necessarily the beauty or ugliness of something that makes us ever ready to receive it as if it were something new, but, rather, the deceptive nature of the form it takes. Forms are not renewed in the open but are contained within the invisible even as their subject matter is forever repeated. So perhaps the forms in art are classical in the same way as is the physical human form, which we make bearable every day by another change of clothing. A naked man would be intolerable in the long run. Clothes were invented so it would be possible to imagine the body underneath.

We can therefore freely change our minds and alter our taste in these matters. Otherwise life and the world would become an unendurable torment. We would be tired of our surroundings if they never changed in appearance, brightness, colour, or style. This is how our world is becoming intellectually bland and monochrome, monotonous and standardized, even though we are tempted to over-look this development. We do not admit that it is our ideas about equality that makes us want everything to be the same, and, at the same time, we are terrified of the consequences. We do not want the ideas to be realized, either emotionally or aesthetically. In this way we are met with the same vision wherever our eyes look.

The torment of modern man is not caused by terror in the usual sense but, rather, by the fact that automatic memory has over-whelmed everything concerning human affairs. Mechanization in life has made our minds mechanical as well: no longer are we held by the need to revolt and understand, but, instead, we find it harder and harder to convince ourselves that new things happen. The only things that take place are those that we have planned and plotted out thoroughly. Our ability to plan and plot does not fail us. Chance is just about outcast, and beauty has become repetitive.

Happiness in life is derived to a large degree from our knack for self-deception concerning things connected with beauty, flattery, beautiful words, beautiful people, and, of course, also from the abil-ity we have of duping ourselves in the hope that something new might happen in our dreams of how to enjoy the variety of life. But in actual fact, we try to make ourselves enjoy and to be content with continuous monotony in forms that are supposed to be good for all, few in number, and easy to learn and to understand. This makes them lightweight over time, and they become easy to dismiss and replace with other, equally impoverished, forms, also effortlessly understood and learned.

If a vigilant man sees something and calls it beautiful, he will be-lieve himself only to a degree. His belief is not unshakeable. But since the sense of beauty runs the risk of being continuously change-able, as witness the above argument that we have a talent for self-deception, then we can change our minds and assert the opposite without blinking or being ashamed of our inconsistency, if we are in the mood to do so or if it is convenient, as when we are discussing the issue with someone who is at odds with us and more clever than he is intelligent. But if we come up against an especially harsh-minded pedant, it might happen that we are unable to answer when this is thrown at us: "You said something else yesterday. You are inconsistent and have no understanding of beauty. I always have my fixed view. It is you who cannot be taken seriously."

I am of a different opinion. Often the act of changing your mind is simply an expediency or a need for change. If we are talking about an artist, then the artist's inconsistency in matters aesthetic could come from what I have called creative inconsistency. This is in contradistinction to what I would call disheartening inconsistency. Disheartening inconsistency occurs when a man shows utter confusion and has no control over his thoughts for psychological reasons. An artist who is in the grip of this latter form of confusion does not possess the control that is required to hold up the silver star of which Nietzsche spoke. An artist who is endowed with creative inconsistency is able to raise the silver star in his works, moulded in the smithy out of the darkness of chaos and the burning waters.

The act of stubbornly holding on to a thing and its beauty, or of insisting on a point of view and claiming that it is the only true perspective, comes close to the religious fervour of Christianity – or the desire to see everything in black and white. This kind of perspective, or, rather, this kind of inner life, sees on the one hand the white – the right view – and on the other hand the black – the wrong view – of the opponent. In these cases the believer is prepared to fight to the death for his position, whatever may come. He will invariably fight with violence and force and will consider both to be proof of his rightness and consistency. If he should be fortunate enough to die in the conflict, then he will be considered holy by his compatriots, who will try to make of him an example of unflinching faith and an absolutely right and beautiful perspective.

With this said, we have come to one of the most important areas of aesthetics and related concerns. That is the relationship between the sense of beauty and cruelty. These two often go together, both in daily life and on special holidays, and they are most noticeable in matters political, social, and religious, and in the raising of children. The ethics and the aesthetics of all of these are closely related. Here we are not only talking abut the ethics of cruelty but also the ethics of the perspective that considers itself to have the right to be cruel, and even to take the life of another in the name of a specific aesthetics.

Most of the cruel acts of man are committed as a consequence of his sense of beauty, of his aesthetic sense. The same can be said of racism, of religious extremism, and of the lack of compassion for others – especially with regard to sexual behaviour. The reason for this is mainly that Christian aesthetics is directed at the idea of improving the world and humankind and of beautifying the spirit of man, by good or ill. This kind of ethical aesthetics is of course attended by violence, which is easy to resort to because a large portion of humankind is blind to some area of its own behaviour, if looked at from a Christian point of view.

I have often dealt with this subject in my works. If someone discovers in himself a need to eradicate entire races of people on account of their heretic beliefs or the colour of their skin, or do away with individuals who are of what we have called the same-sex persuasion, then this person is gripped by a need to cleanse. This is because such people are both mentally and physically ugly to him, and unhealthy as well, if viewed from the Christian perspective, which regards procreation as what defines beautiful sexual behaviour. If such a man is in the grip of this cleansing fever, then he has usually received a "higher calling" and has seen the aesthetic light. This fills him with a "holy rage," and he insists upon beautifying the world by eradicating from it all that is ugly in one fell swoop. He thinks big and never gets bogged down in details: he is engaged in a holy war built on holy force. According to this man's ethics and perspective towards beauty, a huge mass of people only constitutes a blemish on humankind. It is not surprising that violent people are compelled by a certain artistic need or have at least sometime in their youth composed sentimental poems about love and nature. The demand for justice is also borne of a certain aesthetics. It might be ugly, according to some, to be rich or poor or, for example, to behave like an exemplary male or female.

It is not uncommon that aesthetics, and the aggression that it engenders, is especially associated with artists. This argument is made by shallow people who have no understanding of art and who do not understand why artists are prepared to oppose anyone who does not belong to the same artistic movement or who does not verbalize things in the same way they do: who say with them, when they see a photograph of Kjarval, "there is the master Kjarval!" The fanaticism that springs from having different aesthetic tastes is far from being confined to artists. Such fanaticism is much more common with ordinary people than is readily admitted. When on beauty's path, and for no overwhelming reason, mothers are fanatics in the kitchen and fathers in the workplace.

The aversion of the white man towards the black man does not come out of nowhere. The reason for such racism is aesthetic: a person's tastes concerning colour and form in the human body is the beginning of prejudice. The black man may also have an aversion to the white man for the same reasons. The sense of form and taste for colour in each of them has been moulded by circumstance, surroundings, and religion. That is why, when the first white men, the Portuguese, came to Japan and opened the country to foreign influence, Japanese artists painted pictures of the event and gave the foreigners big noses. A big nose was a sign of contempt for foreigners. The Japanese taste and idea of beauty was, among other things, that beautiful people have small, fine noses. In other ways the Portuguese were similar to the Japanese. He who knows nothing about aesthetics does not notice these things and does not see their meaning. Japanese artists could not paint a Portuguese in the same way as could European artists. It was not because of a lack of skill that they could not see other parts of the body that were different, that they were not used to seeing in their own community; rather, because of their taste, their education and tradition, it was enough to emphasize ugliness by making a large nose a symbol of immorality and threat. The Japanese understood this gesture.

Usually terror and beauty are not tied to deeds so grim as the Portuguese invasion of the closed society of Japan; instead, such terror could simply be a part of nature and the changes and tumult in the weather. Such things would mean nothing and be inconsequential if no one followed what was going on. This is because it is man who interprets things and gives things meaning. He sees the elements and tries to determine their nature – or else he gives them a significance that has no bearing on their nature. It would be more accurate to say that the interpretation of nature is wishful thinking on the part of man or that it is really an interpretation of his own nature.

In this connection I would like to tell a short tale of terror and dignity in nature and of different levels of taste regarding both. Both came together when they were translated into art by the British painter Turner.

In the beginning of the nineteenth century a middle-aged aristocratic woman sat in a mail carriage that drove over a deserted, forested area. Through the curtains of the carriage window, a terrifying dark sky could be glimpsed, which frightened the woman. In the seat in front of her sat a rather shabbily dressed man who looked like a beggar because he was unshaven, and he followed closely the changeable sky and landscape. All of a sudden it got very dark and

the rain poured down with thunder and lightning. The passengers
tried to draw the curtains tighter so they would not get wet. All of a
sudden the shabby man excused himelf, rose up, opened the window,
and stuck his head out. There he stood in an awkward position and
glared at the stormy weather. The other people had enough of this
and could not understand his behaviour, but they excused it as part
and parcel of his appearance. The man stared out the window for a
good while and then drew himself back in, completely drenched by
the rain. The woman decided to ask him what he had been looking
at and to say that she herself thought the goings on of the weather
were terrible. He answered her:

"I have seen greater beauty than my eyes have ever before
beheld."

The woman was curious, immediately stuck her head out the window, but saw only more terrible weather. The man said:

"Open your eyes, then you will see the majesty."

The woman followed his advice but she saw only more tumult.

This was a noblewoman, an enjoyer of art and beauty. A year later
she went to an art exhibition in London. There she saw a recognizable, beautiful painting but could not quite place the subject. She was
nonetheless so impressed by the artistry and the beauty of the picture
that she decided to buy it and went to make an offer to the artist.
Then she saw the man she had been sitting with in the carriage.

Each one had seen the same thing in nature: she saw horror and
he saw terrifying beauty. But after the stormy weather had been
transformed into art, they agreed on its aesthetic value.

Where was beauty in this instance: in nature itself, in the woman, or
in Turner's talent? In his eyes or in hers? Or was it only in that part
of his aesthetic sensibility where he could transform it through the use
of colours and tools? Was the beauty built on style or was it in a fleeting taste? That taste was not so fleeting that we are not able to value
Turner's work to this day, but then perhaps we possess not our own
taste but, rather, a learned taste that enables us to value, or pretend to
value, his paintings on the grounds that they are part of art history.

Whatever the answer may be, the anecdote makes it clear that the
painter has been inspired by ordinary events in nature and not by his
"home fields." He has probably been taken by the unusual, terrifying
play of light in the flashes of lightning and by the peals of thunder
because, in his own temperament, similar events were brewing.
When he painted, he combined his memories from the carriage, and

who knows if the woman was impressed by the painting because the memory of the event itself lay buried deep in her mind? Strictly speaking, she may not have been impressed so much by the artistry as by her own sensibility. Or else she was moved by Turner's attitude towards nature and how he could alter its image. The painting was of course not nature itself because both art and nature each have their own laws. What is appropriate in nature is often not so in a painting or in a poem, artistically speaking. The most important aspect of this story is that Turner painted an inner vision rather than what he actually witnessed. He did not say: "Beautiful is the storm, the blazing and ruffled clouds, and out of the postal carriage I will not venture." Instead, he went and created an abstract, classical, and artistic image of nature.

The question arises: What then is beauty? This question is so important that I need to mention a more earthly example than that provided by an artist. I do not know whether everyone has had this experience, but the exemplary parable I am going to tell is meant to address aesthetic experience in a larger sense.

Let us imagine that Jói has gone to a dance but not for any particular reason. This is on a Saturday and nothing is available at home other than television and books he does not care to read. He thinks they are about ugly and boring things. This is a fellow who seeks entertainment and a glass of something to drink.

Now he is at the dance, and he spies a girl not far away. He is not impressed by her at first, mainly because she looks nothing like his own mother. He orders a drink. When he has had another glass and a half, he notices that he likes the girl more. She is beginning to look like his mother, and his father's sister too. He has been very fond of his aunt because she gave him goodies when he was a kid, and now she gives him computer gadgets. Jói is thinking this way until he is positive he has never seen a lovelier girl, and he tells her so. She is in no doubt about the truth of his flattery and goes home with him, which is the custom and the aesthetic attitude of both of them: if someone praises another, or if someone receives praise, then it is quite alright to celebrate this by jumping into bed. They think nothing of the consequences.

When Jói wakes up the next morning, he sees to his horror that beside him lies a snoring woman to whom he has an immediate aversion. It is as if he has gone to bed with his own aunt. He does not comprehend this misunderstanding. His newly awakened good sense

decides that she is an old hag and he wakes her up so he can throw
her out. The woman does not at all like Jói's new-found taste. She
reminds him that just a few hours ago he had told her that she was
the loveliest girl in the world, and it was impossible that she had
grown so much older and uglier in such a short time. Jói claims innocence on the grounds that he was drunk and did not know what
he was doing or saying or seeing. Now the woman regrets that she
did not get his words and his solemn oaths on tape, so she could
prove that she was right, and she contemplates whether it is too late
to charge him with rape, for then she could get her revenge and get
at least something out of the apparent contradictions in his taste. She
figures she deserves as much, since she is almost fifty now.

Jói becomes enraged. He suspects what she is thinking of planning. Besides, now he is positive that his good taste is infallible, especially as it concerns feminine beauty. In this way their argument
grows until they say nasty things and begin to fight for real. Jói is
stronger and gives the woman a black eye. She causes him even
greater harm by calling him a mama's boy, which he knows he is and
he is really hurt by it. At the same moment his mother comes in and
throws the woman out. She knows that this broad is ruining her son
with her ugly behaviour. At this point, Jói's first thought is that he
has done the right and beautiful thing by cleansing his room of this
hag, and now he can go back to his computer games. He blames his
mistakes on the liquor and promises to never taste it again. His
mother says this is a beautiful vow, so like him, and she goes to the
store to buy him a new computer game. She is sure that she can keep
her son with her longer and that, if she does this, he will remain
good. The story ends and Jói re-establishes his good taste, his confidence, and his manhood.

This parable is not just about Jói and the woman but also about
what could be called ordinary behaviour – even though people are
usually moved from admiration to repulsion more slowly – so quick to
go from infatuation to abhorrence. But there are similarities between
this story and marriage and friendship, relating to paintings and art
and our taste in books and music. Few people know what is happening and rarely ever bother to worry about it, and so they endlessly fall
into the same trap. That is how people go forward; either they allow
themselves to be deceived or else they deceive themselves.

But is the sense of beauty actually our inner desires making themselves felt? And when our various needs are fulfilled, each one in turn,

are we then satisfied and have we been satiated mentally and physically? And do we then despise what before we had thought beautiful –
so much so, even, that we are repulsed after we have been satisfied,
and we forcefully push away from us what we before embraced
because of the beauty we saw there, which was only beautiful in the
eyes of a changeable sense of taste, brought on by the hunger of our
yearnings?

Excerpts From *Flatey-Freyr*

For Jón Gunnar Árnason,
who carved Freyr in wood
and woke sound and word

FLATEY AND FREYR

Flatey is a small island in Breiðafjörður, the largest fjord in Iceland. In this fjord there are a thousand small islands, of which Flatey is the biggest. To the north, the sunny shores of Barðaströnd can be seen, and in the south, Snæfellsjökull, the most beautiful of Iceland's glaciers, glistens white. At one time there was a settlement on Flatey, with a harbour, and the small island was a significant point of culture and trade for the western part of the country. Flatey is also known for the *Flateyjarbók* (*Flatey Book*), the largest medieval Icelandic manuscript.

Early in the year the island fills with birds and the fertility of air, sea, and earth. Migratory birds come from all over the world to lay their eggs, waiting until their young hatch before flying off again into the distance.

When I came to Flatey at the end of winter in 1972, the solitary passenger on a little ferry, the island was mostly deserted. Only three houses were inhabited. I chose to stay in a rundown house far off from the others.

A friend of mine from the artist group sÚM, sculptor Jón Gunnar Árnason, came and settled on the island in the middle of that summer. He found a piece of driftwood on the beach and carved from it a statue of Freyr, the Germanic god of fertility.

We set the god up on the remotest part of the island, hidden from all except the birds and flowers.

Every morning I went across the island, through the flocks of birds, to bring the statue a thought, which I left in a jar at its base.

I did this for the whole summer, bringing words, thoughts, single sentences. At first they were handwritten, and later I typed them.

I stayed on the island until well into the winter, under the northern lights. There was no electricity. One morning at the end of August all the birds left, and nothing remained but silence. It was then that I began composing poems with sound.

In that cold house I began to put thoughts and sounds together. Out of this, "Flatey-Freyr" arose, a poem about decay and fertility. Later on, back in Reykjavík, I created a performance incorporating the jar and strips of paper on which the offerings had been written, along with me reading the poem or playing a recording of it from a tape. The show was performed in various cities, such as Amsterdam and Copenhagen. But the tape has all but been destroyed and only fragments of it remain now. Originally the performance lasted an hour.

For a few years, no one would publish "Flatey-Freyr." So, I ended up taking it upon myself in 1978 and saw to everything but the actual printing.

– Guðbergur Bergsson

Freyr, in this jar I honour the spirit of fertility and the progress of art. It used to contain pure Pacific honey that I bought at the health-food store.

The jar will grant good thoughts and fortune to all those who look into it and see the bottom, even when they are in sullen spirits, weakened and worn, stunned by a confining and infertile state of being and limp, up top and down below.

There were two other jars: the happiness jar and the fame jar, but this one, the word-sacrifice jar, is the one in which I place a thought every day, while shouting aloud into the air and recording it to tape.

Freyr

I have said, in your name, to a married couple:

Never use one another in the accusative
never fraternize with a woman in the dative
never regard your children in the genitive

or like an irregular verb.

For the world and everything that lives and breathes in it

is natural in the nominative

in the case of wonder   in the case of love.

But Freyr

from this case come others

through the strength of compulsion

and conjugation.

Freyr, do you believe that absolute justice could rule on Earth if you erased the accusative, the dative, and the genitive from human consciousness?

> Njörður   (Njord)[1]
> örð   (harvest)
> jörð   (Earth)
> er   (is)
> faðir   (the father)
> Freys   (of Freyr)
> ey   (island)
> og   (and)
> Laufey   (Laufey)
> en   (but)
> Loki   (Loki)
> er   (is)
> minn   (my)
> guð   (god)
> Freyr   (Freyr)

---

[1] Translation note: this recurring sequence loses its effect when translated into English, so it appears in the original Icelandic with parenthetical English references.

Freyr

Fertility may not be there to

   please people

but rather displease

awakening a new mood

that pushes other moods off into uncertainty.

Freyr

In the same way, words must be continuously newly spoken

   news.

Freyr

I've heard that a hen has laid a rotten egg.

Freyr

Fertility is, for the most part,

that which must grow under guidance, freely

on the continent of the soul

never reaching the open air through speech and words.

That is the poem.

Don't turn your nose up like that

Freyr.

      Freyr

      I change the word-offering in your jar

                        every day.

      Freyr

      Everything demands change.

Freyr

Why should we not turn time and language

   upside down

try to reverse feeling and thought

and speak in a new way?

Answers are ambiguous. Some questions are double-edged.

But Freyr

If the word is so uniquely validated as it is in Icelandic art

and its value written down

by unwavering poets

writing books that are like well-plucked hens

then the poor word will increase in value at the

national bank

and will be hired out to hacks before Christmas.

Freyr

They say that the word may not be dangerous traffic

between people

flying between fingers, teeth, eyes, winds, flowers

ending up in bad weather, dirtied and kicked away

like a football.

Freyr

We are football players of the word.

Freyr

It does not frighten us that we dare to create each other out of a desire for destruction.

Freyr

The more seclusion, the better. Everything is at its most intense within seclusion. It gives the hand rest from the racket of ideas.

Seclusion strengthens the memory. It is power, and therefore knowledge.

Njörður   (Njord)

örð   (harvest)

jörð   (Earth)

er   (is)

faðir   (the father)

Freys   (of Freyr)

ey   (island)

og   (and)

Laufey   (Laufey)

en   (but)

Loki   (Loki)

er   (is)

minn guð   (my god)

Freyr

What good does it do to invoke old gods here in the eternal
    half-twilight

in the blue wound of the morning frost?

When the sun bleeds the mournful blood

of a violet mist over the mountains of the North

the old man stands by a cabin

and rattles the rings of a broken barrel.

How old and worn-out this world is!

This island: ruins and rot in the once strong timber!

The morning dew covers the man's brows

and his mouth gapes under the fading blue

    of his eyes.

The old man is always in a bad mood and rages

although his vitality is fading.

He clenches his fists at the eternal deafness of his ears to the
world of sounds. And he doesn't know that he's condemned to
death here amidst

    the collapsed fences,

missing cattle, and the burnt plastic garbage

    of summer guests

amidst the tumbledown houses.
He stands alone
all alone
upright and enraged
isolated.

He stands by the cabin and blows his nose abruptly
toward the docks
which have become too flat and worn
    and too small for new ships to land
bringing anything new or exotic to wake thoughts from hibernation.

Freyr
But in the shelter of night and darkness they arrive on the island
and the movement of shadows is seen in
the seaweed.
Who knows what treads there
ghosts or men
arriving on the island in a strange autumn evening.
Freyr
One thing is for sure
Sigurður the dragon slayer rides here neither over meadows
    nor pages.
And no unfamiliar light strikes these
    quiet bays.
Sleep and decay, fundamentally Icelandic, have come over
    every wound and joint.
The dusk is dusky and the Germanic night is dead.
At daybreak the sun doesn't reveal the faces of the gods.
The old man stands by the broken barrel
all alone under the ridge in furious silence.
Oh world!

No longer will it be sung

no magic   no song.

Barren hens waddle arrogantly around

like old poets

screeching and sharpening their beaks, thinking the noise is
singing.

And the raven, melancholy in flight, sends his hiss

   into the distance.

Freyr

What a miserable foretaste of death dwells here in the pale
constellation

   of the nation

of the starfish!

Freyr, illogic is the fundament of all natural science. Freyr, the
time will come someday when man will have to consider his size.
Freyr, the man who stands opposite and outside of you knows
your size. And through him you come to recognize the true size
of your form and thoughts. Freyr, it seems as though you gave
man your thoughts knowingly. The thoughts of a god exist only
in the ideas of his believers.

Freyr

So it is also with my poems and the theatre of the mind,

the interaction between viewer and work.

A question laid before Freyr

   Freyr

   Does man ever love so much

   that his soul merges with another

   like rain that falls in the sea?

Freyr's answer:

   If a man gives his soul to others

another, different one is given to him
just as the sky clouds with evaporated water.

If that is so
Freyr
why is man then neither
cloud, rain, sun, nor the wind in the sky?

Freyr
In the autumn, when the old man sleeps on the beach's
   humid gravel
his head falls into the seaweed
full of dreams.
He dreams in the sea's mud
of a grey cow lying at the teats of a dark brown milk cow
lying helpless on a withered hill.
She chews the teats between green teeth and blows the udder up
like a balloon.
The cow suckles sweet milk eagerly until it is all dried up.

Freyr
The old man then raised his head from the sea's forest, rolled the
cow over and stood her up on tender feet.

But she falls again and bare bones push through her
   skin
as though the summer sun and the autumn have cooked her flesh.

Freyr
At dawn the last journey across dark regions begins.

Freyr
The old man sits in the bow of the boat and embraces the cliff.

Freyr
The winds and weather guide the journey of a headless tongue.

Freyr

Every day is born like a poem.

A poem that wanders on a ship over sea and mind in gloomy light.

And in the helmet of a mind creating, it resounds like a hammer
   on an anvil.

Freyr

Not all heads are at home on a neck.

Freyr

Some heads are free   others are stone.

Freyr

The poem glides on the ship's light feather out in the fishing
grounds

   of the wide fjords

and wanders about the dark sea

carried by the current until a wave takes the old god

in its arms

and brings both head and poem to rest in the dumb embrace
   of the fjord mouth.

Freyr

So poetry wakes out of poetry.

Freyr, the soundshapes, the soundforms of my poems are not
alone but live a life of chastity only in the totality of their
environment.

Freyr, sound is brought into being and exists as soon as it is given
a definite form.

Freyr, there is nothing before form. In the end, everything is
structured around structure.

What, for example, would happen to a house if its form was lost
or if the carpenter forgot how to build it?

Then there would only be the memory of the house, the idea, the
formlessness.

But Freyr, the memory and the idea are nonetheless distinct forms and so is formlessness.

Freyr, why does sugar taste like sugar and not like salt or seaweed?

Freyr, why do we find that sugar tastes bad when salt gets in it, but we would find it good if it were actually salt?

Take note of this Freyr, and consider the reason.

Freyr, human touch, perception, thought, taste, powers of vision and hearing are just distinct forms of particular qualities that combine in a natural way or not at all.

Freyr, the soundshapes, the soundforms of my works are not alone but live a life of chastity only in the totality of their environment.

The pregnant night, Freyr, does not always give birth to day. In the fleeting brightness of a beleaguered winter's day, the old man's constant wailing can be heard. And when it is dim again after midday, Freyr, I see him, howling, wandering in my thoughts amid the deserted houses in the night's light. Why does he howl his sorrows at the sky and moon like someone who has no home or who expects never to find his mother or father again; like a man who has no belief in himself and loses his reason in the sea, Freyr? Or is the old man howling his song of praise, perhaps, for life at the edge of the grave? Yes, that howling born of the darkness into the darkness that strikes man dead, so that he falls, dancing in silence, onto the muddy, frozen earth and dies, Freyr.

Yes.

Freyr
This grassy island's pride comes up so often
on the old man's tongue
that the words of reality are now just
dust in his eyes.

Freyr
And when the vexed old man races, superhumanly,

over the moors and marshes
he sinks in this island's bog.

Freyr
Empty houses stand around the plain
where the collected wisdom of old books now moans
like a foul wind through a heap of paper.
It whirls about like an illusion
and ransacks the roofs of the village houses for the treasures
    of the scummiest corners.
The old man will get so worked up that he won't
    see with his eyes
but with the nape of his neck
his spirit beginning to spin
turning about himself with words and old
    stories
trying to turn in the direction of the pier
so as to greet the arriving ship.
Freyr, from which sea, Freyr?
Freyr, which ship, Freyr? From his spirit?
Perhaps from those puddles that to the old man
have become an unending distance.
Perhaps from those puddles of the imagination
that have become an ocean.
Perhaps ocean liners travel there, submerged
in age and madness.
Perhaps ocean liners travel through tears.

Freyr
In the end the old man stares indifferently
    at the dead sea
and the tears flow lonely over the rocks
    and the path of silence.

Freyr, the stone that was covered in bright green moss in the spring
is once again grey under winter's ice.

But in my mind I can make the stone green again, or blue, bright red
or yellow, even.

Freyr, thus I keep the summer safe

and show reality my power. But I don't paint the stone.

Freyr

When man has become a slave to responsibility

and life weighs upon him like a custom,

how desperate, then, is his search for a future.

He no longer awakens under the pressure of poetry

and lights the lamp.

The moonlight no longer keeps him from sleep

he no longer rushes out into the night

in the frenzy of poetry, insomnia and love.

He does not dream of uncertainty and the sea.

His eyes become cold in the storm

he prefers to sit in solitude.

He seeks no friends and says to himself:

"Shoulder your burden, responsibility's slave,

when life weighs upon you like a duty."

Freyr

Wordless silence is the innermost part of joy

the home of language   where thought is created

formlessness becomes form there colourlessness becomes colour.

Freyr

Wrestling with the desire for silence has no end

just like man's longing to see and perceive

to understand and exist through the wisdom of his eyes.

Freyr
But man has hands and therefore forms
    things
and in the end man gives in to the world of things
even if the silence always enchants him like a lost refuge.

Freyr
We don't miss the soil in which lush flowers
    grow
and where the plants will be as high as mighty giants
fertile fields that do not demand seed.
Our land – Freyr – is spun of other wool.

Freyr
Our desire doesn't seek the crowded regions
those where culture is piling up on culture over
a thick layer of continual murders, punishments and feelings
relics and resistance
and the thought licks itself a way to power with
    a long poison tongue.

Freyr, I no longer feel any regret.
I no longer miss anything in particular, Freyr.

Freyr, has a bird ever flown
has ever a bird flown high, Freyr,
from the surface of the sea, fluttering so far out
fluttering so far out from the surface of the sea in
the wasteland of the air that he forgot that
the sea is
is the sea
that he has become a part of the air's wasteland

that part of the air's wasteland has become him?
Or is that distancing oneself from the mind, Freyr?
Freyr, that is distancing oneself from the mind, or
the mind distancing itself from the body
the body distancing itself from thought
becoming separate from the surface of the sea and fluttering,
Freyr,
alone around the head
around the head alone
over a vague surface out in the wasteland
out in the wasteland over some surface
the spirit alone and sick, itself lost,
Freyr.
Freyr.

> To me it's unclear
> Freyr
> and impossible to understand
> why you
> who are a thing
> or rather
> more accurately
> a piece of wood
> from the sea
> should not be
> worshipped completely
> and turned into a god
> figure
> of the object-worshippers
> of this world
> the worship of objects, their superficiality

always praised
by materialists.

but Freyr   it goes
against your sacredness   and worship in you   that
    you are
not simply   just   a piece of driftwood
an object   but also
a tree of the deep   dragged out of the sea   and formed
from art   from man's spirit   into an image
enriched through the mystery of the deep and the hiddenness
of the unfathomable   and therefore you are the symbol of
conception
and of the spirit's caresses   of fertility.

This belief is avoided by those
who worship the materialized void
and those with hardened spirits
Freyr
you are not just
a thing
but the radiation
of a thing
and its flow
Freyr
therefore
you are the unbound
in the end, the laws of nature
are nothing other than
movement.
Therefore I sit here before you

with a tape recorder, in the flow that renews itself
  in destruction.
Freyr

       Njörður
       örð
       jörð
       er
       faðir
       Freys
       ey
       og
       Laufey
       en
       Freyr
       Loki
       er
       minn
       guð.

Notes

PREFACE

1 Ásgeirsdóttir, *Guðbergur Bergsson*, 16. Unless otherwise indicated, all passages from Icelandic sources quoted in English in *Recesses of the Mind* are translated by Kristjana Gunnars.

2 This view can be explored further in some of the essays in Cazeaux, *Continental Aesthetics Reader*.

3 See Watson, "What Is Art," 8 (review of Kelly, *Encyclopaedia*).

CHAPTER ONE

1 In Guðbergur Bergsson's work, "god" is lowercased.

2 Bergsson, *Mind's Tormented Love*, flyleaf.

3 A great deal has been written about the existentialism of Gunnarsson's novel: its structure as well as its place in Icelandic literary history. See Sæmundsson, *Mynd nútímamannsins* [Image of Modern Man]; Eysteinsson, "Fyrsta nútímaskáldsagan" [First Modern Novel]. See also Sæmundsson, "Á aðra hliðina öskraði dauðinn" [On One Side Death Screamed].

4 Kierkegaard, *Repetition*, 153. When no other text is cited, parenthetical page references to *Repetition* will be to the Hong translation. *Repetition* first appeared in Copenhagen in 1843 under the title *Repetition: A Venture in Experimenting Psychology* by Constantin Constantius (one of Kierkegaard's pseudonyms).

5 Much has been written on this Kierkegaardian concept. See, for example, Þorsteinn Gylfason's introduction to his translation of *Repetition* (Reykjavík: Hið íslenzka bókmenntafélag, 2000), especially 37–42. See

also Kristján Árnason's introduction to Kierkegaard's *Uggur og ótti*, trans. Jóhanna Þráinsdóttir (Reykjavík: Hið íslenzka bókmenntafélag, 2000), 9–44. See also the writings of Joakim Garff, in particular his *Den Søvnløse* [The Sleepless One], 115–56.

6   The novel first appeared in Paris in 1948 under the title *L'Arrêt de mort*. The English translation is by Lydia Davis and is entitled *Death Sentence* (see Blanchot, *Death Sentence*).

7   Blanchot, *Death Sentence*, 32. "J'ai vécu quelque temps avec une personne obsédé de l'ide de ma mort. Je lui avais dit: 'Je crois qu'à certain moments vous avez envie de me tuer. Il ne faut pas résister à cette envie. Je vais écrire sur un paper que si vous me tuez, vous agirez pour le mieux.' Mais, une pensée n'est pas tout à fait une personne, même si elle agit et vit comme elle. Une pensée exige une loyauté qui rend difficile toute ruse. Elle-même est parfois fausse, mais derrière ce mensonge je reconnais encore quelque shose de vrai que, moi, je ne puis pas tromper" (Blanchot, *L'Arrêt de mort*, 55).

8   See Blanchot, "Language of Fiction."

9   In her introduction to her translation of the collection of essays *The Space of Literature*, Ann Smock discusses this matter. Here we are missing names like Luce Irigaray and Hélène Cixous, but they also belong to this group of French thinkers.

10   See Bruns, "Blanchot."

11   Blanchot's "insight" is one of a kind, but, in the discussion of the origins of the work of art, it is not possible to avoid Martin Heidegger. See Heidegger, *Origin*, 17–87.

12   This is not as simple as it sounds. If we, for example, think about a novel like *The Samurai*, we might find it surprising that it is written by Julia Kristeva, one of the most influential theorists of modern times.

13   See Derrida, *Demeure*, 47–8.

14   Blanchot, *Faux pas*, 26. See also Critchley 41.

15   Guðbergur Bergsson, "Two Poems, II," in Bergsson, *Endurtekin orð* [Repeated Words], 20.

16   The essay appears in the collection entitled *La Part de Feu* (Paris: Editions Gallimard, 1949). The present discussion refers to Blanchot, "Literature," 300–44.

17   See Critchley 57–63. It is worth mentioning that Blanchot's essay has been seen as a satire of Hegel's *Phenomenology of Spirit*. Others think that "satire" is not the right word in this regard, that it is not a strong enough term because it does not describe, as it should, the *nature* of Blanchot's

relationship to Hegel. Critchley is of this opinion and claims not only that Blanchot wrote in "the spirit" of Hegel but also that he read Hegel's book as if it were a novel.

18 See Blanchot, "Literature," 321. It should be noted that, with this subject, Blanchot has de Sade in mind. The freedom of death ends for him in the death of God and in an identification with God.

19 See Critchley 63. And what are the possibilities? Blanchot writes: "Literature is a concern for the reality of things, for their unknown, free, and silent existence; literature is their innocence and their forbidden presence, it is the being which protests against revelation, it is the defiance of what does not want to take place outside. In this way, it sympathizes with darkness, with aimless passion, with lawless violence, with everything in the world that seems to perpetuate the refusal to come into the world" ("Literature," 330).

Literature's search for this moment can, however, exact a high toll: "Literature, a blind vigilance which in its attempt to escape from itself plunges deeper and deeper into its own obsession, is the only rendering of the obsession of existence, if this itself is the very impossibility of emerging from existence, if it is being which is always flung back into being, that which in the bottomless depth is already at the bottom of the abyss, a recourse against which there is no recourse" (332).

CHAPTER TWO

1 "Es ist gleich tödlich für den Geist, ein System zu haben und keins zu haben. Er wird sich also wohl entschliessen müssen, beides zu verbinden" (*Athenäum* 1, 2 [1798]: 66).

2 "Man kann nur Philosoph werden, nicht es sein. Sobald man es zu sein glaubt, hört man auf, es zu werden" (*Athenäum* 1, 2 [1798]: 66).

3 "Was in der Poesie geschieht, geshiet nie, oder immer. Sonst ist es keine rechte Poesie. Man darf nicht glauben sollen, das es jetzt wirklich geschehe" (Schlegel and Schlegel, *Athenäum* 1, 2 [1798]: 72).

4 "Eine Definition der Poesie kann nur bestimmen, was sie sein soll, nicht, was sie in der Wirklichkeit war und ist: sonst würde sie am kürzesten so lauten: Poesie ist, was man zu irgendeiner Zeit, an irgendeinem Orte so genannt hat" (Schlegel and Schlegel, *Athenäum* 1, 2 [1798]: 74).

5 "Die romantische Poesie ist eine progressive Universalpoesie. Ihre Bestimmung ist nicht bloss, alle getrennte Gattungen der Poesie wieder zu vereinigen und die Poesie mit der Philosophie und Rhetorik in Berührung

zu setzen. Sie will und soll auch Poesie und Prosa, Genialität und Kritik, Kunstpoesie und Naturpoesie bald mischen, bald verschmelzen, die Poesie lebendig und gesellig, und das Leben und die Gesellschaft poetisch machen, den Witz poetisieren und die Formen der Kunst mit gediegnem Bildungsstoff jeder Art anfüllen und sättigen und durch die Schwingungen des Humors beseelen ... Nur sie kann gleich dem Epos ein Spiegel der ganzen umgebenden Welt, ein Bild des Zeitalters werden. Und doch kann auch sie am meisten zwischen dem Dargestellten und dem Darstellenden, frei von allem realen und idealen Interesse auf den Flügeln der poetischen Reflexion in der Mitte schweben, diese Reflexion immer wieder potenzieren und wie in einer endlosen Reihe von Spiegeln vervielfachen ... Die romantische Dichtart ist noch im Werden; ja, das ist ihr eigentliches Wesen, dass sie ewig nur werden, nie vollendet sein kann: Sie kann durch keine Theorie erschöpft werden, und nur eine divinatorische Kritik dürfte es wagen, ihr Ideal charakterisieren zu wollen. Sie allein ist unendlich, wie sie allein frei ist und das als ihr erstes Gesetz anerkennt, das die Willkür des Dichters kein Gesetz über sich leide" (Schlegel and Schlegel, *Athenäum* 1, 2 [1798]: 75–6).

6 For example, Jónas Hallgrímsson never turned his back on poetry and its possibilities and, unlike Schlegel, did not become a bourgeois official who ate cream cakes on the Continent. Instead he fell down a staircase in Copenhagen, dirt poor and in a shabby state, and died shortly thereafter. About the demise of Hallgrímsson, see Valsson, *Jónas Hallgrímsson*, 485–8.

7 Cf. Eysteinsson, *Double Speak*.

8 Þórir Óskarsson has also written on this. See Óskarsson, "What Is Romanticism?"

9 Apart from Óskarsson's essay "What Is Romanticism?" I point to his *Undarleg tákn á tímans bárum: Ljóð og fagurfræði Benedikts Gröndals* [Strange Signs on the Waves of Time: The Poetry and Aesthetics of Benedikt Gröndal]. There Óskarsson discusses the poetry as well as the aesthetic ideas of Benedikt Gröndal.

10 In the introduction, Jakobsdóttir mentions an important point concerning ideas about continuity in Icelandic literature. She talks about her literary studies at Smith College in the United States and how important it was for her, as an Icelander schooled in a "particular Icelandic world view," to have teachers of Medieval literature who placed medieval Icelandic literature within the tradition of the literature of the Middle Ages in Europe "as if nothing were more self-evident." See the introduction to Jakobsdóttir, *Glimpse*.

11 I am referring to the poem "Ísland" by Hannes Pétursson:
    Minn staður er hér, þar sem Evrópa endar
    og auðnir hnattarins taka við.
    Eldgröf í sæ, með ísbláan múrinn
    á aðra hlið.

    Örlagastaður sem stundirnar markar.
    Hér stendur rótum í gleði og sorg
    mitt sveitamannslíf, mín hálfgildings hugsun
    í hálfgildings borg

    og er viðspyrna, farg; það fellur hér saman–
    flækjuleg reynsla. Hvort nýtist hún mér
    til fullnaðarsöngva? Útmörk. Evrópa
    endar hér.
    (Rímblöð 88–9)

    "Iceland"
    My place is here, where Europe ends
    and wastelands of earth appear.
    A grave of fire beside an ice-blue wall
    in the sea.

    A fateful place, leaving its mark.
    Here it stands, both in joy and in sorrow,
    my provincial life, my halfway thought
    in a semi-city

    a resistance, burden, it is here the two collide –
    complicated experience. Does it harbour seeds
    of perfection? The edge. This is where Europe
    ends. (Trans. Birna Bjarnadóttir)

12 Some of Thomsen's essays have appeared in Icelandic. See Thomsen,
    Íslenskar bókmenntir og heimsskoðun [Icelandic Literature and
    Philosophy].

13 We might mention in passing that, much later, another foreign scholar,
    Theodore M. Anderson, writes an article on the difference between the
    way emotions are expressed in Homer and in the Sagas of Icelanders.
    There we read, for example: "Whereas the Saga authors lavish loving de-
    tail on the gestures that are the products of emotion, Homer looks at the

emotion itself." His closing words are: "Homer, composing two thousand years before the Sagas were written, is closer to our taste. What the Homeric heroes experience, the Saga heroes tend to deny, and since we do not believe that such a denial is possible and suspect therefore that the attempt verges on a sterile posture, we are likely to feel more comfortable with the less high strung but more resonant tones of Homer's heroism" ("Heroic Postures" 8–9).

14 Charles Taylor's *A Secular Age* (2007) does provide a path for the question: What does it mean to exist within a secular period, seen from the perspective of the history of humankind?

15 Page numbers given in parentheses in the following refer to Kristjana Gunnars' translation of Gröndal's essay (see Gröndal, "Some Fragments").

16 See Gröndal, "Some Fragments," 71n30.

17 Here I am of course making a great leap, historically speaking. It is a fact that Sigurður Nordal's thoughts on the history of Icelandic literature, philosophy, and culture in the twentieth century are irrefutably influential. Much has been written and said about this. But with new times come new interpretations. In the year 1999, the Sigurður Nordal Institute staged a conference on Nordal's book *Icelandic Culture*. Three of the papers delivered there appear in *Tímarit Máls og menningar* 1 (2000): "Dagrenning norrænnar sögu" by Ármann Jakobsson, "*Íslenzk menning* og evrópsk þjóðernisstefna" by Sigríður Matthíasdóttir, and "Fúlsað við flotinu" by Kristján B. Jónasson. All these papers show, each in its own way, a new attitude towards Nordal's contribution.

18 This is spoken by Ugla in Halldór Laxness' novel *Atómsstöðin* [*The Atom Station*], 24.

19 Daðason, "Defence of Poetry," 26. Hereafter, this essay is referenced in the main text with page numbers in parentheses.

20 See also Daðason, "Defence of Poetry," 31. My quote from Nordal's essay is longer than that provided by Daðason.

21 See *Þjóðviljinn* [*The Nation's Call*], 2 November 1951.

22 Dagný Kristjánsdóttir has discussed the postwar cultural battles in Reykjavik. See her *Kona verður til* [*A Woman Comes into Existence*], 358–419.

23 These words are reminiscent of the words of Gestur Pálsson in his lecture "Life in Reykjavík," which he delivered at the end of the nineteenth century. There Pálsson talks about how books are not enough for the "education of the young person," who needs to have "a varied and amazing life around him" and to get to know "the poetic arts of the cultures of the world" (343–4). About the literary scene in Reykjavík he writes: "Icelandic literary life is non-existent here, as it is elsewhere in the country; although there may be a

few stray individuals in this town who buy up whatever little is printed in
Icelandic – not in order to read it but, rather, to put it up in their cabinet so
others can say of him when he is dead that he was a great friend of books. It
is as if Icelandic literary life is just now dying out" (366–7). About the cultural life in the same town, Pálsson writes: "Culture in this town is just like the
town itself in the evenings, when it has become dark: in most houses there is
a small flicker of light for those living there." And, aside from that, "nothing
but pitch darkness, and coal-black night, where nothing is known of any
light or even that any heaven exists" (368–9). See also Ástráður Eysteinsson's
commentary on Pálsson's lecture in his article "Menningarfræði í ljósi
bókmennta" ["Cultural Studies in the Light of Literature"].

24 In 2001, a large collection of the writings of avant-garde movements of
the early twentieth century finally appeared in Icelandic. See Hjartarson,
Yfirlýsingar [Declarations].

CHAPTER THREE

1 This summary of Augustine's position in Western literary culture is based
on Stock 2–3.

2 "Alle Analogien zwischen diesen Denkern bezeugen die Tiefe der
Erregtheit, die Fähigkeit zu äussersten Erfahrungen, die Gewalt der
Persönlichkeit, die 'Modernität' Augustines" (Jaspers, *Die Grossen
Philosophen*, 375).

3 Here the editors cite a brief essay Hannah Arandt wrote on Augustine and
Protestantism. It was published in the *Frankfurter Zeitung*, 4 December
1930.

4 Cf. Jaspers' observation in *Die Grossen Philosophen*, where he writes: "Es
ist eine unheimliche Atmosphäre der hochmütigen Demut, der sinnlichen
Askese, der ständigen Verschleierungen und Umkehrungen, die durch die
christlichen Gehalte wie durch keine andere gehen. Augustine hat sie als
erster durchgeschaut. Er kannte die Qual des Nichtstimmens, der falschen
und verborgenen Motive, – das Dogma von der Erbsünde hat dieses
Unheil für das Weltdasein absolut gemacht und gleichsam gerechtfertigt.
Dieses Selbstdurchschauen ging weiter durch die christlichen Denker bis
zu Pascal, bis zu Kierkegaard und Nietzsche" (396).

5 Cf. Bjarnadóttir, "Í mótsögn tilfinninga" [Contradicion of Emotions], 224.

6 Augustine, *Confessions*.

7 "In Augustine's doctrine, the intimacy of self-presence is, as it were, hal-
lowed, with immensely far-reaching consequences for the whole of
Western Culture" (Taylor 140).

8 See Stock 15. Here Stock again mentions this particular company of ideas. It is something other than us, but it reminds us that we live our lives inside what Plato calls "a zone of unlikeness."

9 See also Blanchot, "Literature and the Right to Death," in which he discusses the following fragment of Hegel, taken from his 1805–06 Jena writings: "Adam's first act, which made him master of the animals, was to give names, that is, he annihilated them in their existence (as existing creatures)." God, Blanchot writes, "had created living things, but man had to annihilate them. Not until then did they take on meaning for him, and he in turn created them out of the death into which they disappeared" (322–3). See also Harris's *Hegel's Development*, 467–522.

10 This passage by Wittgenstein is cited in Thompson, "Wittgenstein's Confessions," 152.

11 At the time, Þorgeir Þorgeirsson wrote a review of *Repeated Words*, in which he notes the author's "manifestation" and finds it in another poem marked XXI: "art is / by nature observation" (Þorgeirsson, "Endurtekin orð," 419).

12 In the following I cite from the second edition of the book (Reykjavík: Forlagið, 1994).

13 See, for instance, Þorgeirsson, "Endurtekin orð," 420.

14 Here I am referring to groundbreaking changes in the foundations of this society; namely, the part faith plays and the shrinking power it has over people's lives. I wish to thank Guðbergur Bergsson for pointing out this element of the story in a discussion concerning its form and content. These discussions took place at a cultural festival in Grindavík in the summer of 2000.

15 This sausage-licking episode is reminiscent of the "sin" of the young man in Philip Roth's novel *Portnoy's Complaint*. That young man masturbates on a piece of liver that was in the refrigerator, and his mother unkowingly cooks it up in the evening. The story concerns a young man who is on the verge of adulthood. As in *The Mouse That Skulks*, the idea of sin plays a prominent part in Roth's novel, although its setting differs from the one played out in the era of watered-down Lutheranism on the outskirts of Europe.

CHAPTER FOUR

1 See Eyjólfur Kjalar Emilsson's introduction to his Icelandic translation of Plotinus's "Beauty" [Um fegurðina], 463–4.

2 Perhaps Shakespeare's *A Midsummer Night's Dream* is an exploration of this same movement from pleasure to revulsion.

3 For a while there was an interesting debate in the journal *Skírnir* concerning the role of the writer in modern society and the relationship between life and writing – a debate that began with philosopher Páll Skúlason's "Is Poetry Helpful?" First Bergsson responded with "Is Literature the Path to Salvation?" then the writer and professor Álfrún Gunnlaugsdóttir followed with "To Deceive and Not to Deceive," and, finally, the writer Sigurður A. Magnússon chimed in with "Is Fiction Useful?"

4 In "The Saga and Morality: Thoughts on the Interpretation of the Ethics of the Sagas of Icelanders," Vilhjálmur Árnason discusses the importance of considering the context of the ideological reality of the time of the sagas if one wishes to understand the ethics expressed within them. He makes a point of noting the difficulty of distinguishing the influence of Christian ethics on the sagas. This is natural, he says, "because Christian ideas were known in Iceland long before the circumstances that were necessary in order for them to take root in the ideological reality of the nation" (141). If this is right, the madness exposed in the sagas is not necessarily related to what is described in their modern equivalents.

5 See *Þjóðviljinn*, 20 October 1985.

6 See for example, Guðmundur Andri Thorsson's review of Bergsson's *The Search for the Beautiful Land*, which is entitled "Oh, He Hides His Depths." There the reviewer points to Tómas R. Einarsson's interview with Bergsson and says: "What is noteworthy about Guðbergur's notions is that nowhere is the reader accounted for as an individual. He does not expect the reader to be creative and does not consider reading to be a creative activity; does not allow for the fact that this reading individual's imagination is active, but instead just absorbs what is there to absorb, and even perhaps admire" (114–15).

7 Nietzsche, *Svo mælti Zaraþústra* (*Thus Spake Zarathustra*), (trans. Jón Árni Jónsson), 110.

8 Here the review by Guðmundur Andri Thorsson comes to mind since he says that Bergsson does not appear to relish the close proximity between narrator and reader, and that this is why the narrative voice in his books is so "brusque and derisive and the ideology so nihilistic. He is constantly afraid that someone might suddenly agree with something in the book, and he tries to wiggle out of any kind of readerly embrace" (115).

9 Cf. Critchley in *Very Little ... Almost Nothing*. In a chapter that bears the beautiful title "Travels in Nihilon," the author discusses the circumstances

for disappointments that seem to be indicative of contemporary modern times. He also discusses the notion of nothingness in a wider context and how thoughts of the project of living are (and have been) closely aligned with humanity's relation to death.

10 See Clive Cazeaux's discussion of Nietzsche in *Continental Aesthetics Reader* 13.

11 The emphasis here is on the setting of this novel in relation to the creation of an "inner space." What remains is that the story raises equally insistent questions about "space" in general. See Egilsson, "Náin kynni Guðbergs og Málfríðar [The Close Acquaintance between Guðbergur and Málfríður].

CHAPTER FIVE

1 In *Synspunktet for min Forfatter-Virksomhed* (which Kierkegaard wrote in 1848 but which appeared in 1859, four years after his death), Kierkegaard discusses his own view of his works, with an emphasis on the distinction between religion and aesthetics.

2 See also the discussion in Bjarnadóttir, "Contradiction of Emotions," 219.

3 Perhaps *Fear and Trembling* is the most challenging of all the books written by Kierkegaard. See the introduction to the Icelandic translation of *Fear and Trembling* by Kristján Árnason (30).

4 In her book *The Broken Middle* Gillian Rose writes about the part Regine plays in Kierkegaard's existentialism.

5 With regard to the title of this short story, please note that, in keeping with Bergsson's usage, the word "bible" is lowercased.

6 The Holy Bible, King James version. Genesis 22: 1–12.

7 See *The Gift of Death* 7, where Derrida points to the writings of the Czech philosopher Jan Patočka (d. 1977), who discusses the Christian self and argues that Christianity has not thought through its own kernel, for which it is nonetheless responsible.

8 Cf. Bjarnadóttir, "Contradiction of Emotions," 219–20.

9 In this context, Derrida mentions several well-known philosophers. In addition to the Czech twentieth-century philosopher Patočka, he names "a certain" Kant and "a certain" Hegel, Kierkegaard, and, "for provocative effect", Heidegger, all of whom thought in different ways about the possibility of religion without religion. However, as Derrida poins out, this list does not have any clear demarcations.

10 Árnason's afterword to the Icelandic translation of *Fear and Trembling* 271.

11 It could be added that the theologian whom Kierkegaard harshly criticizes in *Fear and Trembling*, the aforementioned Martensen, had, in his position

towards faith and Christianity, departed from Saint Augustine's rigorous sense of sin and viewed faith as an understandable part of a human being's existence. As Þráinsdóttir further notes in the close of her summary, Martensen had thereby, in Kierkegaard's estimation, "abandoned all right to be aligned with true Christianity."

12 The question of the *genre* of Kierkegaard's writings is, of course, a vast subject. See Joakim Garff's discussion in *Søren Kierkegaard: A Biography* (552). This is where he discusses a familiar theme – the way in which Kierkegaard's *Point of View* could be said to hover between autobiography and literary testament. Augustine's *Confessions* spring instantly to mind. However, Garff is of the opinion that the book in question is neither autobiography nor literary testament. If we believe Garff, what we are faced with in *The Point of View*, genre-wise – and this in a book that is supposed to explain Kierkegaard's point of view of his own work – is a "chameleon."

13 See Ray, "Experiment in Strength."

CHAPTER SIX

1 Cf. Guðmundsdóttir, "Approaching Nearness."

2 Cf. Hermann Stefánsson's 2001 interview with Bergsson, which appeared in *Kistan.is*, a web journal on art and culture.

3 See Berkowitz 44–66.

4 See Nietzsche's foreword, "Versuch einer Selbstkritik," 8. See also Berkowitz 47.

5 Here we could mention *Ecce Homo*; *The Geneology of Morals*; *Nachlassene Fragmente*; *Beyond Good and Evil*; *and Thus Spake Zarathustra*, along with "On Truth and Lie."

6 See afterword by Baldursson and Þorgeirsdóttir in Nietzsche, "On Truth and Lie," 32.

7 In his review of Simon Schama's *Rembrandt's Eyes* in the *New York Review of Books* E.H. Gombrich discusses the aesthetics of the individual as found in Rembrandt. Schama makes himself guilty – to Gombrich's great surprise – of seeing the work of Rembrandt more or less in the reflection of another master painter: Rubens.

CHAPTER SEVEN

1 In his short story collection *Boredom's Toys*, which appeared in 1964 (and was republished in 1997), we see the "beginning" of this fictional world. There we find not only the setting, or "the ever-present Grindavík," as

Þorsteinn frá Hamri calls it in a review of the book, but also the characters who have yet to "reappear" in the Tangi stories.

2 See Bergsson's "Ideas on Beauty," 111–12.

3 Cf. Jóhansson, *Guðbergur Bergsson*, 18.

4 See, for example, Ólafur Jónsson's review of *Tómas Jónsson Bestseller*,
   which is reprinted in *Also Life*. See also Sigfús Daðason's review,
   "Expression of Negativity."

5 Bergsson's novel *The Swan* (1991) is of interest in this connection for here
   we see Bergsson's "abilities" in this area. This book has not been associated with parody of form, but in it we find the emotions and desires of a
   young girl interwoven with the nature of the land, which is something that
   characterizes the aforementioned fusion of realism and romanticism in the
   works of the "golden authors." *The Swan*, as Milan Kundera writes,
   "breathes the Icelandic landscape from every line." But the reader needs to
   be cautious. As Kundera says: "please, do not read it as an 'Icelandic
   novel,' as an exotic oddity. Guðbergur Bergsson is a great European novelist. His art is primarily inspired not by some sociological or historical, still
   less a geographical, curiosity, but by an existential quest, real *existential
   insistence*, which places his book at the very centre of what could (in my
   view) be termed the modernity of the novel" ("Secret of the Ages of Life"
   28.) As such, it bears the trademark of the *Mind's Tormented Love, The
   Heart Still Dwells in Its Cave*, and other writings by Bergsson; therefore,
   it cannot be confined to what the Icelandic poet Jóhann Jónsson once defined, in opposition to "the language of humanity" (i.e., the language of
   world literature), as the "dialect of eccentricity." This is from Jónsson's
   article on Gunnar Gunnarsson, Bergsson's forerunner in the ranks of
   Icelandic existentialist writers (Jónsson "Gunnar Gunnarsson í Berlín").

6 See, for example, Þorsteinsson's short story "Blástör" in the collection
   Blessed Week. The story begins as follows: "It was a cold August morning.
   A weak ray from the rising sun pressed itself in through the window, and
   it was as if the sunray were the breast of a young woman, modest in its
   smallness, half-hesitant and weak and helpless" (29).

7 It should be noted that, in a discussion of form and meaning in *Tómas
   Jónsson Bestseller*, Eysteinsson ("Fyrsta nútímaskáldsagan og Vefarinn
   mikli" 56–91) talks about this subject in connection to literary history and
   also discusses *The Great Weaver of Kashmir* by Halldór Laxness and
   Letters to Lára by Þórbergur Þórðarson.

8 The folk tale about Katrín is a tempting citation in this context. According
   to this story, the part played by the Icelandic singer during the Second
   World War is considerable: the day before Hitler invades Poland,

1 September 1939, Katrín turns him down in the name of art and her loyalty to Iceland. At the same time, the interpreter knows the citation is not "certain" and could just as well be evidence of a warning. What remains is that the folk tale creates a space where the boundaries between reality and fiction, the individual and society, and Iceland and Europe are fluctuating.

9 Bergsson had received the "silver horse" award (i.e., the critics' award) for *The Love Life of a Compatible Couple*.

10 See Guðmundsson, "I Whine over the Icelandic Poet," an article on Hallgrímur Helgason's novel *The Author of Iceland* and the discussions surrounding it on the radio program "Víðsjá."

11 Perhaps the short story by Gunnar Benediktsson entitled "Guðrún in the Gestur Farm" is one of those "romantically styled" works.

12 In addition to the critiques that have been discussed, there are quite a few that are accepting of Bergsson's aesthetics. Ólafur Jónsson wrote more than one review of Bergsson's novels in the 1970s and 1980s (e.g., "Pure Nonsense, Tómas?" in *Also Life*, 100–13). As well, I could mention the reviews of Árni Bergmann ("He Even Heard Them Whine"); and Pétur Gunnarsson ("On the Trail of a Primitive Tribe." The last mentioned wrote the following in his review of Bergsson's *It Rises from the Deep*: "In Guðbergur Bergsson's latest novel … we meet as main characters personages that appear already in *Tómas Jónsson*." At the end of his review, Gunnarsson says of the Tangi stories: "We are dealing with the most interesting and noteworthy staging of the reality of Iceland since [Halldór Laxness] wrote *Salka Valka* and *Independent People*. At that time Iceland was on its way up; now it is in a stage of humiliation and decay." See "On the Trail of a Primitive Tribe."

Bibliography

Augustine. *The City of God against the Pagans*. Trans. and ed. R. W. Dyson. New York: Cambridge University Press, 2010 [1998].

– *Confessions*. Trans. Henry Chadwick. New York: Oxford University Press, 1998.

– *Játningar* [Confessions]. Trans. Sigurbjörn Einarsson. Reykjavík: Bókaútgáfa Menningarsjóðs, 1962.

Ágústsson, Símon Jóh. *List og fegurð* [Art and Beauty]. Reykjavík: Hlaðbúð, 1953.

Anderson, Theodore M. "Heroic Postures in Homer and the Sagas." In *Sjötíu ritgerðir helgaðar Jakobi Benediktssyni* [Seventy Essays in Honour of Jakob Benediktsson]. Vol. 1. Ed. Einar G. Pétursson and Jónas Kristjánsson, 1–9. Reykjavík: Stofnun Árna Magnússonar, 1977.

Arendt, Hannah. *Love and Saint Augustine*. Trans. Hannah Arendt and E.B. Ashton. Ed. Joanna Vecchiarelli Scott and Judith Chelius Stark. Chicago and London. University of Chicago Press, 1996. (This is E.B. Ashton's revised translation of the manuscript of Hannah Arendt's doctoral dissertation, "Liebesbegriff bei Augustine," 1929.)

Árnason, Kristján. "Inngangur" [Introduction]. In Søren Kierkegaard, *Uggur og ótti: Prætubókarljóð* [Fear and Trembling: Dialectical Lyric]. Trans. Jóhanna Þráinsdóttir, 9–44. Reykjavík: Hið íslenzka bókmenntafélag, 2000.

– "Sjálfsþekking og sjálfsval" [Self–Examination and Self–Realization] *Tímarit Máls og menningar* [Journal of Language and Literature] 4 (2000): 6–14.

Árnason, Vilhjálmur. "'Deyðu á réttum tíma'": Siðfræði og sálfræði í ljósi dauðans" [Die at the Right Moment: Ethics and Pschycology in the Light of Death]. *Skírnir* 164 (Fall 1990): 293–5.

– "Á rauðu ljósi" [On a Red Light]. In *Hvers er siðfræðin megnug? Safn ritgerða í tilefni tíu ára afmælis Siðfræðistofnunar* [What Is Ethics Capable

Of? Collection of Essays on the Tenth Anniversary of the Institute of Ethics], ed. Jón A. Kalmansson, 219–38. Reykjavík: Háskólaútgáfan, 1999.

– "Að velja sjálfan sig: Tilraunir Kierkegaards um mannlífið" [To Choose Oneself: Kierkegaard's Experiments on Human Life] *Tímarit Máls og menningar* 4 (2000): 17–32.

– "Eftirmáli." In Søren Kierkegaard, *Endurtekningin* [Repetition]. Trans. Þorsteinn Gylfason, 209–12. Reykjavík: Hið íslenzka bókmenntafélag, 2000.

– "Grímur manns og heims" [Masks of Man and World]. *Tímarit Máls og menningar* 3 (1997): 51–9.

– "Hvers er siðfræðin megnug?" [What Is Ethics Capable Of?]. In *Hvers er siðfræðin megnug? Safn ritgerða í tilefni tíu ára afmælis Siðfræðistofnunar* [What Is Ethics Capable Of? Collection of Essays on the Tenth Anniversary of the Institute of Ethics], ed. Jón A. Kalmansson, 145–68. Reykjavík: Siðfræðistofnun and Háskólaútgáfan, 1999.

– "Leikreglur og lífsgildi: Hugleiðing um hlutverk siðfræðinnar" [Rules and Values: Reflection on the Role of Ethics]. In *Broddflugur: Siðferðilegar ádeilur og samfélagsgagnrýni* [Gadflies: Moral and Social Criticisms], ed. Geir Sigurðsson, 194–204. Reykjavík: Rannsóknastofnun í siðfræði and Háskólaútgáfan, 1997.

– "Saga og siðferði: Hugleiðingar um túlkun á siðfræði Íslendingasagna" [Sagas and Morals: Reflections on Interpretation in Relation to the Sagas of Icelanders' Ethics]. In *Broddflugur: Siðferðilegar ádeilur og samfélagsgagnrýni* [Gadflies: Moral and Social Criticisms], ed. Geir Sigurðsson, 128–47. Reykjavík: Rannsóknastofnun í siðfræði og Háskólaútgáfan, 1997.

– "Við rætur mannlegs siðferðis: Siðagagnrýni og heilræði Friedrichs Nietzsche" [At the Roots of Human Morals: Nietzsche's Criticism and Advice]. *Skírnir* (Spring 1993): 34–65.

– *Broddflugur: Siðferðilegar ádeilur og samfélagsgagnrýni* [Gadflies: Moral and Social Criticisms]. Ed. Geir Sigurðsson. Reykjavík: Rannsóknastofnun í siðfræði and Háskólaútgáfan, 1997.

Artaud, Antonin. *The Theatre and Its Double*. Trans. Mary Caroline Richards. New York. Grove, 1958 [1938].

Ásgeirsdóttir, Þóra Kristín. *Guðbergur Bergsson metsölubók* [Guðbergur Bergsson Bestseller] (Þóra Kristín Ásgeirsdóttir talks with the writer). Reykjavík: Forlagið, 1992.

Baldursson, Magnús Diðrik, and Sigríður Þorgeirsdóttir. "Eftirmáli þýðenda" [Translators' Epilogue]. In Friedrich Nietzsche, *Um sannleika og lygi í ósiðrænum skilningi* [On Truth and Lie in an

Extra–Moral Sense]. Trans. Magnús Diðrik Baldursson and Sigríður Þorgeirsdóttir. *Skírnir* 167 (Spring 1993): 29–33.

Bataille, Georges. *Inner Experience*. Trans. Leslie Anne Boldt. New York: SUNY Press, 1988.

Benediktsson, Bjarni. "Vaxtarbroddurinn" [Growth] (review). *Þjóðviljinn* [The Nation's Call], 17 July 1949.

Benediktsson, Gunnar. "Guðrún í Gesthúsum" [Guðrún in the Gestur Farm]. *Tímarit Máls og menningar* 2 (1959): 156–7.

– "Þrjú ung sagnaskáld" [Three Young Novelists] (review). *Tímarit Máls og menningar* 1 (1968): 83–94.

Bergmann, Árni. "Hann heyrði þá meira ad segja jarma" [He Even Heard Them Whine] (review). *Þjóðviljinn*, 27 October 1974.

Bergsson, Guðbergur. "Andinn sem ríkti í Súm" [The Spirit That Reigned in Súm]. In *Súm 1965–1972*, 105–15. Reykjavík: Listasafn Reykjavíkur/ Kjarvalsstaðir, 1989.

– *Anna*. Reykjavík: Helgafell, 1969.

– *Anna: Íslenska ævintýrabókin* [Anna: The Icelandic Book of Fairy Tales]. Reykjavík: Forlagið, 2001.

– *Ástir samlyndra hjóna: Tólf tengd atriði* [The Love Life of a Compatible Couple: Twelve Related Themes] Reykjavík: Forlagið, 1989 [1967].

– *Endurtekin orð* [Repeated Words]. Reykjavík: Heimskringla, 1961.

– "Eftirmáli" [Epilogue]. In Gabriel García Márquez, *Hundrað ára einsemd* [One Hundred Years of Solitude]. Trans. Guðbergur Bergsson, 361–5. Reykjavík: Mál og menning, 1978.

– "Eftirmáli" [Epilogue]. In *Lazarus frá Tormes* [Lazarus from Tormes]. Trans. Guðbergur Bergsson, 101–26. Reykjavík: Mál og menning, 1972.

– "Eftirmáli" [Epilogue]. In *Ástir samlyndra hjóna: Tólf tengd atriði* [The Love Life of a Compatible Couple [The Love Life of a Compatible Couple: Twelve Related Themes], 271–82. Reykjavík: Forlagið, 1989.

– *Eins og steinn sem hafið fágar: Skáldævisaga* [Like a Stone the Sea Polishes: Fictional Autobiography]. Reykjavík: Forlagið, 1998.

– "Er skáldskapurinn leið til hjálpræðis?" [Is Literature a Path to Salvation?] *Skírnir* 165 (Fall 1991): 438–49.

– *Faðir og móðir og dulmagn bernskunnar: Skáldævisaga* [Father and Mother and the Mysterious Power of Childhood: Fictional Autobiography]. Reykjavík: Forlagið, 1997.

– "Formáli fyrir þýðingu minni á *Don Kíkóta*" [Preface for My Translation of *Don Quixote*], 15–27. Reykjavík: JPV útgáfa, 2006.

– "Formáli" [Preface]. In *Hið eilífa þroskar djúpin sín: Úrval spænskra ljóða 1900–1992, í þýðingu Guðbergs Bergssonar* [The Eternity

Ripens Its Depths: A Selection of Spanish Poems from 1900–1992], 7–9. Reykjavík: Forlagið, 1992.

- "Formáli" [Preface]. In *Tómas Jónsson metsölubók* [Tómas Jónsson Bestseller], 3–6. Reykjavík: Forlagið, 1987.
- "Fyrirbrigðafræði nútímabókmennta" [The Phenomenology of Modern Literature]. *19 Júní* 2 (1994): 18.
- "Gagnrýni á gagnrýnina" [A Critique of Criticism]. *Tímarit Máls og menningar* 5 (1982): 556–61.
- "Hafa kvennabókmenntir sérstöðu?" [Does Feminist Literature Hold a Special Place?]. *Tímarit Máls og menningar* 3 (1981): 325–35.
- *Hermann og Dídí* [Hermann and Dídí]. Reykjavík: Forlagið, 1999 [1974].
- *Hjartað býr enn í helli sínum* [The Heart Still Dwells in Its Cave]. Reykjavík: Mál og menning, 1982.
- "Hugmyndir um fegurð" [Ideas on Beauty]. *Tímarit Máls og menningar* 3 (1996): 111–21.
- "Hvað er eldi guðs? [What Is God's Kindling?]. Tímarit Máls og menningar 3 (1964): 229–32.
- *Jólasögur úr samtímanum* [Current Christmas Stories]. Reykjavík: Forlagið, 1995.
- *Kenjarnar – Los Caprichos – eftir Francisco Goya y Lucientes í túlkun Guðbergs Bergssonar* [*Caprichos by Francisco Goya y Lucientes* in Guðbergur Bergsson's Interpretion]. Reykjavík: Forlagið, 1998.
- *Leikföng leiðans* [Boredom's Toys]. Reykjavík: Forlagið, 1997 [1964].
- *Leitin að landinu fagra* [The Search for the Beautiful Land]. Reykjavík: Mál og menning, 1985.
- "Maður sem varð fyrir óláni" [The Man Who Suffered a Misfortune]. In *Maðurinn er myndavél* [Man Is a Camera], 39–49. Reykjavík: Forlagið, 1988.
- "Maðurinn í náttúrunni" [Man in Nature]. *Tímarit Máls og menningar* 2 (1997): 73–87.
- "Mannsmynd úr biblíunni" [An Image of Man from the bible]. *Maðurinn er myndavél* [Man Is a Camera], 7–21. Reykjavík: Forlagið, 1988.
- *Músin sem læðist* [The Mouse That Skulks]. Reykjavík: Forlagið, 1994 [1961].
- "Ómurinn, ofsinn og mildin" [The Echo, the Ferocity, and the Mildness]. In *Íslensk list* [Icelandic Art], 130–9. Reykjavík: Bókaútgáfan Hildur, 1981. (An article on Jón Gunnar Árnason.)
- "Sæmundur fróði hinn nýi reiðir selinn til höggs gegn bókinni" [The New Sæmundur the Wise Lashes Out against the Book]. *Tímarit Máls og menningar* 4 (1993): 91–102.

- *Sannar sögur* [True Stories]. Reykjavík: Forlagið, 1999.
- "Skáldsagnahöfundurinn og textinn. "'Óttinn' við textann" [The Novelist and the Text: The Fear of the Text]. *Tímarit Máls og menningar* 1 (1993): 51–61.
- *Stígar* [Paths]. Reykjavík: JPV Forlag, 2001.
- *Sú kvalda ást sem hugarfylgsnin geyma* [The Mind's Tormented Love]. Reykjavík: Forlagið, 1993.
- *Svanurinn* [The Swan]. Reykjavík: Forlagið, 1992.
- "'Tíminn' í listaverkinu" [Time in the Work of Art]. *Tímarit Máls og menningar* [Journal of Language and Literature] 2 (1989): 160–8.
- *Tómas Jónsson metsölubók* [Tómas Jónsson Bestseller]. Reykjavík: Forlagið, 1987 [1966].
- "Um ásthneigð í bókmenntum og lífinu eins og hún er runnin undan rifjum Adams" [Love's Inclination in Literature and Life According to Adam]. *Skírnir* 163 (Spring 1989): 41–53.
- *Það rís úr djúpinu* [It Rises from the Deep]. Reykjavík: Forlagið, 1999 [1976].
- *Það sefur í djúpinu* [It Sleeps in the Deep]. Reykjavík: Forlagið, 1999 [1973].

Berkowitz, Peter. *Nietzsche: The Ethics of an Immoralist*. London: Harvard University Press, 1995.

Biblían [The Bible]. Reykjavík: Hið íslenzka biblíufélag, 1981.

Bjarnadóttir, Birna. "Endurfæðing harmleiks: Um skapandi mörk lífs og listar í skáldævisögu Guðbergs Bergssonar" [The Rebirth of Tragedy: On the Creative Boundaries between Life and Art in the Fictional Autobiography of Guðbergur Bergsson]. *Andvari* 124 (1999): 141–56.
- "Hvers vegna er dauðinn besta gjöfin, Kierkegaard?" ["Why Is Death the Best Gift, Kierkegaard?"]. *Tímarit Máls og menningar* 4 (2000): 47–62.
- "Í guðlausu fjaðrafoki: Um sambönd og innra líf í sögum Guðbergs Bergssonar" ["In a Godless Flurry: Relationships and Inner Lives in the Stories of Guðbergur Bergsson]. *Tímarit Máls og menningar* 1 (1998): 34–52.
- "Í mótsögn tilfinninga: Um játningar Ísaks Harðarsonar" [In Contradicion of Emotions: On the Confessions of Ísak Harðarson]. *Skírnir* 172 (Spring 1998): 219–37.
- "Möglichkeiten der Kreativität am Rande Europas: Über die Dichtung Guðbergur Bergssons" [Possibilities of Creativity on the Edge of Europe]. In *Präsentationen: Isländische und faröische Gegenwartsautoren – Steinunn Sigurðardóttir, Guðbergur Bergsson, Jens Pauli Heinesen* [Presentations: Icelandic and Faroese Contemporary Literature

– Steinunn Sigurðardóttir, Guðbergur Bergsson, Jens Pauli Heinesen].
Trans and ed. Gert Kreutzer, 102–26. Köln: Seltmann and Hein Verlag,
2002.

– "Þegar spurt er um tilfinningar? *Sú kvalda ást sem hugarfylgsnin geyma*," [And the Emotions? *The Mind's Tormented Love*] in *Heimur
skáldsögunnar* [The World of the Novel]. Ed. Ástráður Eysteinsson, 93–
102. Reykjavík: Bókmenntafræðistofnun Háskóla Íslands, 2001.

– "Tími Íslands? Fáein orð um ritgerð Sigfúsar Daðasonar 'Til varnar
skáldskapnum' og tíma fagurfræðinnar á Íslandi" [What's the Time in
Iceland? Reflections on Sigfús Daðason's "In Defence of Poetry" and
Aesthetic Sense of Time in Iceland]. *Lesbók Morgunblaðsins*, 6 October
2001.

Blanchot, Maurice. "*Adolphe*, or the Misfortune of True Feelings." In
Blanchot, *Work of Fire*, 240.

– *Death Sentence*. Trans. Lydia Davis. Barrytown: Station Hill Arts, 1998
[1948].

– *Faux pas*. Paris: Gallimard, 1943.

– *The Infinite Conversation*. Trans. Susan Hanson. Minneapolis and
London: University of Minnesota Press, 1993.

– *The Instant of My Death*. Trans. Elizabeth Rottenberg. Stanford:
Stanford University Press, 2000 [1994].

– "Kafka and Literature." In Blanchot, *Work of Fire*, 1–26.

– "Kafka and the Work's Demand." In Blanchot, *Space of Literature*,
57–83.

– *L'arrêt de mort*. Paris: Gallimard, 1999 [1948].

– "Literature and the Right to Death." In Blanchot, *Work of Fire*, 300–44.

– "On Nietzsche's Side." In Blanchot, *Work of Fire*, 287–99.

– "The Language of Fiction." In Blanchot, *Work of Fire*, 74–84.

– "The Original Experience." In Blanchot, *Space of Literature*, 234–47.

– "Reading Kafka." In *Work of Fire*, 1–11.

– *The Space of Literature*. Trans. Ann Smock. Lincoln and London:
University of Nebraska Press, 1989.

– *Thomas the Obscure* (rev. ed.). Trans. Robert Lamberton. In *The
Station Hill Blanchot Reader*, 51–128. Barrytown: Station Hill, 1999.

– *The Work of Fire*. Trans. Charlotte Mandell. Stanford: Stanford
University Press, 1995.

Bollason, Arthur Björgvin. "Inngangur" [Introduction]. In Friedrich
Nietzsche, *Handan Góðs og ills* [Beyond Good and Evil]. Trans. Arthur
Björgvin Bollason and Þröstur Ásmundsson, 9–72. Reykjavík: Hið
íslenzka bókmenntafélag, 1994.

- "Stefnumót við Díonýsos" [Date with Dionysius]. *Tímarit Máls og menningar* 3 (1997): 60–8.

Bruns, Gerald L. "Blanchot, Maurice." In *Encyclopedia of Aesthetics*, ed. Michael Kelly, 283–6. New York and Oxford: Oxford University Press, 1989.

Cazeaux, Clive, ed. *The Continental Aesthetics Reader*. London and New York: Routledge, 2000.

- "Introduction." In Cazeaux, *Continental Aesthetics Reader*, xiii-xvii.

Cervantes. *Don Kíkóti*. Trans. Guðbergur Bergsson. Reykjavík: JPV útgáfa, 2006.

Cixous, Hélène. "Blanchot, the Writing of Disaster: Nothing Is What There Is." In *Readings*, 19–27. Hemel Hempstead: Harvester, 1992.

Critchley, Simon. *Very Little … Almost Nothing*. London and New York: Routledge, 2004 [1997].

Daðason, Sigfús. "Til varnar skáldskapnum" [In Defence of Poetry]. In *Ritgerðir og pistlár* [Essays and Epistles], prepared by Þorsteinn Þorsteinsson, 25–48. Reykjavík: Forlagið, 2000.

- "Útmálun neikvæðis" [The Expression of Negativity] (review). *Tímarit Máls og menningar* 4 (1966): 423–6.

Dante. *The Divine Comedy of Dante Alighieri*. Vol. 1: *Inferno*. Trans. and ed. Robert M. Durling. New York and Oxford: Oxford University Press, 1996.

- *The Divine Comedy of Dante Alighieri*. Vol. 2: *Purgatorio*. Trans. and ed. Robert M. Durling. New York and Oxford: Oxford University Press, 2004.

- *The Divine Comedy of Dante Alighieri*. Vol. 3: *Paradiso*. Trans and ed. Robert M. Durling. New York and Oxford: Oxford University Press, 2011.

Derrida, Jacques. *Demeure: Fiction and Testimony*. Trans. Elizabeth Rottenberg. Stanford: Stanford University Press, 2000.

- *The Gift of Death*. Trans. David Wills. Chicago: University of Chicago Press, 1995 [1992].

Egilsson, Sveinn Yngvi. "Náin kynni Guðbergs og Málfríðar: Um *Hjartað býr enn í helli sínum*" [The Close Acquaintance between Guðbergur and Málfríður: On *The Heart Still Dwells in Its Cave*]. In *Heimur skáldsögunnar* [The World of the Novel], 301–13. Reykjavík: Bókmenntafræðistofnun Háskóla Íslands, 2001.

- *Arfur og umbylting: Rannsókn á íslenskri rómantík* [Heritage and Upheaval: Icelandic Romanticism]. Reykjavík: Hið íslenzka bókmenntafélag and Reykjavíkurakademían, 1999.

Einarsson, Sigurbjörn. "Kristin trú á tækniöld" [Christianity in the Age of Technology]. *Skírnir* 161 (Fall 1987): 337–55.

Einarsson, Tómas R. "Íslendingar losna ekki við Lútherskuna" [The Prevailing Lutheranism among Icelanders] (interview with Guðbergur Bergsson). *Þjóðviljinn*, 20 October 1985.

Emilsson, Eyjólfur Kjalar. "Um Plótinos og verk hans" [On Plotinus and His Work]. *Skírnir* 169 (Fall 1995): 462–5.

Eysteinsson, Ástráður. "Að gefa í boðhætti: Módernismi og kvennapólitík í *Gefið hvort öðru* eftir Svövu Jakobsdóttur" [To Give in the Imperative: Modernism and Feminist Politics in *Give unto Each Other* by Svava Jakobsdóttir]. In Eysteinsson, *Umbrot*, 122–36.

– "Baráttan um raunsæið: Um módernisma, raunsæi og hefð" [The Battle of Realism: On Modernism, Realism, and Tradition]. In Eysteinsson, *Umbrot*, 30–55.

– "Formgerð og frásögn: Um skáldsagnagerð á níunda áratugnum" [Structure and Narrative: On Fiction Writing in the Nineties]. In Eysteinsson, *Umbrot*, 92–100.

– "Fyrsta nútímaskáldsagan og módernisminn" [The First Modern Novel and Modernism]. In Eysteinsson, *Umbrot*, 56–91.

– "Í svartholi eða svanslíki: Heilabrot um tvær skáldsögur" [In a Dungeon or in the Guise of a Swan: Thoughts on Two Novels"]. In Eysteinsson, *Umbrot*, 320–34.

– "Menningarfræði í ljósi boókmennta" [Cultural Studies in the Light of Literature]. In Eysteinsson, *Umbrot*, 430–49.

– *The Concept of Modernism*. Ithaca and London: Cornell University Press, 1990.

– *Tvímæli: Þýðingar og bókmenntir* [On Translations and Translation Theories]. Reykjavík: Háskólaútgáfan, 1986.

– *Umbrot: Bókmenntir og nútími* [On Literature and Modernity]. Reykjavík: Háskólaútgáfan, 1999.

Faulkner, William. *Go Down Moses*. New York: Vintage, 1991.

Fjölnir, vols. 1–9. 1835–47 (photocopied 1943).

Gaarder, Jostein. *Vita Brevis*. Oslo: Aschehoug and Co., 1996.

Garff, Joakim. *"Den Sövnlöse": Kierkegaard laest aestetisk/biografisk* [The Sleepless One: An Aesthetic/Biographical Reading of Kierkegaard]. Copenhagen: C.A. Reitzel Forlag, 1995.

– *Søren Kierkegaard: A Biography*. Trans. Bruce H. Kirmmse. Princeton and Oxford: Princeton University Press, 2005.

Gombrich, E.H. *"Rembrandt's Eyes." New York Review of Books*, 20 January 2000, 6–10.

Gröndal, Benedikt Sveinbjarnarson. "Some Fragments Concerning the Poetic." In *Steingrímur Eyfjörð: The Golden Plover Has Arrived*. Trans. Kristjana Gunnars, 59–72. Reykjavík. Centre for Icelandic Art, 2007.

– "Nokkrir greinir um skáldskap" [Some Fragments Concerning the Poetic]. *Ritsafn* 3. Reykjavík: Ísafoldarprentsmiðja, 1950.

Guðmundsdóttir, Gunnþórunn. "Að hafa fjarlægð á nálægðina" [Approaching Nearness from a Distance] (review of *Like a Stone the Sea Polishes*). *Tímarit Máls og menningar* 3 (1999): 108–12.

– "'Það að lifa er að setja tæting saman'" [To Live Is to Reside in Chaos] (review). *Tímarit Máls og menningar* 4 (1998): 132–6.

Guðmundsson, Eiríkur. "Ek em hið íslenska skáld" [I Am the Icelandic Poet]. Útvarpsþátturinn "Víðsjá," *Ríkisútvarpið-Rás* [Cultural Program, Iceland's National Broadcasting Service], 1 December 2001.

Gunnarsson, Gunnar. *Sælir eru einfaldir* [Blessed Are the Simple]. Reykjavík: Almenna bókafélagið, 1981 [1920].

Gunnarsson, Pétur. "Á vit frumstæðs ættbálks?" [On the Trail of a Primitive Tribe?]. *Vísir*, 10 January 1977.

Gunnlaugsdóttir, Álfrún. "Ad blekkja og blekkja ekki" [To Deceive and Not to Deceive]. *Skírnir* 168 (Fall 1994): 479–91.

Gylfason, Þorsteinn. "Inngangur" [Introduction]. Søren Kierkegaard, *Endurtekningin* [Repetition]. Trans. Þorsteinn Gylfason, 9–42. Reykjavík: Hið íslenzka bókmenntafélag, 2000.

Hamsun, Knut. *Gróður jarðar* [Growth of the Soil]. Trans. Helgi Hjörvar. Reykjavík: Almenna bókafélagið, 1987.

Haraldsson, Róbert. "Einræða, umræða og samræða" [Monologue, Discussion and Dialogue]. In *Hvers er siðfræðin megnug? Safn ritgerða í tilefni tíu ára afmælis Siðfræðistofnunar* [What Is Ethics Capable of? Collection of Essays on the Tenth Anniversary of the Institute of Ethics]. Ed. Jón A. Kalmansson, 169–88. Reykjavík: Siðfræðistofnun og Háskólaútgáfan, 1999.

Harris, H.S. *Hegel's Development: Night Thoughts (Jena 1801–1806)*. New York: Oxford, Clarendon Press, 1983.

Hegel, Georg W.F. *Gesammelte Werke* [Collective Works]. Vol. 8. Hamburg: F. Meiner, 1968.

– *Phenomenology of Spirit*. Trans. A.V. Miller. Oxford and New York: Oxford University Press, 1977.

– *Vorlesungen über die Ästhetik* [Lectures on Aesthetics]. Vols. 1–3. *Sämtliche Werke* [Collected Works]. Stuttgart: Hermann Glockner, 1953–54.

Heidegger, Martin. *The Origin of the Work of Art: Poetry, Language, Thought*. Trans. Albert Hofstadter. New York: Harper and Row, 1975.

Helgason, Hallgrímur. *Höfundur Íslands* [Iceland's Author]. Reykjavík: Mál og menning, 2001.

Hjartarson, Benedikt, ed. *Yfirlýsingar: Evrópska framúrstefnan* [Declarations: The European Avant-Garde Movement]. Trans. Áki G. Karlsson, Árni Bergmann, and Benedikt Hjartarson. Reykjavík: Hið íslenzka bókmenntafélag, 2001.

Homer. *Kviður Hómers* [Homer's Epics]. Vols. 1 and 2. Trans. Sveinbjörn Egilsson. Reykjavík: Bókaútgáfa Menningarsjóðs, 1973.

Íslendingasögur [Sagas of Icelanders]. Vols. 1–3. Ed. Bragi Halldórsson, Jón Torfason, Sverrir Tómasson, and Örnólfur Thorsson. Reykjavík: Svart á hvítu, 1987.

Jakobsson, Ármann. "Dagrenning norrænnar sögu" [The Dawn of Nordic History]. *Tímarit Máls og menningar* 1 (2000): 3–9.

James, William. *The Varieties of Religious Experience*. New York and Bombay: Longmans, Green and Col, 1908.

Jaspers, Karl. *Die Grossen Philosophen* [The Great Philosophers]. Vol. 1. München: R. Piper and C.O. Verlag, 1959.

– *Nietzsche und das Christentum* [Nietzsche and Christianity]. Hameln: Verlag der Bücherstube Fritz Seifert, 1938.

Jimenez, Juan Ramon. *Plateró og ég. Harmljóð frá Andalúsíu 1907–1916* [Platero and I]. Trans. Guðbergur Bergsson. Reykjavík: JPV Forlag, 2000.

Jakobsdóttir, Svava. *Skyggnst á bak við ský* [A Glance behind the Clouds]. Reykjavík: Forlagið, 1999.

– "Veizla undir grjótvegg" [Under a Stone Wall]. In *Sögur handa öllum* [Stories for Everyone], 3–103. Reykjavík: Íslensku bókaklúbbarnir, 2001.

Jónasson, Kristján B. "Einn a sínum hól" [Alone and Above] (review). *Tímarit Máls og menningar* 2 (1978): 281–300.

– "Fúlsað við flotinu: *Íslenzk menning* eftir Sigurð Nordal á árinu 2000" [No Thanks: *Icelandic Culture* by Sigurður Nordal in the Year 2000]. *Tímarit Máls og menningar* 1 (2000): 17–25.

Jónsson, Jóhann. "Gunnar Gunnarsson í Berlín" [Gunnar Gunnarsson in Berlin]. *Lesbók Morgunblaðsins*, 6 April 1930.

Jónsson, Kristján Jóh. "Í ætt við andlega rúst" [A Kind of Mental Rust] (review). *Þjóðviljinn* [The Nation's Call], 2 December 1982.

Jónsson, Ólafur. *Líka líf: Greinar um samtímabókmenntir.* [*Also Life: Essays on Contemporary Literature*]. Reykjavík: Iðunn, 1976.

Kafka, Franz. *The Castle*. Trans. Mark Harman. New York: Schocken Books, 1998.

Kalmansson, Jón A. "Hlutverk siðfræðinnar?" [The Role of Ethics] In
Hvers er siðfræðin megnug? Safn ritgerða í tilefni tíu ára afmælis siðfræðistofnunar [What Is Ethics Capable Of? Collection of Essays on the
Tenth Annniversary of the Institute of Ethics]. Ed. Jón A. Kalmansson,
189–217. Reykjavík: Siðfræðistofnun og Háskólaútgáfan, 1999.

Kaufmann, Walter. Nietzsche: Philosopher, Psychologist, Anti-Christ.
Princeton: Princeton University Press, 1991.

Kelly, Michael, ed. Encyclopedia of Aesthetics. New York and Oxford:
Oxford University Press, 1998.

Kierkegaard, Søren. Endurtekningin: Sálfræðileg tilraun [Repetition: A
Psychological Experiment]. Trans. Þorsteinn Gylfason. Reykjavík: Hið
íslenzka bókmenntafélag, 2000.

– Enten-Eller: Et Livs-Fragment, Søren Kierkegaards Skrifter [Either/Or:
Life's Fragment, Søren Kierkegaard's Writings]. Copenhagen: Søren
Kierkegaard Forskningscenteret/Gads Forlag, 1997.

– Fear and Trembling. Trans. Sylvia Walsh. Cambridge: Cambridge
University Press, 2007.

– Repetition. Trans. Howard E. Hong and Edna H. Hong. Princeton:
Princeton University Press, 1983.

– Om min Forfatter-Virksomhed: Søren Kierkegaards Skrifter [The Point
of View: Søren Kierkegaard's Writings]. Binde [Vol.] 13. Copenhagen:
Søren Kierkegaard Forskningscenteret/Gads Forlag, 2009.

– The Point of View. Trans. Howard V. Hong and Edna H. Hong.
Princeton: Princeton University Press, 1998.

– Uggur og ótti: Þrætubókarljóð [Fear and Trembling: Dialectical Lyric].
Trans. Jóhanna Þráinsdóttir. Reykjavík: Hið íslenzka bókmenntafélag,
2000.

Kristeva, Julia. The Samurai. Trans. Barbara Bray. New York: Columbia
University Press, 1992.

Kristinsson, Þorvaldur. "Þetta eru vorir tímar" [These Are Our Times] (review.) Tímarit Máls og menningar 3 (1983): 337–40.

Kristjánsdóttir, Dagný. Kona verður til: Um skáldsögur Ragnheiðar
Jónsdóttur fyrir fullorðna [A Woman Comes into Existence: On
Ragnheiður Jónsdóttir's Novels]. Reykjavík: Bókmenntafræðistofnun
Háskóla Íslands and Háskólaútgáfan, 1996.

Kundera, Milan. "The Secret of the Ages of Life (Guðbergur Bergsson:
The Swan)." In Encounter, 28–31. Trans. Linda Asher. New York:
Harper Collins, 2010.

Laxness, Halldór. Af menningarástandi [Cultural Condition]. Reykjavík:
Vaka-Helgafell, 1986.

– *Atómstöðin* [The Atom Station]. Reykjavík: Helgafell, 1961 [1948].

– *Gerpla* [*The Happy Warriors*]. Reykjavík: Vaka-Helgafell, 2011 [1952].

– *Sjálfstætt fólk* [*Independent People*]. Reykjavík: Vaka-Helgafell, 2001 [1934–35].

– "Úr drögum til Gröndals stúdíu" [Sketches of Gröndal]. *Morgunblaðið* [Morningpaper], 20 March 1924.

– *Vefarinn mikli frá Kasmír* [The Great Weaver from Kashmir]. Reykjavík: Vaka-Helgafell, 2002 [1927].

Lazarus frá Tormes [Lazarus from Tormes]. Trans. Guðbergur Bergsson. Reykjavík: Mál og menning, 1972.

Magnússon, Sigurður A. "Er gagn að skáldskap?" [Is Literature Useful?]. *Skírnir* 169 (Fall 1995): 478–88.

Marquez, Gabriel Garcia. *Hundrað ára einsemd* [One Hundred Years of Solitude]. Trans. Guðbergur Bergsson. Reykjavík: Mál og menning, 1978.

Matthíasdóttir, Sigríður. "*Íslenzk menning* og evrópsk þjóðernisstefna" [*Icelandic Culture* and European Nationalism]. *Tímarit Máls og menningar* 1 (2000): 10–16.

Morgunblaðið, "Halldór Kiljan Laxness" (news story), 26 April 1926, 3.

Musil, Robert. *Der Mann ohne Eigenschaften* [Man without Qualities]. Hamburg. Rowolt, 1999 [1930–32].

Nehamas, Alexander. *Nietzsche: Life as Literature*. Cambridge, MA: Harvard University Press, 1985.

Nietzsche, Friedrich. *Beyond Good and Evil: Prelude to the Philosophy of the Future*. Ed. Rolf-Peter Horstman and Judith Norman. Trans. Judith Norman. New York: Cambridge University Press, 2007.

– *Ecce homo*. In *Nietzsche Werke: Kritische Gesamtausgabe* [Nietzche's Works: Critical Edition], pt. 6, vol. 3, ed. Giorgio Collini and Mazzino Montinari, 253–372. Berlin and New York: Walter de Gruyter, 1969.

– "On Truth and Lie in an Extra-Moral Sense." In *The Continental Aesthetics Reader*, trans. Daniel Breazeale, ed. Clive Cazeaux, 53–61. London and New York: Routledge, 2000.

– *The Birth of Tragedy*. Trans. Ronald Speirs. Cambridge: Cambridge University Press, 2007.

– *Svo mælti Zarathústra: Bók fyrir alla og engan* [Thus Spake Zarathustra: A Book for All and None]. Trans. Jón Árni Jónsson. Reykjavík: Háskólaútgáfan, 1996.

– "Versuch einer Selbstkritik" [An Attempt at Self-Criticism]. In *Die Geburt der Tragödie* [The Birth of Tragedy]. In *Nietzsche Werke: Kritische Gesamtausgabe*, pt. 3, vol. 1, ed. Giorgio Collini and Mazino Montinari, 5–16. Berlin and New York: Walter de Gruyter, 1972.

Nordal, Sigurður. "Frá meistaraprófi Gríms Thomsen" [From the
Master's Thesis of Grímur Thomsen]. *Landsbókasafn Íslands. Árbók*
[National Library of Iceland's Yearbook] 1946–47, 3rd-4th year. 151–6.
– *Íslenzk menning* [Icelandic Culture]. Reykjavík: Mál og menning, 1942.
– "Samhengið í íslenzkum bókmenntum" [Continuity in Icelandic
Literature]. In *Ritverk: Samhengi og samtíð* [Writings: Continuity and
Contemporary Times], 1:15–38. Reykjavík: Hið íslenzka bókmennta-
félag, 1996.
Novalis (Heinrich von Hardenberg). *Heinrich von Ofterdingen, Novalis:
Gesammelte Werke* [Henry Von Ofterdingen, Novalis: Collective
Writings]. Vol. 1. Ed. Carl Seelig. Herrliberg-Zurich: Buch-Verlag, 1945.
Ólafsson, Sigurður, and Sölvi Björn Sigurðsson. "Hið djúpa yfirborð:
Viðtal við Guðberg Bergsson og Thor Vilhjálmsson" [The Deep Surface:
Interview with Guðbergur Bergsson and Thor Vilhjálmsson]. In
Blóðberg, 34–43. Reykjavík: Sigurður Ólafsson and Sölvi Björn
Sigurðsson, 1998.
Óskarsson, Þórir. "Hvað er rómantík? Hugleiðingar um vandmeðfarið orð í
íslenskri bókmenntasögu" [What Is Romanticism? Reflections on a Tricky
Term in the History of Icelandic Literature]. *Andvari* 124 (1999): 104–25.
– *Undarleg tákn á tímans bárum: Ljóð og fagurfræði Benedikts Gröndals*
[Strange Signs on the Waves of Time: The Poetry and Aesthetics of
Benedikt Gröndal]. Studia Islandica 45. Reykjavík: Bókaútgáfa
Menningarsjóðs, 1987.
Pálsson, Gestur. "Lífið í Reykjavík" [Life in Reykjavík]. In *Ritsafn: Sögur-
kvæði-fyrirlestrar-blaðagreinar* [Collected Works: Stories, Poems,
Essays, Columns], 341–72. Reykjavík: Þorsteinn Gíslason, 1927.
Pétursson, Hannes. *Rímblöð* [A Book of Poems]. Reykjavík: Helgafell,
1971.
Platon. *Ríkið* [The Republic]. Trans. Eyjólfur Kjalar Emilsson. Reykjavík:
Hið íslenzka bókmenntafélag, 1997.
Plotinus. *The Enneads*. Trans. Stephen MacKenna. New York: Larson,
1992.
– "Beauty." In Plotinus, *Enneads*, 64–72.
– "The Intellectual-Principle, the Ideas, and the Authentic Existence." In
Plotinus, *Enneads*, 498–508.
– "Um fegurðina" [Beauty]. Trans. Eyjólfur Kjalar Emilsson. *Skírnir* 169
(Fall 1995): 466–77.
Ray, Matthew. "Tilraun um styrk: Trúin í túlkunarsálarfræði Nietzsches"
[An Experiment in Strength: An Outline of Nietzsche's Metapsychology
of Religion]. Trans. Birna Bjarnadóttir. *Hugur* 10–11 (1998–99): 50–65.

Rose, Gillian. *Love's Work: A Reckoning with Life*. London: Chatto and
  Windus, 1995.
- *The Broken Middle: Out of Our Ancient Society.* Oxford: Blackwell,
  1992.
Roth, Philip. *Portnoy's Complaint.* New York: Random House, 1969.
Rulfo, Juan. *Petro Paramo (Pétur heiði)* [Petro Páramo]. Trans. Guðbergur
  Bergsson. Reykjavík: Iðunn, 1985.
Sæmundsson, Matthías Viðar. "'Á aðra hliðina öskraði dauðinn; brjálæðið
  hló á hina': Um menningaskil og nútímavefara" [On One Side Death
  Screamed; Insanity Laughed on the Other: On Cultural Rift and
  Modern Weavers]. In *Myndir á sandi* [Reflections in the Sand], 495–
  598. Reykjaviík: Mál og menning, 1996.
- *Íslensk bókmenntasaga* [A History of Icelandic Literature]. Vol. 3.
  Reykjavík: Mál og menning, 1996.
- *Mynd nútímamannsins: Um tilvistarleg viðhorf í sögum Gunnars
  Gunnarssonar* [The Image of Modern Man: Existentialist Perspectives
  in Gunnar Gunnarsson's Stories]. Studia Islandica 41. Reykjavík:
  Bókaútgáfa Menningarsjóðs, 1982.
- *Myndir á sandi* [Images in the Sand]. Reykjavík: Bókmenntafræðistofnun
  Háskóla Íslands, 1991.
Sigurjónsson, Steinar. "Blandað í svartan dauðann" [Mixed with the Black
  Death]. In *Ritsafn* [Collected Writings]. Ed. Eiríkur Guðmundsson.
  Reykjavík: Ormstunga, 2008 [1967].
Schilpp, Paul Arthur, ed. *The Philosophy of Karl Jaspers.* Library of Living
  Philosophers. La Salle, IL: Open Court, 1981.
Schlegel, August Wilhelm, and Friedrich Schlegel. *Athenäum* vols. 1–3. Ed.
  Gerda Heinrich. Leipzig: Reclam, 1984.
Schlegel-Schelling, Caroline. "Lieber Freund, ich komme weit her schon an
  diesem frühen Morgen" [Dear Friend, I Arrive from Afar into This Early
  Morning]. In *Caroline Schlegel-Schelling in ihren Briefen* [Caroline
  Schlegel–Schelling in Letters]. Ed. Sigrid Damm. Darmstadt:
  Luchterhand, 1984.
Shakespeare, William. *Draumur á Jónsmessunótt* [A Midsummer Night's
  Dream]. Trans. Helgi Hálfdanarson (rev. trans.). Reykjavík: Mál og
  menning, 1987.
Skúlason, Páll. "Spurningar til rithöfunda" [Questions for Writers]. *Skírnir*
  164 (Fall 1990): 96–8.
- "Tilvistarstefnan og Sigurður Nordal" [Existentialism and Sigurður
  Nordal]. *Skírnir* 161 (Fall 1987): 309–36.
Smári, Jakob Jóh. "Óleyfileg mök við framliðna menn" [Prohibited
  Intercourse with the Deceased]. *Vísir*, 17 February 1923.

Smith, Robert. *Derrida and Autobiography.* Cambridge: Cambridge University Press, 1995.

Smock, Ann. "Translator's Introduction." In Blanchot, *Space of Literature,* 1–15.

Södergran, Edith. "Kristin trúarjátning" [Christian Confession]. In *Landið sem ekki var til* [The Land That Is Not]. Trans. Njörður P. Njarðvík, Seltjarnarnes: Urta, 1992.

Stefánsson, Hermann. "Stígar: þriðja ljóðabók Guðbergs" [Paths: Guðbergur's Third Book of Poems]. Interview. *www.kistan.is,* 2001.

Stock, Brian. *Augustine the Reader.* Cambridge, MA: Harvard University Press, 1996.

Svansson, Geir. "Ósegjanleg ást: Hinsegin sögur og hinsegin fræði í íslensku samhengi" [Unspeakable Love: Queer Stories and Queer Theory in Icelandic Context]. *Skírnir* 172 (Fall 1998): 476–527.

Sveinsdóttir, Jóhanna. "Guðbergsk siðbót" [A Bergssonian Regeneration]. *Tímarit Máls og menningar* 3 (1972): 281–300.

Sveinsson, Einar Ólafur. "Íslenzkar bókmentir eptir siðskiptin" [Icelandic Literature after the Reformation]. *Tímarit Þjóðræknisfélags Íslendinga* [Journal of the Icelandic National League], 127–71, Winnipeg: Þjóðræknisfélag Íslendinga, 1929.

Sveinsson, Gunnar. "Músin sem læðist" [The Mouse That Skulks] (review of *The Mouse That Skulks*). *Skírnir* 136 (1962): 236–7.

Taylor, Charles. *A Secular Age.* Cambridge, MA: Harvard University Press, 2007.

– *Sources of the Self: The Making of the Modern Identity.* Cambridge, MA: Harvard University Press, 1994.

Teresa of Ávila. *Interior Castle.* Trans. and ed. Allison Peers. New York: Random House, 2004 [1961].

Thompson, Caleb. "Wittgenstein's Confessions: A Study of the Influence of Augustine's and Tolstoy's Confessions on the Philosophy of Wittgenstein." PhD diss., University of Virginia, 1994.

Thomsen, Grímur. *Íslenskar bókmenntir og heimsskoðun* [Icelandic Literature and Philosophy]. Trans. Andrés Björnsson. Reykjavík: Bókaútgáfa Menningarsjóðs, 1975.

– *On the Character of the Old Northern Poetry.* Studia Islandica 31. Reykjavík: Bókaútgáfa Menningarsjóðs, 1972.

– "Sérkenni íslenskra bókmennta" [The Character of Icelandic Literature]. In Thomsen, *Íslenskar bókmenntir,* 51–82.

– "Um sérkenni fornnorræns skáldskapar" [On the Character of the Old Northern Poetry]. In Thomsen, *Íslenskar bókmenntir,* 83–105. Reykjavík: Bókaútgáfa Menningarsjóðs, 1975.

Thorsson, Guðmundur Andri. "Benedikt Gröndal (1826–1907)." In
    Þjóðskáldin, Úrval úr bókmenntum 19. aldar. [The National Poets: A
    Selection from Nineteenth-Century Literature]. Reykjavík: Mál og men-
    ning, 1992. 415.

– "Ó, hann felur djúpin sín" [Oh, He Hides his Depths](review). *Tímarit
    Máls og menningar* 1 (1987): 114–19.

– ed. *Þjóðskáldin. Úrval úr bókmenntum 19. aldar* [The National Poets:
    A Selection from Nineteenth-Century Literature]. Reykjavík: Mál og
    menning, 1992.

Tolstoi, L.N. *My Religion.* Trans. Huntington Smith. New York: Thomas
    Y. Crowell and Co., 1885.

Tulinius, Torfi H. "Æviatriðið og augnablikið: Um sjálfsævisögur frans-
    kra nýsöguhöfunda" [Life and the Fleeting Moment: Autobiographies
    by Nouveau Roman Writers]. *Tímarit Máls og menningar* 1 (1991):
    81–93.

– "'Gægur er þér í augum: Alain Robbe-Grillet, formbylting og kynórar"
    [Lust Is In Your Eyes: Alain Robbe–Grillet, Revolution of Form and
    Sexual Fantasies]. In *Bjartur og frú Emelía* [Bjartur and Mrs Emelía]
    (special issue of *Erlendir höfundar* [Foreign Writers] 13, 4 (1993):
    17–27.

Valsson, Páll. "Dýrðardæmi Abrahams: Grátittlingur Jónasar
    Hallgrímssonar" [On Abraham and Jónas Hallgrímsson's Pipit] *Tímarit
    Máls og menningar* 3 (1996): 50–63.

– *Jónas Hallgrímsson: Ævisaga* [Jónas Hallgrímsson: Biography].
    Reykjavík: Mál og menning, 2001.

Watson, Kendall L. "Is 'What Is Art?' Really the Question?" *Times
    Literary Supplement,* September 2000.

White, Edmund. *The Married Man.* London: Vintage, 2001.

Wittgenstein, Ludwig. *Philosophische Untersuchungen* [Philosophical
    Investigations]. Frankfurt am Main: Suhrkamp Verlag, 1977.

Þórðarson, Þórbergur. *Bréf til Láru* [Letters to Lara]. Reykjavík: Mál og
    menning, 1995.

Þórðarson, Þórir Kr. "Akedah: Freisting Abrahams" [Akedah: The Tempta-
    tion of Abraham]. In *Trú og þjóðfélag: Afmælisrit dr. Þóris Kr.
    Þórðarsonar prófessors* [Faith and Society: Festschrift for Dr. Þórir Kr.
    Þórðarson, Professor]. Studia Theologia Islandica 8. Reykjavík:
    Guðfræðistofnun-Skálholtústgáfa, 1994.

Þorgeirsdóttir, Sigríður. "Lygin um sannleikann og sannleikurinn um ly-
    gina" [On Truth and Lie in an Extra–Moral Sense]. *Tímarit Máls og
    menningar* 3 (1997): 38–50.

– *Vis Creativa: Kunst und Wahrheit in der Philosophie Nietzsches* [Vis Creativa: Art and Truth in Nietzsche's Philosophy]. Würzburg: Köningshausen and Neumann, 1996.

Þorgeirsson, Þorgeir. "Endurtekin ord: Músin sem læðist" [Repeated Words: The Mouse That Shulks]. *Tímarit Máls og menningar* 4–5 (1962): 418–20.

– "Um tussuna á klettinum og klerklegan yfirgang" [About the Cunt on the Cliff and Clerical Aggression"]. *Frjáls Þjóð* [Free Nation], 11 July 1968.

Þorsteinn frá Hamri. "Grindavík" (review). *Tímarit Máls og menningar* 4 (1964): 403.

Þorsteinsson, Indriði G. "Blástör." In *Sæluvika* [Blessed Week], 29–45. Reykjavík: Iðunn, 1951.

Þráinsdóttir, Jóhanna. "Er trúin þverstæða? Gagnrýni Magnúsar Eiríkssonar á trúarskoðunum Kierkegaards í *Ugg og ótta*" [Is Faith a Paradox? Magnús Eiríksson's Criticism of Kierkegaard's Views on Religion in *Fear and Trembling*]. *Tímarit Máls og menningar* 4 (2000): 35–45.

– "Sögulegt baksvið" [A Historical Backdrop]. In Søren Kierkegaard, *Uggur og ótti: Prætubókarljóð* [Fear and Trembling: Dialectical Lyric]. Trans. Jóhanna Þráinsdóttir, 231–44. Reykjavík: Hið íslenzka bókmenntafélag, 2000.

Index